romantically challenged

Sami Lukis is one of Australia's most versatile media personalities, with a career spanning more than twenty years in Australian media. Sami also runs her own successful travel business, hosting unique getaways for women in New York.

In radio, Sami has co-hosted *The Sami Lukis & Yumi Stynes Show* and *The Ant & Sami Lukis Show* on Mix FM. Sami co-hosted *The Grill Team*, *The Ugly Phil & Sami Show* and *The Cage* at Triple M, and *The Merrick & Rosso Show* at Nova 969.

In television, Sami has worked as a host/reporter on the *Today* show, *The Morning Show*, *The Daily Edition*, *Studio 10*, *Dancing on Ice*, *Loves Me, Loves Me Not*, *20 to 1*, *Big Brother*, *Totally Wild*, *The Blue Planet*, *Shipwrecked*, *Good Morning Australia*, the *TV Week Logie Awards* Red Carpet, the New Year's Eve telecast and *Fox Sports News*. Sami also featured in the documentary *Sami's Baby* on Foxtel and she has worked as a regular host/red carpet reporter for Event Cinemas and Cinema Live.

Sami graduated from the Queensland University of Technology with a Bachelor of Business Communication (with Distinction). She is the proud Patron for Kids Rehab at the Children's Hospital at Westmead and the Australian Ambassador for global beauty brand L'Occitane.

instagram.com/samilukis
twitter.com/samilukis
facebook.com/samilukistravel
samilukis.com

romantically challenged

sami lukis

VIKING
an imprint of
PENGUIN BOOKS

VIKING

UK | USA | Canada | Ireland | Australia
India | New Zealand | South Africa | China

Penguin Books is part of the Penguin Random House group of companies
whose addresses can be found at global.penguinrandomhouse.com.

First published by Penguin Random House Australia, 2018

13 5 7 9 10 8 6 4 2

Text copyright © Samantha Lukis 2018

The moral right of the author has been asserted.

Cover design by Louisa Maggio © Penguin Random House Australia Pty Ltd
Cover photographs: author: Julian Kingma; brick wall: BsWei/Shutterstock
Song lyrics to 'No Sami' © Mark Stewart
Typeset by Midland Typesetters Australia
Colour separation by Splitting Image Colour Studio, Clayton, Victoria
Printed and bound in Australia by Griffin Press, an accredited ISO AS/NZS 14001
Environmental Management Systems printer

 A catalogue record for this
book is available from the
National Library of Australia

ISBN: 9780143785804 (paperback)

penguin.com.au

To Oma
who gave me
my name
my strength
and my weakness for gin

Romantically Challenged

I don't count sheep. I count lovers.

I've been a hopeless insomniac my whole life. But at some point in my early forties, I finally found a remedy that works. I lie in bed, staring into the darkness, doing a mental count of the number of men I've slept with.

The exact number? I honestly don't know. That's *why* I fall asleep. The strain of trying to remember every single one is quite tiring. I usually get to around forty-something before I lose count. Or drift off.

Mission accomplished.

Now before you start questioning the possibility that I might be a tad – *promiscuous* – I want you to know that I'm not the least bit bothered by what you think of my 'number'. Just like I don't care how many people *you've* slept with. All those studies and surveys about what an acceptable 'number' *should be* are just sancti-monious noise.

As I write this, I am a 47-year-old single woman who's been having sex since the age of seventeen. I am aware that my 'number' is considerably higher than most of my friends'. I also know that it's much, much lower than many others'. Plus, the ratio of men I've *shagged* versus men I've *dated* is surprisingly low. I've been on *hundreds* of dates in my search for Mr Right. Hundreds. This is not an exaggeration.

Aside from a handful of long-term relationships, I've been a serial dater for the better part of *thirty friggin' years*. But, while all those years of dating did provide me with an unusually effective insomnia cure (and, thankfully, no STIs), they have, so far, failed to locate my Mr Happily Ever After.

It's not like I haven't tried to find Prince Charming. I've given it a bloody good go. My frog-kissing game is strong. I've dated guys on almost every continent. I've been on more blind dates than is reasonable for anyone to endure in one lifetime.

However, despite my best efforts, and the fact that I was once voted 'TV's most spankable personality'*, I have always been romantically challenged.

I'm challenged in quite a few areas, actually. I'm completely useless in the kitchen. I've never been able to solve a Rubik's cube. I'm crap at tennis. And I cannot, for the love of Oprah, understand how the stock market works.

But above all, I'm challenged in the romance department.

Some people are lucky enough to meet their soul mate randomly, effortlessly, and perfectly by chance. For others, it's a full-time job. For me, it has, so far, proven impossible.

I swear, if one more person says to me, '*I just don't understand why you're single*', I'll claw my own bloody eyes out.

My own parents even decided to have the we-don't-mind-if-you're-a-lesbian chat with me sometime in my early thirties. I imagine they were confused about why their little girl hadn't settled down with a lovely man and started popping out babies. And the only viable reason they could think of was that I didn't like boys. When Mum sat me down to have a serious conversation, it went something like this:

---

*   (Interpret this as you wish.)

Mum: All your father and I really want is for you to be happy. So we want you to know that it's totally fine with us if you find that happiness with a man . . . or with a woman. Okay?
Me: Thanks, Mum. Good chat. And PS I'm not gay.

I guess I could simplify it by saying the reason I'm single is because I just haven't met the right guy. And I have steadfastly refused to settle.

It has also become blaringly obvious, during my three disastrous dating decades that I am a weirdo magnet. For reasons I do not entirely understand, I often find myself in ridiculously bizarre and sometimes extraordinary interactions with the opposite sex. I'm the girl everyone turns to at a dinner party, keen to hear about my latest dating drama (which usually results in cries of, 'He did *what*?' as everyone roars with laughter at my expense). My married friends have been living vicariously through me for years. I once penned a weekly magazine column documenting the perils of single life. Hell, I even made a career out of sharing my deepest, darkest dating disasters on my own radio show.

I have also considered the possibility that I'm just not the marrying kind (if anything, I've realised that marriage can make some people very, very unhappy).

And so, with no imminent wedding to plan, I decided to write this book: a collection of my most memorable and unintentionally entertaining courting encounters.

I would really like this book to be a celebration of all the smart, self-sufficient and self-respecting kickarse single gals who also refuse to settle. In a world that still loves to measure a person's happiness based on their relationship status, we know there are plenty of *other* ways to have fabulous and fulfilling lives. Being single doesn't mean there's something wrong with us. We don't feel like we're 'on the shelf' or that we're unlovable. 'Single' isn't some kind of unbearable holding pattern we begrudgingly exist in, *between* relationships. And we're certainly not living in a state of limbo, waiting despondently for Prince Charming to come rescue us from our singledom.

No, we're *not* looking for 'Mr Perfect' – we all know he's hanging out in Middle Earth somewhere with Santa Claus and the Easter Bunny. And please stop assuming we're all just 'too picky'. We are not too picky. We're *choosey*. There's a difference. We've already managed to create valuable and meaningful lives *without* a significant other, so we're only interested in meeting someone who adds to what we already have, not someone who detracts from it.

I will concede, however, that all of the above does make us pretty ruthless on the dating front. I guess that's why people like me, who have been single for so long, seem to have the most difficulty finding love.

On the upside, it *has* enabled me to accumulate this vast and mostly humorous assortment of dating anecdotes.

I share my romantic misfortunes in sympathy with anyone else who's experienced more lows than highs on the always nerve-racking, sometimes horrifying and often stomach-churning dating roller-coaster. This is for you unwavering romantics who have found yourselves *in* dating hell or *on* a date from hell. I trust *my* dating disasters will help you feel a little better about your own.

As you read the following stories, some of you might think at times, 'Oh come on, she *must* be making this shit up.' But I assure you, as outrageously ludicrous and shockingly unbelievable as some of these encounters might seem, this is not a work of fiction. Everything I have written about *actually* happened (although some names have been changed to protect me from the wankers).

And please don't mistake my intentions. I am not a man hater. Never have been. Never will be. I *adore* men. Most of my closest mates are men. I've just been exceptionally unfortunate with them in a *romantic* capacity.

And so, to all the men I've loved, and dated and slept with. Thanks for the memories – and the following yarns.

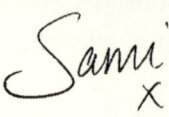

Ruck Off

I had my first 'real' date with a boy when I was fourteen years old. And by 'real' I mean chaperone-free. It was a big deal and I was equal parts excited and petrified.

I thought Jake was the most babelicious boy in Brisvegas. He was one of those sporty types – tall and super fit with a square rugby head and wide swimmer's shoulders. We went to different schools but I'd see him every Friday night at swimming club, where I couldn't keep my eyes off his rock-hard sixpack as he pranced around poolside in his dick stickers.

He'd been flirting with me for months, which consisted of flicking me on the back of my legs with his towel whenever I walked past. And giving me Chinese burns whenever I was close enough for him to reach a forearm.

So, basically, I knew he liked me.

About seventy-five towel flicks and twenty Chinese burns later, he finally asked me out on an actual date.

We agreed to meet at Timezone in the Queen Street Mall on Saturday afternoon. Which might sound like the lamest date ever, except that it was the eighties, so an afternoon of playing video games was, in fact, a totally bitchin' idea. I couldn't wait to impress Jake with my mad Galaga skills.

In the days leading up to our rendezvous, I was on a massive high. I told all my friends about it. I knew *exactly* what I was going to wear (my favourite 'Choose Life' t-shirt, of course!) and I even splashed out on a brand-new fluro scrunchie for the occasion. But on the day of our date, Jake's mother called my house and informed my mum that he wouldn't be able to meet me at Timezone, because he'd been trampled at the bottom of a ruck during a school rugby game that morning and was laid up in hospital with a broken leg.

I was devo.

I'd been psyching myself up for that date all week. But all it took was one phone call . . . and drats! My dreams were crushed and I felt like my life was over. I was heartbroken, wondering if I'd ever see him again.

Jake was a no-show at swimming club – der, broken leg! – and I really missed him. And his dick stickers. And those annoying towel flicks.

And then, bingo! Three weeks later Jake called my house to ask if he could reschedule our date. He was still on crutches and not very mobile, so would I like to go over to his place and sign his cast and watch a VHS and enjoy some Chinese burns, for old times' sake?

Yepparooni! What took you so long? (Also, yay!)

And, just like that, I was on top of the world again. My date was back on, like Donkey Kong. I couldn't wipe the smile off my face.

My excitement level reached fever pitch by the time date-day rolled around. Mum dropped me off at his place and Jake's mum met me at the door and led me down to the basement rumpus room, where my dreamboat was sitting on the couch, his right leg in plaster, looking very forlorn (mainly because he'd already missed three weeks of rugby and it didn't look like he was getting back on the paddock any time soon). He was wearing tracksuit pants and I remember noticing that he didn't seem to be wearing any underpants underneath.

That was weird.

We chatted for a bit about the hospital and his broken leg and the cast and how itchy it was, and I told him I was there to cheer him up and I tried not to look at the dubious bulges in his trackie dacks. And then I put the cassette into the VCR, ready to settle in and watch the movie with my little lovebug. In that moment, life couldn't get any better.

I realised very quickly that Jake had absolutely no intention of watching a movie. We didn't even get through the opening credits before he launched himself at me. He wasn't going to let a silly thing like a broken leg slow him down. His tongue was down my throat before I knew it and his hands were all over me. We'd already enjoyed a few sneaky pashes under the grandstand at swimming club, but this was the first time I'd let him (or any boy) touch my boobs. He was awkwardly grabbing them and kind of squishing them like you do with those rubber stress balls and I couldn't understand where the enjoyment was for him in that whole situation. There was zero enjoyment in it for me.

That was weird.

It was also my first ever body contact with a hard penis. I didn't actually touch it (gross!) but I could feel it through his flimsy pants. He kept pushing that thing up against me. We might not have made it to the video arcade, but Jake was still determined to score as many points with his joystick as he possibly could.

Despite numerous dexterous attempts on his behalf, I wouldn't let Jake put his hand down my pants. I was afraid he might think I was frigid, but I just wasn't ready to go to third base. He tried valiantly throughout the movie, and by the end credits, he'd given up and completely lost interest. He said I should probably go home.

I couldn't believe our date was over already. Had I done something wrong? Was it because I wouldn't let him touch my bits? But I thought he liked me?

Boys are weird.

So I left my first ever real date feeling inadequate and frigid and humiliated. And I had the physical scars to remind me of that heartbreaking afternoon for days. Jake had given me the worst pash rash ever (oh my god, we pashed for *two hours straight*). My boobs were sore from all the squishing and squashing. And the next day I noticed an actual bruise next to my hipbone, from where he'd been poking that *thing* into me all afternoon.

Best. Date. Ever. Not.

I guess Jake was looking for a home run, because he never asked me out again and he pretty much ignored me when he eventually returned to swimming club. He attempted the odd towel flick now and then, but I could tell his heart wasn't in it.

I couldn't believe how confusing this whole dating caper was. How could something that had initially brought me so much excitement and happiness turn out to be such a big fat fucker of a disappointment? One minute I was the happiest girl in the world: I'd met a spunky boy, he gave me butterflies in my belly, I thought he was the perfect guy! But our date was a disaster. And Jake turned out to be a massive jerkwad.

So that was my introduction to the highs and lows of 'dating' and the roller-coaster of emotions that go with it. A taste of things to come . . . for the rest of my friggin' life!

Congratulations, Jake. I don't want to give you a big head or anything, but you hold the esteemed title of being *number one* on the list of countless disappointments in my dating life.

But don't worry, buddy. You're not alone. This single woman has plenty of other equally disastrous dating stories to tell.

Hanky Panky

Mum says I came home from kindergarten one day and proudly announced that I was going to marry my classmate Troy. And when she asked me how I knew Troy was The One, I said it was because he always lay on the mat next to me during nap time. There was no hanky panky going on, just some kind of invisible love current drawing us together as one. The mere fact that a boy was lying beside me obviously meant that we were destined to live happily ever after.

I'm not sure if Troy was aware of our life plan, but that really didn't matter. I knew exactly what I wanted in a man when I was just four years old.

I also knew exactly what I *didn't* want, apparently: a man with a smelly lunchbox.

Let me explain.

Mum found herself on the receiving end of an awkward phone call from another classmate's mother one day, regarding a sensitive situation that had been distressing her son Darren. Every lunchtime, I would forbid Darren from sitting next to me because I couldn't stand the smell of the hard-boiled eggs in his lunchbox. Poor old Dazza was longing to sit with me, but I told him he could only do so if he was sans egg.

Shunned and rejected, Darren would go home each afternoon and *beg* his mother to stop putting eggs in his lunchbox. But every morning, she'd throw those little stink bombs in, unwittingly exposing him to rejection in front of the entire class.

Day after humiliating day.

Bless his little, broken-hearted, cotton socks.

Okay, I *know* this makes me sound like a bratty four-year-old ballbreaker, but I was never one of the mean girls. My folks were actually quite proud of the fact that I was a bit of a bleeding heart. When I found out the school was dishing out punishments to any snotty-nosed kid who forgot to carry a handkerchief, I insisted on taking extra hankies with me to school every day, so I could distribute them to anyone in need.

Hanky Panky Sami to the rescue!

My reason for shunning Dazza at lunch wasn't coming from a nasty place. I just had an overwhelmingly visceral reaction to the smell of egg. It's been a problem all my life. The slightest whiff of it – boiled, fried, scrambled, otherwise – still makes me dry-retch more than forty years later.

My overly sensitive olfactory actually produces an intense reaction to all kinds of unpleasant odours (you'll discover the extent of it later, in the chapter 'Putrid Phermones').

Anyhoo, Darren eventually broke down and explained to his mum that the eggs were turning him into a social pariah and preventing him from getting the girl of his dreams (i.e. *moi*). Which is when his mother reached boiling point and called mine to discuss.

My dear mum explained to me that my behaviour was upsetting poor Darren and she tried to persuade me to reconsider my egg-free zone. But I stubbornly refused to relax my no-eggs-near-me-at-lunch policy.

So, instead, she gave me the best advice she possibly could at the time. Rather than brutally rejecting Daz so mercilessly, I could try to gently reassure him: 'I'm really sorry to upset you, Darren. It's not you. It's just your smelly lunchbox.'

Which, as it turns out, has been solid advice I've used through-out my entire dating life. Just replace 'your smelly lunchbox' with 'your thin shoulders'*, 'your wave machine'*, 'your warm sushi escape clause'*, 'your weird text message'*, 'your two pugs'*, or any other appropriate wording for the particular man and/or situation.

Thanks, Mum! (They really do always know best.)

---

*   All are actual excuses I have used over the years.

Kissing Frogs

Okay, so I might be romantically challenged. But I'm a *really* great kisser. That's what three decades of dating does for a girl. Plus, I had pashing lessons when I was just ten.

I had just started 'going around' with a boy when the most popular girl in school, Kylie, told me that if I was 'going around with someone' it meant I had to kiss him . . . with an open mouth. I had never kissed a boy like that before and my ten-year-old, Type A personality was petrified that I might do it all wrong and that I would be a really bad kisser. So Kylie agreed to meet me and my boyfriend each lunchtime behind the school dental clinic and teach us how to pash.

I'm not talking any girl-on-girl action here. Kylie would literally just talk us through the actions, step by step, as we did it. 'First, he has to turn his head this way. And you have to turn your head that way. Good, now your lips need to touch. Open your mouths. Keep your lips soft. Okay, move your head slowly left and right. And move your heads up and down. Now he has to put his tongue into your mouth and move it around a little. Softly. Now touch his tongue with yours . . .'

And that's how it went, daily, for two weeks, until we perfected the pash. The irony of being taught the finer points of tonsil hockey behind the school dental clinic was completely lost on me at the time.

I don't know how or why Kylie became such an expert on kissing, but she was a very good teacher. And we were obviously outstanding students because we eventually graduated from Kylie's 'pashing lessons' to her 'pashing sessions'.

We were one of three couples invited to Kylie's secret after-school pashing project. As soon as the school bell rang each afternoon, we'd all race down to meet in the giant concrete pipe in the playground, where there was enough space for us all to get it on, but remain hidden from any sneaky onlookers. We would assume pashing position. Kylie would look at her watch and yell, 'Go!' and we would all have to suck face for a full minute. Then, when the minute was up, we'd stop pashing, jump on our BMX bikes and ride home.

Strangely, it's more humiliating for me to share this now than I remember it actually being at the time.

I also look back and think, how hilarious was Kylie? Teaching pashing at the age of ten. What a legend! I wonder what she's doing now? Probably managing a brothel. Or directing porn.

In spite of my early smooching escapades, I'm not a random pasher. Never have been. I need to be attracted to a guy both physically *and* mentally before I want to feel his lips on mine. That first kiss is a precious moment I might just want to remember for the rest of my life. What if he turns out to be my Mr Happily Ever After, and that first kiss is the last first kiss I'll ever have?

Some of my girlfriends have no qualms about going straight in for the pash within seconds of meeting a guy. My dearest friend Angela is known as the Pash and Dash Queen for this very reason. I've never seen anyone sidle up to a complete stranger on a dancefloor and get their tongue down his throat faster than Angie. She would go in for the kill, suck face with the guy for a couple of minutes and then rejoin our group to continue dancing around our handbags as if nothing had happened.

I don't know how Angie managed to get away with it so often. A certain naughty twinkle in her eye, perhaps? Or her flaming copper-coloured hair, which practically screamed 'I'm a randy red-head'? Or maybe it was just the simple fact that no man on the planet can resist a random kiss from a gorgeous girl on a dancefloor.

Angie is now a respectable married woman, so her P&D days are well and truly behind her. But, good Lord, we had some fun watching her in action back in the day.

Anyhoo, with a little help from Kylie and her expert pashing tuition, I now pride myself on my kissing ability. And I've certainly put that training to very good use over the years during my decades-long, frog kissing crusade.

Where the Men Are

When it comes to dishing out advice on how and where to meet men, I'd like to respectfully ask my smug married friends to please shut the fuck up. Especially if you feel the need to share this particularly unhelpful pearl of wisdom: 'Listen, darl, you've just got to stop *looking*. Because that's when love will find you.'

I've heard this one from my married girlfriends over the years, collectively, no less than around 4 million times. And each time I hear it, I sit there smiling at my dear friend's smug little face and nodding politely, while secretly thinking about how to break into her smug little house while she's sleeping, find her smug little wedding dress and rip it to shreds. Yes, it can be surprisingly easy to call off the search party *if you have made the decision to take a break from dating and you have absolutely zero interest in meeting anyone*. But it's a completely different story *if you really, really, really would like to find your person*. We might tell you we're not looking. Hell, we might even tell *ourselves* we're not looking. But the fact is, we are *always* looking.

You cannot simply flick your internal 'seeking love and companionship' switch to the off position. Anyone who's ever been single for an extended period of time knows it's impossible to just stop looking. You are always on alert. Every time you leave the house.

This does not imply a sense of desperation. It's simply (and feel free to blame this on every rom-com ever made) about remaining optimistic that you just might just stumble across your future husband anywhere, anytime, in a moment of perfect serendipity. Perhaps even when you least expect it. Maybe in the unlikeliest of places.

Which is why I spent two hours blow-drying my hair and painstakingly applying a full face of makeup before arriving at the hospital to have my gall bladder removed. I convinced myself that this was perfectly acceptable behaviour.

It was also the first time I'd ever had any type of surgery and I had no idea how many people, or who, might be staring down at me while I lay there unconscious on the operating table. What if my anaesthetist was single and he looked like Patrick from *Offspring*? Why shouldn't I look my best while having an organ removed?

My makeup actually looked pretty good that day, too. And my hair sat just the way I like it, even *post*-surgery (miracles *can* happen). But I left the hospital the following day, with one less organ and no new love in my heart.

My gorgeous girlfriend Shelley *never* leaves the house without a full face of makeup. If she's going for a run around the park at 7 a.m., she's up at 6 a.m. to blow-dry her hair, fix her face and apply fake lashes. I always thought it was a touch ambitious to think you could meet someone while out running. I mean, how is he even supposed to notice you or get your attention as you whiz past? But this actually happened to another friend as she was enjoying her power walk along the Bondi to Bronte scenic coastal track. A man walked up beside her and said, 'I notice you walking here every morning and I'd really like to take you out. Here's my number. Call me if you're interested.' And she did. And they ended up dating for a few years.

My friend Nina once met a guy at a wake. It was a funeral for an old schoolfriend, and a guy she hadn't seen in twenty years showed up looking much finer than she remembered. They ended up sharing what they agreed was an entirely appropriate, if somewhat overly affectionate, send-off for their old mate.

See – it *can* happen. Anywhere. Anytime.

If you've ever been a single woman in Sydney or Brisbane for any extended period of time, someone has probably suggested that the best place for you to meet men is . . . in Melbourne. Yeah, thanks. Like *that's* helpful.

I discovered, quite by accident, that the cute little town of Portsea (ninety minutes' drive *south* of Melbourne) might just be the pick-up capital of Australia. More men hit on me during one eventful night at the local pub in Portsea than in some entire years in Sydney.

First there was 'Sandy', the young surfer dude. After he flicked his blond dreadlocks in my direction, his opening lines were a) Are you that girl from the telly? and b) Come here often? Not a good start, but at least he had a go. He was young. He'd learn.

'Randy', the fitness trainer with an awkward sense of dress, offered to take me sailing. I was willing to overlook the fact that he had his jeans pulled up too high. I even turned a blind eye to the matching snakeskin shoes and belt (bless). But I declined his kind offer after discovering that a) he had a girlfriend and b) she'd been standing 3 metres from us the whole time he'd been chatting me up.

'McSleazy' was a handsome guy in his forties who had an obvious love affair with his own chest. Too many buttons undone for my liking. He also talked too much. In less than five minutes, he told me that a) he'd just had the 'best conversation of his life' with two large-breasted women and b) they'd been discussing porn. I moved on.

'Mr Big' was a late yet promising arrival. Tall, dark, kind of handsome. We chatted for only fifteen minutes before he a) told me I was going to be his 'future wife' and b) offered to fly me to Fiji first class the following weekend for our first date. Tempting, I agree (especially if I suddenly discovered a thirst for kava). But a little too intense. And kind of desperate.

'Bob' the builder from Ballarat, was the cute guy with the cheeky smile who engaged me in the most witty and charming conversation I'd had with a bloke in a long time. He had me in stitches for two hilarious hours, before a) asking ever so politely for my number and b) asking even more politely for a kiss under the full moon.

Bob from Ballarat definitely won the contract that night.

My Mok Moment

There's another charming little saying every single gal has heard during extended periods of singledom, usually by some well-meaning smug married friend or a parent. 'You really need to get out there, darl. Mr Right is not going to come knocking on your front door.'

Of course, I realise this is 100 per cent true. I live in an apartment on the eighth floor of an inner-city building with fortress-like security. There's security to get into the building, second-level security to make it into the lift, and third-level security to get through my front door. So the chance of my dream guy somehow making it through Fort Knox and randomly knocking on my door on the eighth floor are slim to none.

Okay. More like none.

Unless he moves in next door. Or, if he's the Thai delivery guy, who actually appears at my front door once a week. The Thai delivery guy is really lovely. He's kind of cute. His name is Mok. But, sadly, he's not my guy. He's too young. We have zero chemistry. And, over the years, I do feel like I've spent enough time with him in that brief exchange of food and money to know.

While I haven't found my Happy Ever After with the guy who delivers my vegetarian laksa, Mok has taught me a valuable lesson about love (other than reinforcing that my dream guy will *not* come knocking on my front door). My beloved furchild, Lolli, gets *crazy* excited whenever Mok arrives. It's the same ritual every time. She hears the security buzzer to signal his arrival at the building and she starts barking. It's a bark I've come to recognise as different to the others. It's a bark of pure anticipation.

There are many people who ring my buzzer each week (clearly not a metaphor), so I'm not sure how Lolli knows it's Mok. But she does. She must hear a unique tone in my voice when I answer the buzzer – something that subliminally says, 'Yippee, the delicious Thai dinner that I didn't have to cook myself is here. Get. In. My. Belly!'

So after I've let Mok into the building, Lolli barks and barks and barks at the top of her little lungs until I let her out into the hallway where she sits, on the edge of her paws, staring at the lift door, willing it to open. She sits there waiting as if her little life depends on it. Body upright. Tail wagging. Laser-like focus. Waiting for the lift door to open. And Mok to appear.

And when that lift door finally opens to reveal Mok (with my tasty Thai treats), Lolli literally jumps for joy. I love watching this interaction. It always makes me smile. Mok's arrival fills Lolli with the kind of happiness and pure joy I imagine you feel for a great romantic love.

So this is what I've learned: my dream guy will never randomly come knocking at my front door. But when I do meet a guy and I'm standing in my hallway on the eighth floor waiting for him to step out of the lift, I hope to be feeling the level of excitement and anticipation and happiness and joy that Lolli feels in that moment, when she's waiting for Mok.

Speculums and Sliding Doors

While I've never had a handsome stranger come knocking at my front door, I did have one randomly knock on my car window once.

I'd just returned to my car after running errands in the busy business district of North Sydney. I was about to drive off when I heard a tap on my window. A stranger was standing there, motioning with his hands for me to wind down the window. I immediately thought there was a problem with my engine or I'd left my handbag on the roof. Why else would a complete stranger be knocking on my window? So I rolled it down and, rather timidly, the man leaned in and said, 'Hello, I was just wondering if I could take you to lunch?'

No introduction. No small talk. Just a knock on the window and an invitation to eat. Very forward, indeed! I'd never seen the guy before in my life. He was dressed in a nice suit and he looked professional and harmless (and handsome) enough, but there was no way in hell I was going to just saunter off and have lunch with a complete stranger. So I freaked out and drove off at high speed. As if the guy had actually leaned in and said, 'Hello, Samantha I would very much like to cut your body up into little pieces and eat your intestines with some fava beans and a nice chianti.'

*

One of the most memorable TV commercials from my childhood was an ad for antiperspirant, in which a girl walks past a stranger, and he is so captivated by the delicious scent coming from her underarms that he chases her down the street to give her a bunch of flowers. I remember being totally enchanted by such a wonderfully spontaneous and mysteriously romantic gesture and at the same time thinking something like that would never happen in real life.

But when it *did* happen to me (well . . . sort of), it just felt creepy. In fact, the more I thought about it, the more I started to panic. Had the guy been following me? And, if so, for how long? How did I know he wasn't a serial killer? Or a Scientologist?

It takes a brave woman to go on a date with a total stranger. I'll only accept a date with someone I've already met, or researched online or been introduced to through mutual acquaintances. I like to know at least *something* about that person (age, interests, job) that might indicate we have some kind of connection. When the guy who approaches you has never met you and knows absolutely nothing about you, you can only assume that it is based on physical attraction alone. Which should probably be really flattering.

But instead, I saw it as disconcerting and a little desperate.

Later, I wondered if I did the wrong thing by driving away so hastily. Should I have been impressed by a man who had the balls to take a risk, in that spontaneous, 'sliding door' moment, rather than let the moment pass him by, as so many of us do? We've all had a sliding door moment (or three), haven't we? When you feel an inexplicable, undeniable attraction to a complete stranger and for one fleeting moment, you wonder, Should I say something? Should I get their attention? If I let this moment pass, I may never see that person again. Your decision, in that moment, could change your destiny. But instead, you do nothing, and your destiny is just a dirty big 'what-if'. Most of us choose the second option, because

I guess living with a dirty big 'what-if' is easier to deal with than a big fat rejection.

Maybe the reason I've been single so often and for so long is because I don't take enough chances. That stranger knocking on my car window might have turned out to be the greatest love affair of my life.

But in my defence, he caught me at an especially unfortunate moment. I'd just walked out of my GP's office after getting a pap smear. So I was feeling about as desirable as a warm glass of champagne. And to make matters worse, it was one of those really hideous paps, where the doc missed on her first attempt so she had to have a *second* try. Lucky me! If this has ever happened to you, you'll know that you don't leave the doctor's office feeling fabulous and flirty after you've had a giant speculum shoved up your vag. Twice.

That stupid speculum may just have ruined the most spectacular sliding door moment of my life. I guess I'll never know.

Pads Are a Passion Killer

I once felt that unexpected, inexplicable and yet undeniable spark of chemistry with a guy I met randomly in a café. The conversation started veering into some oh-so-subtle flirty territory, but then we reached the 'so what do you do' part of the exchange. And, suddenly, the hot guy was talking to me about pads.

Without a hint of embarrassment or inhibition, he told me that he owned a company that made sanitary napkins.

I pretended not to be totally weirded out by it all. Like I talk about pads with hot guys every other day. We actually had a fairly lengthy discussion about them and he seemed very knowledgeable about all things of a sanitary nature. He explained that his company produced more of the adult nappy–type pads than the regular, straight-up period pads. There's more money to be made with the oldies, he told me. Supply could barely keep up with demand from retirement villages and hospitals.

And it was sometime around *that* point, while we were discussing lady periods and old peoples' poo, that I realised . . . this guy's just not into me. Everyone knows pads are a passion killer. The fact that this guy was discussing pads with me so openly clearly indicated that he was not interested in getting into *my* pants at all.

Maybe my assumption was wrong. I mean, if the guy really did own a sanitary pad company, why should he lie about it? It actually sounded like a very profitable venture. But can we all please agree that it's an incredibly unsexy business for a man to work in? How would I possibly tell my friends that I was dating the 'pad guy'? Imagine the nicknames they'd give him? Menstrual Man. The Pad Prick. Sami's Sanitary Sexbomb. They would dine out on that one for years. (Oh yes, rest assured my friends have had *way* too much fun making up naughty monikers for all the guys I've dated over the years. They treat it like some kind of sport.)

'Director of The Pad Factory' is not even the most bizarre occupation I've heard from a guy in the dating arena.

I found myself at a cosy little bar in Sydney's CBD after a long boozy lunch, where I met a tall, handsome (in a nerdy way) stranger. This time, when we reached the 'so what do you do' part of the exchange, he said, 'I'm a butterfly doctor'.

I laughed in his face and called bullshit on his occupation, although I was secretly impressed that he'd come up with such a creative twist on the more commonly used 'dolphin trainer'.

But, straight-faced and perfectly sober, the guy insisted that he was, in fact, a *butterfly doctor*.

I simply could not process what he was telling me. And I couldn't stop giggling at how ridiculous it sounded. It just didn't seem possible. Is there really a need for butterfly specialists in the veterinary profession? Do they need tiny little operating tables? Did butterflies even live long enough to require medical assistance? Why would anyone bother?

But he wasn't laughing. 'I'm actually not a vet,' he explained. 'I have a PhD specialising in the study of butterflies.'

Okaaaay then, so you're *that* kind of doctor.

Actual job title: 'Lepidopterist', he told me. A person who studies the nature, behaviour and habitats of moths and butterflies.

He said he thought 'lepidopterist' didn't sound sexy enough and most people didn't know what it was anyway (you got that right, buddy!), so he just went with the much simpler job description of 'butterfly doctor' instead.

Not terribly sexy either, if you ask me. But at least it's better than Menstrual Man.

So, in my slightly buzzed, post-long-lunch state, I decided to have some fun. 'So you're the guy who really can make butter fly?' I laughed. 'That's actually a really fly job.' Ha ha ha ha ha! 'So when you walk into a bar, is it easy for you to spot the *most* social butterflies?' I thought I was hilarious.

Conversation with the Butterfly Doc sort of stalled when it became embarrassingly clear that we didn't share the same sense of humour. I decided to move on. The lovely lepidopterist didn't give me butterflies anyway. (Boom-tish!)

Fake Jobs

My girlfriends and I went through a phase of making up fake jobs when we were out on the town meeting men. Yes, it was every bit as silly as it sounds and we found it wildly amusing. However, what started out as harmless fun developed into a really interesting social experiment and an intriguing study in human nature. The way people react and respond to you when you tell them what you do for a living can tell you a lot about them.

I've told guys I'm a dog catcher for the city council. That one always gets a raised eyebrow – they usually don't believe me. I've said I'm the person who sits at the end of the production line at the Cadbury's Chocolate Factory in Tasmania, measuring the Picnic bars to make sure they're not one millimetre longer than they're supposed to be (I've heard that was a real job, by the way). Some guys actually believe that one.

I especially enjoyed watching men's reactions when I told them I was a heart surgeon. Usually, they'd straight up laugh in my face, which was actually pretty rude. Why couldn't I be a heart surgeon at face value? My tertiary entrance score was *almost* high enough to get me into Medicine at uni. The one time a guy didn't react when I told him I was a cardiovascular surgeon was when he told me that he was one too (a *real* one, I assume). I reckon I held up my end of the conversation fairly convincingly until he started asking for my opinion about invasive versus non-invasive surgery. That was my cue to leave.

I decided to stop telling guys I was a heart surgeon after I casually mentioned it to a fellow once and his eyes filled with tears as he spent the next five minutes praising me with gratitude for my profession, because a triple bypass had just saved his father's life. Seeing the admiration and respect in his eyes and hearing all that tender emotion in his voice after I had just flat out lied to him for shits and giggles was not a pleasant experience. I'm a terrible person, I thought to myself. And now the only thing worse than telling him I'm a heart surgeon would be confessing that I'm not a heart surgeon at all. I bought him a beer and did a runner.

Surprisingly, one of my most convincing fake jobs has been hostage negotiator. I was inspired to give this one a go after a lawyer I know attended a course at Harvard, where one of her lecturers was an *actual* hostage negotiator. Apparently lawyers can learn all kinds of valuable skills and awesome tools from the experts in this field. Who knew?

Well I thought hostage negotiator sounded like an especially awesome and glamorous profession, so I decided I would quite like to be a fake one. Now and then.

I must be really convincing in the role too, because no one has ever questioned it. They usually seem super interested. I've even made up a whole fake backstory to go with my fake job, about how I used to be a lawyer so it was a natural transition into this field for a master negotiator like myself. See, I'm a terrible person.

There's another profession I'm apparently quite convincing at. One night I was out with a few girlfriends when a young pup sat down and tried valiantly to chat us up. He wasn't focused on any one of us in particular. He was just putting it out there and having a crack at anyone who might be silly (or desperate) enough to take the bait. We told him we were flattered by his attention but we were

'Oh, okay,' I said. 'Yep, it's me.'

Then he said, 'Wow. I can't believe it's Sami Lukis. I used to watch you on the *Today* show . . . back when you were hot!'

I took it as a compliment.

The Ex Files

One of the most dangerous predators I've encountered in the dating jungle is 'the troublemaker ex-girlfriend'.

I'd just started dating a guy who was A-grade, ten-out-of-ten, five-star boyfriend material. He ticked *all* the boxes. Handsome and charming and funny and sexy and an all-round nice guy. We fell madly in love and things got serious pretty quickly.

Unfortunately, one of his exes got her knickers in a twizzle when she heard we were dating, and she embarked on some evil shenanigans to try to win him back.

Her first attempt was apparently to call my boyfriend and inform him that I was a total slutguts because she'd heard that I was dating *three* different guys and he, like, really needed to know, so he wouldn't get hurt.

Well, this ridiculous high-school melodrama was complete bullshit. I was not dating three guys. Bitch, please! Gag me with a spoon!

Luckily it didn't turn into a game of 'she said, she said' because my gorgeous fella agreed that the ex was just jealous and talking total bollocks.

I brushed it off at the time and thought, Wow, that girl really needs to take a chill pill. But girlfriend clearly forgot to get her prescription filled because she then turned up the crazy, tenfold. My boyfriend was mortified when Miss Ex called his *sister* to warn her that old slutguts Sami had been sprung giving a blow job to a colleague under the table during the live telecast of the TV Week Logie Awards. That is what the ex-girlfriend apparently told *my new boyfriend's family*. What a completely heinous thing to do!

Look, I can appreciate that seeing the man you love with someone new can be tough. And, yes, sometimes women do desperate things to try to rekindle a lost love. But on a scale of one to the-astronaut-who-was-so-desperate-to-get-to-her-lover-that-she-drove-across-America-in-an-adult-nappy-so-she-didn't-need-to-stop-for-toilet-breaks kind of desperation, Miss Ex was sitting at around an eight. Nudging a nine, even.

To make matters worse, I hadn't even met my boyfriend's family yet. The idea of meeting the parents made me nervous enough already, without having to worry about them thinking I was some kind of Sami Lewinsky freak as well.

And just in case you're wondering about the whole blow job under the table caper? It *never* happened. At the Logies or anywhere else, for that matter!

The craziest thing I've ever done at the Logies was taking off the million-dollar flawless diamond ring I'd been lent for the night and passing it around the table for everyone to try on. Because who *doesn't* want to know what it feels like to wear a million-dollar sparkler, right? It was all fun and games until the security guard who'd been assigned to keep me and the ring company for the evening quietly whispered in my ear, 'If anyone drops that ring or scratches it, it will no longer be flawless. I suggest you put it back on your finger and stop sharing it around like a bag of chips.'

Oops. My bad.

I guess my boyfriend's family must have already suspected that Miss Ex was telling porkies, because I was welcomed into the family from the moment I met them.

This ridiculous ex devilry all happened a very long time ago, but it still saddens me to think about it. Mainly because I just don't understand how a woman could be so despicable to another woman, regardless of how hopelessly lovesick she might be. It's a bit of a shock to realise that mean-spirited, crazy-arse women don't only exist as characters in far-fetched daytime TV soaps. Sometimes they are *real* people who appear in your *real* life and create *real* problems that you cannot prevent. It's how you deal with them that counts.

I've run into Miss Ex several times over the years, and I've never once confronted her about her inexcusable behaviour. That's just not my style. I figure it was revenge enough for her to see me and the tall, handsome stud muffin together and happy for all those years after her pathetic attempts to break us up.

In the end, I got the guy (and I *really* hope she got some help).

The Invisible Love Current

One of the most memorable dates I ever went on was the one where I watched that gorgeous five-star boyfriend fall in love with his future wife.

And I was probably partly responsible.

After three enjoyable years together, my fella went and ruined everything when he started mentioning the 'M' word. He told me he was ready to settle down with a white picket fence and a couple of rugrats in the suburbs. I was not. I loved him deeply and I thought we probably would get married *one day*, but I couldn't ignore a gut feeling that I just wasn't ready to tie the knot.

We had plenty of intense discussions about it and it was the same old argument every time. He'd ask why I didn't want to get married. I'd say it was just a piece of paper and it wasn't going to prove anything. He'd say it would prove that I loved him. I'd say that piece of paper wouldn't make me love him any more than I already did, so why bother? And he'd say if marriage didn't mean anything to *me*, why not just do it because I knew how much it meant to him?

He had a point.

But in a textbook case of passive-aggressive, completely dysfunctional manipulation, I'd suggest that *he* must be the one with the problem, not me. We lived together. We travelled together. We had great jobs, gorgeous friends, a wonderful relationship. We already had a perfect life. Why couldn't he just be content with the way things were? If he needed to be married to feel secure, maybe *he* actually wasn't happy in the relationship in the first place.

So I guess the relationship was already on shaky ground when we went to a birthday dinner for one of his work colleagues. The night kicked off with drinks in the bar. Just as everyone was invited to sit down for dinner, I popped into the bathroom to pee and freshen up. By the time I'd returned, most people were already seated at a long communal table, with about fifteen seats on either side. I was surprised to notice that my boyfriend was already seated and he hadn't saved a seat beside him for *me*. I didn't make a fuss about it because I knew most of his colleagues and friends anyway, so I just plonked myself down in the empty seat diagonally across from him and started chatting to the folks around me.

I wonder if it was fate stepping in with my bladder function that night because those seating arrangments gave me a front-row seat to the love affair unfolding before my very eyes . . . between my boyfriend and the tall, attractive blonde sitting beside him. She was a colleague of his, so they already knew each other. But whenever I'd glance across, I couldn't help noticing that this wasn't just two workmates having a chat. There was a subtle chemistry between them I couldn't ignore. Like an invisible electric love current, drawing them together. I saw the way his eyes lit up as he looked at her. And there was something quite beautiful about the way he focused on her mouth as she spoke. Like he desperately wanted to know what it would feel like to put his lips on hers.

It was such an odd feeling as I sat there watching them, mostly because I didn't feel an ounce of jealousy. I actually felt a bizarre sense of calm about the whole scenario. By the end of the night, the same gut feeling that had been telling me I didn't want to marry him was now telling me that the tall, pretty blonde sitting beside my boyfriend was supposed to be his wife. And I was totes okay with it.

I told my best friend the next day that I was ready to break up with my boyfriend, because I'd just met his future wife. She thought I'd fallen out of the stupid tree and hit every branch on the way down. 'That's insane, Sam. He loves *you*. It's so obvious. He wants to marry *you!*'

'Nope,' I insisted. 'He *thinks* he wants to marry me. But he's meant to be with *her*. Trust me!'

I broke up with him a few weeks later. And I wasn't the least bit shocked when I found out that he had started dating the tall, pretty blonde from the birthday dinner not long after. Just as I'd predicted.

It did briefly occur to me that they might have been having an affair already when I saw them together that night. But, to be honest, I couldn't care less. It seemed perfectly inevitable that they would end up together anyway. He didn't look at me the way he looked at her.

A couple of years later he married her. Last I heard, they're still together with a couple of gorgeous kids. And I'm genuinely happy for him, and for her.

It must be super inconvenient to meet 'The One' when you're already with somebody else. This also happened to a friend's mum back in the 1960s when she agreed to attend a premarital counselling course at the local church with her fiancé and ended up falling in love with the counsellor. The very thing that was supposed to provide the young couple with a strong foundation for their future was the catalyst for their breakup.

She simply couldn't deny the strength of that invisible love current, so she dumped the fiancé, cancelled the wedding and married the marriage counsellor instead. And they're still together fifty years, four kids and eleven grandkids later.

Lucky she didn't let an unfortunate inconvenience, like the fact that she was engaged to someone else, stand in the way of her happiness.

You really can't fight the strength of that invisible love current.

True love for the win, right?

Dating Hand Grenades

If life occasionally throws you curve balls, I think it's fair to say the dating process can sometimes lob hand grenades at you.

If you're lucky, you'll be able to dodge those nasty missiles. But if you end up directly in the line of fire, they can blow up, rather awkwardly, in your face.

A girlfriend of mine once nervously turned up to a blind date, to discover she'd been set up with a dwarf. She was shocked, to say the least. At no stage throughout the entire set-up process had anyone thought to mention that her blind date was, in fact, a little person. You know, like 'Tom is thirty-five. He works in finance. Loves to travel. He's been single for nine months. Oh, and he's three foot four. You're cool with that, right?'

After briefly toying with the idea of leaving, she realised that would be insanely rude and downright offensive. She told herself to stop being so judgemental. He was probably a lovely guy. So she decided to go ahead with the date. He bought her a drink. They chatted. He seemed fun. She was quite enjoying his company. And then, out of the blue he said, 'Yeah. I'm going to be really honest with you. I'll only fuck girls who are a size six to eight. And I quite like Asian.'

My friend is a healthy size ten to twelve. And she looks about as Asian as Cameron Diaz.

She never saw him again.

My gorgeous friend Danielle was getting understandably frustrated by her fella's casual attitude to dating. Despite seeing each other for almost twelve months, they still only caught up once a week. Sometimes she'd go a week or two without hearing from him at all. Then one night, when she was lying in his arms after some especially awesome sex, he hit her with this grenade: 'You know, Danielle, if your weight didn't fluctuate so much, I might be able to get serious about you.'

She lay there stunned and humiliated, in total disbelief that the man she had just been so intimate (and naked) with, could be so rude, crude and insensitive. She didn't hear from the fuckbucket for a week. And when he called her to beg for forgiveness, it pains me to tell you that Danielle accepted his apology and took him back! I know, right? Sometimes love isn't just blind. It's deaf as well.

Four months later, he left her for another woman, who was a size 2.

I found myself on the receiving end of a memorable foot-in-mouth moment while on a blind date with a not-so-charming fella named Dan. Dan's sister Dee offered to set us up. I didn't know Dee really well, but I'd met her a few times and she seemed like a cool chick. So I agreed to meet her brother for dinner, on the proviso that Dee and her boyfriend join us as well.

On the day of the date, I bought a new dress but then I still couldn't decide what to wear so I called a friend several times to workshop my outfit. Then I spent another hour doing my hair and makeup so I could look as desirable as possible. I hadn't been on a date in forever and I really wanted to impress.

Dan arrived for our date forty-five minutes late, completely dishevelled and hammered. Not quite Charlie Sheen wasted, but he did proudly confess to coming straight from a seven-hour 'business' lunch. We all laughed about the fact that he'd arrived in that state for our date, and Dee warned her little brother to be on his best behaviour. But just after main course (and another four vodka sodas), Dan started ranting about how he really wished he'd been set up with *another* friend of Dee's – a girl he'd apparently fancied for a while. 'Whatever happened to that hottie friend of yours, Michelle?' he asked Dee. 'When are you going to set me up with *her*, like you promised? She's such a babe.'

Dee tried to tactfully change the subject, but little bro wouldn't let up. He went on and on and on about how smoking hot her *other* friend was and how he *really* wanted to go on a date with *her* and why wouldn't she just make it happen already?

Meanwhile I sat there feeling completely invisible. I was mortified.

Um, buddy, can you fucking not? I wanted to scream. Because I'm the girl she *did* set you up with. And I'm not sure if you've noticed, but I'm sitting *here*. On a *date*. With *you*. Right *now*.

But dear old Dan wouldn't stop carrying on until Dee finally, sheepishly, agreed to set him up with the hottie. And then she very quickly changed the subject.

I had somehow found myself on a blind date with Sydney's rudest, most passive-aggressive man, but his message couldn't have been any clearer. Dan just wasn't into me. He was either too drunk, too rude or just too clueless to see how awkward the situation was for me. Or maybe he just missed the memo on how to be a decent person.

I certainly wasn't going to cause a scene or let the idiot know how much he'd hurt and humiliated me. Luckily, I'd had a few wines by that stage, so I was sufficiently buzzed to see the funny side of it. And as I sat there, amused, for the remainder of dinner, I couldn't decide who I felt more sorry for: his sister Dee or the poor girl she was setting Dan up with next.

Yeah, good luck with that, Michelle!

A Moment of Clarity

There are certain things a guy should *never* do on a date. Openly admit that he'd rather be on a date with someone else, for starters.

Also, he should not pick his nose. Eat it. Fart. Perve at other women. These actions should only be attempted in front of the opposite sex after you've known each other a *really* long time (and even then guys, please don't pick your nose and eat it in front of me. Ever.)

I discovered something else men shouldn't do during the early getting-to-know-you phase, courtesy of a guy I'd been out with a few times. After dinner on our third date, Jack suggested we head to one of his favourite bars. Imagine my surprise, upon entering the venue, to discover it was a strip joint.

At first glance, it could have been any other club, with pumping music, trendy leather lounges and dim lighting. But that was before I spotted the *completely naked* woman on the stage, demonstrating her impressive flexibility, rather enthusiastically, on a pole.

We got a drink and I sat there awkwardly, trying to work out why on earth a guy would bring me to a strip club on our third date (and how on earth Kristal could possibly get her foot behind her ear like that). I noticed some other half-dressed women leading guys through a little hidden side door. Jack told me that was the 'private room', where the dancing is performed in a more personal setting. 'A bit of touching's allowed,' he said, 'but no sex.'

After initially trying to pretend he'd only 'heard' about the special room from some of his mates, he fessed up to being in there himself. A few times. 'Bucks' nights.'

Yeah. Sure. Whatevs.

Sometimes, in the early stages of dating, a guy says or does something that's a major no-no. It's in that moment that you just know this guy will never, ever see you in the big white dress. A moment of perfect clarity. A moment of 'You and Me. Will Never Be'. Different strokes for different folks, and all that. But taking me to a strip club on our third date is a very good indication that you and me are not meant to be.

My friend Kerry's moment of clarity came on her third date with a 26-year-old backhoe driver. He'd suggested they grab some takeaway and watch a movie at home. He chose *Top Gun* and then he sat on the couch next to her making aeroplane noises, loudly, throughout the entire movie. She felt like she was on a date with a toddler. She never saw him again.

Another friend was invited by a guy to his favourite Mexican restaurant in Bondi for their second date. When the bill came, he produced a Shop A Docket with a two-for-one voucher and used it to pay for *his* half of the bill. She knew, in that moment, that there was no future for them.

One of the most unsavoury turn-offs happened to my dear friend Penny, on her very first date with a high-profile Sydney businessman. After a lovely dinner at a posh restaurant, he drove her home in his Porsche convertible. But, as he pulled up outside her apartment building, he boldly asked if she would prefer to go back to his place instead. She laughed it off and said, 'No, thank you. Not tonight. But thanks for a lovely evening. And thanks for dropping me home.'

Now, instead of jumping out of the car and racing around to open her car door and say a gentlemanly good night, he just sat there in the driver's seat and said, 'Are you absolutely *sure* you don't want to come home with me?'

'Yes, I'm very sure,' she replied politely.

And that's when she noticed that somehow, during that brief exchange, he had managed to unzip his trousers. And he was sitting there, with his right hand in his pants, slowly stroking his exposed, semi-erect penis. He watched her gaze down at his dick, so *he* knew that *she* knew exactly what he was doing. But he didn't stop. He just sat there in the driver's seat of his Porsche convertible, wanking, before he leaned across to her and said, 'How could you *possibly* leave me now?'

'Um. Quite easily,' she replied. 'Watch me!' And she bolted.

As completely feral as that whole experience was for poor Penny, I guess the really positive thing to come out of this story is confirmation that Porsche drivers really are wankers. Because, ladies, now we know for sure.

The Business Lunch/Date

I'd been invited out to lunch by one of the bosses at the TV station where I was working at the time to discuss my 'future at the network'.

This was a *major* deal. I'd been working my little butt off, hoping the television superpowers would notice me and decide I was most definitely destined for bigger and better things. So that lunch invitation was a promising indication that my career was heading in the right direction.

I wore the Cue suit I'd bought specially for the occasion. Back then, Cue was the go-to store for the trendiest female corporate attire. I had never worked in the corporate arena, but I hoped my new suit would exude a Jana Wendt level of professionalism, ambition and credibility.

Lunch got off to a cracking start. We discussed my job, the show I was working on and the general goings-on at the network. Just after main course, the mood changed slightly as Mr TV leaned across the table and with a weird smirk, said 'So . . . you're a journalist?'

'Yes, I am,' I replied, wondering why he didn't already know that. 'I graduated with a Bachelor of Business Communication with majors in Journalism and Film and Television Studies from the Queensland University of Technology.'

'Impressive,' he purred. 'So I guess that means you're good with words?'

'Well, I hope so.' I laughed. 'My career kind of depends on it.'

By this stage, I was convinced that my Jana Wendt Cue suit was working its magic and he was about to offer me a job reading the prime-time news.

But instead, he leaned a little closer, like he wanted to tell me a really big secret, and said, 'Do you know what my *favourite* word is?'

Awkward silence.

I mean, what sort of question is that? There are more than 170 000 words in the English dictionary. How could I possibly guess his *favourite*? Was it a trick question? Did my future at the network depend on knowing the answer? Would Jana Wendt know the word? Good god! What could it be? 'Television'? 'Winklepicker'? 'Kakorrhaphiophobia'?

But instead, I just said, 'Umm. No, I don't know what your favourite word is.'

And then he leaned even further across the table, leered at me intently and, in a deep, suggestive, growling voice, said, '*Moist*.'

Yikes.

That's a word that makes most women cringe. It's up there alongside 'discharge' in the repulsive zone.

So why the hell was this guy forcing it into our conversation over a *business lunch*? Was he deliberately trying to make me feel uneasy? Or was it an attempt to steer our conversation down that suggestive little path towards his casting couch? Was he just throwing it out there to see if I might bite? I know for sure he wasn't about to invite me for a game of Scrabble.

After clearing the little bit of vomit that had surfaced in the back of my throat, I laughed out loud, like it was the funniest joke I'd ever heard. And then I quickly changed the topic. I'm a nervous talker. When I don't know what to say, I somehow manage to talk incessantly.

I'm not even sure how the words come out of my mouth. But they just keep coming. I guess it's my superpower (my other superpower is making champagne disappear, by the way).

We finished lunch without further incident. He didn't bring it back up and we never spoke about it again.

A friend had a similar experience after she'd just started working at a popular radio station. A well-known announcer at the station, who also happened to be much older, invited her out to lunch. She was flattered and honoured to spend time with a man she had respected for so long. But as their business lunch was winding up, the dirty old man leaned over to her and said, 'I get the feeling our relationship could be like a ride in a Ferrari. Fast, exciting and fun while it lasts. I've booked us a room at the hotel around the corner. Let's go.' Ewwwwww.

I was too embarrassed to tell anyone about my lunch experience for a long time. I felt like a fool for even agreeing to the meeting in the first place. Maybe it wasn't a business lunch at all. Had I been on a *date* with my boss without even realising it? Was I somehow supposed to know that 'let's discuss your future at the network' is television-executive-code for 'let's discuss your future in my bedroom'?

I never called the guy out over his inappropriate 'business' lunch chat. At the time I tried to brush it off by convincing myself he'd done nothing wrong. It was just one little word, after all. But I couldn't deny that that one little word had made me feel . . . I guess the best word to describe how I felt in that moment is . . . 'icky'.

So I walked away from that lunch feeling icky and vulnerable and a little bit confused, which was in stark contrast to the excitement, pride and optimism I'd felt when I'd arrived that day in my brand-new, perfectly pressed Cue suit.

But it also made me determined to work even harder and be noticed for all the *right* reasons. Which I most certainly was.

Big Brother

My TV prime time break was when I was offered the gig as the roving reporter on the very first Aussie series of *Big Brother*. During each Sunday night eviction show, I'd report live from *BB* parties around the country or from the family homes of the housemates as Gretel Kileen hosted the show from the studio on the Gold Coast.

That role gave me the opportunity to really hone my skills in live television and I loved it. At first I was petrified, knowing that if something went wrong, I wouldn't be able to just stop, press rewind and do it again. But I quickly became addicted to the adrenaline rush of live TV and I discovered the best way to do my job was to always expect the unexpected.

One thing I *never* expected to happen on that show was to fall in love with one of the housemates.

One of my few long-term boyfriends became an 'accidental' celebrity when he appeared on that first series of the show. Pete Timbs was one of the earliest alumni of reality television. They had no idea they were about to become household names. Pete didn't go on *Big Brother* to be famous. He was just a guy working in a bottle shop who was a bit bored one day so he applied for some random radio competition.

And, next thing he knew, he was living with eleven strangers in a fake house at Dreamworld.

That first *BB* series was a huge hit. Australian TV audiences had never seen anything like it. Viewers either loved or loathed the housemates, especially the stand-out star, Sara-Marie, and her kooky bunny ears. It was also the year that introduced us to the first series winner, Ben, the hunky runner-up, Blair, who propelled himself into an acting gig on *Neighbours*, and the gorgeous Jemma, who launched her own line of lip gloss. Pete made a name for himself by engaging in some very public 'doona dancing' with another housemate, Christina.

Pete and I met the night he was evicted from the house and we struck up a friendship immediately. Despite hooking up and then breaking up with Christina while they were on the show (awks!), he was an instantly likeable guy.

It took us both by surprise, a few months later, when our friendship developed into a romantic relationship. I can't even remember exactly how it happened. It was just a natural progression for two people who were already great mates and really enjoyed each other's company.

We were together for almost two years and Pete was one of the loveliest boyfriends I've ever had. He was kind and attentive and always a true gentleman.

While we were dating, I got the gig as the weather presenter on the *Today* show at Channel Nine, which meant I was out of town, on location, up to five days each week. But Pete would always go over to my apartment before I got home from another long work trip and ensure the place was clean and tidy and the fridge was stocked with my favourite things. 'Cause that's just the kind of delightfully thoughtful human being he is.

When the Sydney gossip writers found out we were dating, we became the focus of some pretty serious media attention. People started calling us a 'celebrity couple' and we suddenly found ourselves being invited to every red carpet event in town. For a while there, you couldn't scan the Sydney social pages without seeing a photo of us arm in arm, smiling like goofballs and scoffing champagne at some fancy soiree. Someone even wrote an article naming us the couple you most needed to have at your event if you wanted guaranteed press coverage. I mean, seriously? A weather girl and a *Big Brother* housemate? It was completely ludicrous.

I'm probably not supposed to admit it, but I think we both secretly enjoyed the attention. It made us feel a bit like Brad and Ange (pre-splitsville) at times. Thankfully, it didn't affect our relationship. Not one little bit. Not even after Pete scored a modelling gig in a national campaign for Jeanswest and was plastered half naked on huge billboards all over the country. He was a handsome guy to begin with, but his sex appeal was only amplified by his *Big Brother* fame and that modelling campaign. He was mobbed by horny female fans at every appearance, and I watched on with a bizarre sense of pride as countless women begged my boyfriend to sign their boobs.

I'd never had a boyfriend who had his own groupies. And I'm surprised it didn't turn me into the green-eyed 'you said you'd call at seven and it's now 7.02, so who is she?' type. But Pete always made me feel 100 per cent secure.

I know some people might assume that anyone on *Big Brother* would be a fame-hungry fool, but I can honestly say that Pete is one of the smartest, sharpest, most outgoing, down-to-earth people I've ever known. This became even clearer to me one night when we attended a black tie charity fundraiser. I was seated with Pete to my left and a well-respected brain surgeon to my right. The three of us chatted all night and at the end of the evening, just before the brain guy got up to leave, he leaned across me, handed his business card to Pete and said, 'It was so great to meet you. Please let me know if you would ever consider donating your brain to science.'

Yes, you read that right. The surgeon actually leaned across me (deliberately bypassing *my* brain in the process), to ask my boyfriend for *his* brain. And it wasn't a joke. The guy was fucking serious.

It's one of the most hilariously humiliating things that's ever happened to me. I was totally insulted that the guy didn't want my brain for research – *I* thought I'd engaged in some fabulously interesting and witty repartee.

But I also felt the same level of intense pride for my fella as I did when women begged him to sign their boobs. Weird, huh?

So why wasn't Pete my Mr Happily Ever After? There was no cheating or lying or celebrity scandal to divulge. We just agreed that we didn't have that 'great love' for one another and we'd be better off as friends. Seriously, no pun intended when I say he felt more like my big brother than my boyfriend.

We're still mates to this day. Pete married a gorgeous woman and they're happily married with two adorable daughters.

I really hope Pete does donate his brain to science one day. Future generations of young men could learn an awful lot from that guy about how to be an all-round awesome bloke.

The Cashed-Up Prince Charming

The most enjoyable and rewarding job I've ever had was working as the travelling weather presenter on the *Today* show for three wonderful years. It was also a deceivingly demanding role. Viewers would only see my happy, smiling face as I presented the weather for a few minutes every hour, but it could be incredibly stressful behind the scenes. The early mornings, long days and hours of travel between locations, combined with the pressure of trying to create six different entertaining and enjoyable segments each day, was a huge challenge for me. A couple of minor-meltdowns aside, I loved my job. And I saw more of Australia in those three years than most people get to experience in a lifetime.

It also came to my attention pretty quickly that when you're beaming into people's homes daily on a national breakfast TV show, the viewers either adore you or they despise you. I received some hilarious hate mail. Like the scathing letter from the woman who told me I was the worst presenter on TV because she didn't like my hair. Or the guy who wrote in to tell me I looked 'grotesque'. Or the person who sent me this typewritten letter, which actually resembled a ransom note:

```
Listen Samie Lucas (sic) and take serious
note. For no valid reasons you always laugh
```

> and giggle like a kookaburra none stop (sic).
> When you do such acts you give us very big
> shits. We are sick and tired to watch.
> So stop this as much as possible. Get another job
> where your laughing is useful and justified.

My favourite was from someone named Jo (I couldn't work out if Jo was a man or a woman) who wrote directly to the Executive Producer of the *Today* show with a very serious concern about my presenting ability.

> Sami Lukis, your weather presenter, would have to
> be the most flat-chested woman on television. She
> looks revolting. Surely you can find someone out
> of 20 million people in Australia with a normal
> set of breasts. Get her off TV. You'd think that
> with all the money she's making she could afford
> $5000 to pay for breast implants.

So it turns out that the five years I spent at university getting my Bachelor's Degree in Communication (with distinction) was a complete waste of time. I could have saved myself a lot of unnecessary study if I'd known that the only thing that would truly matter in my career as a journalist was having ginormous tits.

I was delighted to receive my fair share of lovely fan mail as well, which included a large number of requests from men asking me out on dates. I was really appreciative that these guys had taken the time to write to me and I was incredibly flattered that they thought I was date-worthy, but I never accepted any of their offers. (Although I was tempted by the charming invitation I received from a young fella asking if I would accompany him to his Year 10 formal. It was scribbled on the back of his chemistry homework and he'd dotted the 'i' in Sami with a love heart. Bless.)

I never felt comfortable with the idea of going on a date with a 'fan'. I'm sure for the most part they were perfectly lovely gentlemen, but there was always the chance that one might turn out to be a freak who would cut me up into small pieces and store me in his freezer.

One morning I rocked up to the *Today* show office to find the biggest, most breathtakingly beautiful bunch of flowers I'd ever seen from an anonymous admirer. There was one hundred glorious, gigantic red roses and one spectacular single white rose. And the card said: 'Sami, I can think of 100 reasons to call you. I'm hoping you can think of one reason to call me.'

Oh. My. God.

I know, right?

Original. Clever. Sweet.

There was phone number on the card but no name, so I couldn't Google-stalk the guy. I probably should have just dialled the number anyway and found out who this (cashed-up) Prince Charming was immediately. I could certainly think of more than one reason to call him. But I didn't.

Nothing that mysteriously romantic had ever happened to me before. And I was pretty sure it would never happen again. It was the most over-the-top anonymous gesture I'd ever experienced. The effort. The thought that had gone into the card. The extraordinary expense (unless he owned a rose farm?).

Still, this was just another fan. And I felt like if I *did* call him, it would be unfair to the other men who had tried to get my attention by writing me a simple letter. Just because this guy could afford the expensive, extravagant gesture shouldn't guarantee him the date. Should it?

So I didn't call.

But I *did* take the flowers home and fill every vase I owned. And every time I walked in the door, I felt like a complete bitch. Some guy had sent me 101 roses and I didn't even have the decency (or guts) to call him and say thank you.

So imagine my surprise when, exactly one week later, he sent me *another* bunch, with *another* 101 roses. This time, the card said, 'Second attempt at getting your attention.'

I couldn't believe it! This guy sure was persistent (it also seemed a little more likely at this stage that he did, in fact, own a rose farm).

I *knew* I had to call him and say thank you. But that's all. I wouldn't engage him in conversation and I certainly wouldn't go on a date with the guy.

So when I finally got the courage to call and thank him for the flowers, I apologised profusely for not calling sooner and we laughed about the fact that I was probably responsible for a rose shortage across Sydney (he said he did not own a rose farm, by the way).

He told me he'd seen me working out at the gym at the Crown Hotel in Melbourne (I stayed there whenever I was in town on location for the show) but he didn't want to interrupt my workout so he asked one of the gym attendants who I was. She recognised me from the *Today* show and suggested he contact me through Channel Nine. I had assumed he was a fan who'd seen me on TV, but he said he didn't even watch breakfast television. He said he was surprised to find out I was a TV presenter, but relieved that it made it so easy to find me . . . yada yada yada . . . magnificent OTT flower delivery (times two).

I was impressed by the fact that he didn't want to meet me just because he'd seen me on TV. I was flattered by his tenacity. And I was intrigued by his story. Who sends 202 roses to someone they've only ever seen walking on a treadmill? (I also made a mental note to buy three more pairs of the workout pants I was wearing at the time.)

I argue that it would be near-impossible for *any* single woman to walk away from this situation without wanting to know more about the guy who sent her 202 roses. So I momentarily relaxed my 'don't date fans' policy and agreed to meet him for coffee. We lived in different states and I was travelling a lot with the *Today* show at the time so we agreed to meet in the Qantas Lounge at the airport on a day when he was flying into Sydney and I was flying out. In more than thirty years, this is the only date I've ever had in an airport lounge. I actually thought it was a little bit fabulous (and what a hilarious story it would be to tell at our wedding).

As I sat there on date-day, my nerves turned to excitement. I couldn't believe I was doing this. I suddenly couldn't wait to meet the anonymous Prince Charming who'd spotted me at the gym and sent me 101 roses . . . twice. This might turn out to be a pretty epic love story.

However, I realised this *wouldn't* be my fairytale romance from the moment he arrived. It was a total shit soda. He turned up wearing board shorts and thongs. It would have been nice if he'd made some kind of effort in the wardrobe department. I mean, is it too much to expect a guy to wear shoes on a first date?

Plus, there was no spark. Zero chemistry. The conversation was incredibly awkward. For someone who wanted to be anonymous at first, he sure did speak about himself at great length. And he didn't ask me a single thing about myself. Surely if you felt compelled to send 202 roses to a stranger after simply watching her walk on a treadmill, you might actually want to find out a little something about her? I mean, anything?

The entire date was excruciating and weird. I've had more chemistry with my neighbour's pet lizard. He also made sure to drop into conversation early on that his driver had met him at the gate and taken his bags and was waiting for him in his limo downstairs. That turned me off. The completely gratuitous use of the words 'driver' and 'limo' indicated that he was a bit of a muppet. Probably a very wealthy muppet. But a muppet, nonetheless.

The date was so bad that I excused myself at one stage to go and make sure my flight was leaving on time. I'm usually the last person to board the flight (the Sydney Airport boarding announcement people are *very* familiar with my name). But on that day, I was the first person on the plane.

I remember sitting on that flight feeling completely deflated. I knew there was no point in a second date. My cashed-up Prince Charming had the best pre-game of any guy I'd ever met, but his on-field performance was appalling. What had unexpectedly appeared in my life as something so extravagant and promising and romantic had turned out to be yet another big fat fucker of a disappointment.

I was impressed when he told me he owned a very successful company, but I also realised this meant the excessively generous flower delivery probably wasn't a big deal for him. Wealthy guys can spend whatever it takes to try to get what they want.

Well, money might be able to buy you a ridiculously large bunch of roses (or two). But money can't buy you humility. Or a personality. Or, apparently, shoes.

Get a Dingo Up Ya

I've experienced a variety of unique approaches from men over the years. Two hundred and two roses was certainly one way to get my attention. Another was an email sent to the radio station where I was working at the time. It read: 'Sami, I'm the guy who fell on you on the dancefloor on Friday night. Just wondering if I could take you out for dinner sometime?'

Of course I remembered a brief interaction at a bar the previous weekend when a totally wasted guy fell over, on top of me, in the middle of the dancefloor. It's not a moment I could easily forget. I was trapped under him briefly while everyone around us laughed hysterically. He apologised profusely as people peeled him off me, and then he disappeared and I never saw him again. Our entire encounter only lasted about thirty seconds, but I guess he saw that moment as something too precious to ignore. Hence, the 'I fell on you on the dancefloor' email on Monday morning.

I politely declined his invitation, but I had to give the guy credit for a) recognising me in his heavily inebriated state, b) working out how to contact me, and c) seeing the humour in the situation.

Some guys think money talks. One Friday arvo I'd popped into the Char Char Char bar in Brisbane for a few drinks with friends. A rowdy table of well-lubricated suits nearby had clearly enjoyed an extended lunch and were in no rush to get back to the office or home to their wives. One of the guys came over, presented me with two fifty-dollar notes and said, 'Hey, Sami, I'll give you a hundred bucks if you come and talk to my friends.'

Seriously, buddy? Go rent a hooker. What kind of fuckbucket thinks splashing a hundred bucks in a girl's face will make her do whatever he wants? I later found out from the maitre d' that they were a group of lawyers.

Alcohol seems to be a common factor when it comes to random men approaching me. The result can sometimes be hideously offensive. But mostly it's pretty humorous.

My all-time favourite fan moment occurred when I was presenting the weather for the *Today* show on location in the small mining town of Cobar in central western New South Wales. We were set up on the balcony of the local Heritage Centre and I was already aware that a bunch of blokes were having a pretty raucous drinking session about a block away at the Grand Hotel – even though it was only 7 a.m. The local tour guide told us they were probably a group of miners grabbing a cold one (or six) on their way home from the night shift. Well, the boys must have seen the *Today* show on the TV in the pub. And, bloody hell, mate, throw me against the wall and call me a gecko if those blokes didn't notice that the weather girl was right there in Cobar, just up the street!

Which must have been what prompted one of the local lads to poke his head out of the pub just after I finished my weather cross and scream at the top of his lungs, 'Hey, Sami, get a dingo up ya!'

I heard it loud and clear. But I wasn't quite sure how to respond. I can't say I was familiar with that particular turn of phrase, so I couldn't work out if it was intended as a compliment or an insult. Or a proposition from a guy who called himself Dingo?

So I just waved and smiled and gave him the thumbs up. As if random men suggest to me that I shove a wild dog where the sun don't shine, all the time.

Call 1800 Sami

I received more date requests while I was working on the *Today* show than at any other time in my life. Someone screaming, 'Get a dingo up ya' was certainly the most baffling proposition, but it wasn't the only one.

I received mostly letters and emails from viewers, which were sent to Channel Nine. Many of the letters were handwritten, which was a lovely touch, but the way these men presented themselves on paper was often as questionable as the various wooing methods they used.

It did, however, give me an intriguing and often unsettling insight into what men think women are looking for in a mate. I've included some examples below, which we can use as a kind of social experiment to examine the dating psyche of the modern man. They've been grouped into sub-categories, according to the various approach methods deployed.

1800 Sami

In an effort to prove just how serious his adoration was, one guy wrote to tell me he'd applied for the number 1800 SAMI LU (1800 726 458) for his business. I kid you not. I don't know what he was expecting me to do with this information. Or how my name was in any way relevant to his business. I think he fixed air conditioners.

I have noticed that the number is now disconnected, so either old mate never actually registered it or he cancelled it when he realised we were not going to connect in this lifetime.

Paint my face on a rock

One guy expressed his love for me by painting my image on a massive rock at Port Macquarie. He sent me a photo to prove it. The rock was about the size of a washing machine.

Anyone is welcome to paint a rock on the southern breakwall of the Hastings River on the mid New South Wales coast, in what has become a public outdoor art gallery. Most of the rocks are dedicated to deceased family members. The 'Sami' rock featured a painting of a blonde woman holding a *Today* show microphone. I could definitely see some resemblance from the neck up, however I looked a lot more like Pamela Anderson from the neck down (#titsonarock).

Celebrity shag notification

One charmer wrote to inform me that I was one of his three wife-approved celebrity shags. He said that while I was only number two on his list (wedged between Natalie Imbruglia at number one and Avril Lavigne at number three), I should feel pretty good about it, because I had firmly held the number two position for the best part of a decade. He must have thought I provided the best chance out of the three of ever actually happening, so he included his phone number and email address and urged me to contact him anytime because, in his words, 'If it's my celebrity shag, it wouldn't be cheating, after all.'

Write me a song

I was really chuffed when a guy from a band called Carpe Diem wrote to tell me he'd written a song about me, called 'No Sami', and he was hoping for an opportunity to perform the ballad on the *Today* show one morning during my weather cross. I'm not sure why the producers declined his request, considering the song included such profound lyrics as:

> *The weather is atrocious but I really don't care*
> *'Cause it's being presented by the girl with the long blonde hair*
> *The queen of the isobars is standing right there*
> *And I'm sure that is where most other men stare*
> *But there's no Sami, no Sami*
> *There's no Sami Lukis at the weekend.*

Bizarre, right? But in a totally fabulous way!

The song had three more verses, with equally compelling lyrics. Why it never became a number-one hit is beyond me.

Mr Irresistible

Many of the guys felt the need to include details of an important personal trait or skill in their letters. I guess they hoped it would make them irresistible, thereby compelling me to accept their date invitation and get in touch. (All are *actual* excerpts from letters I received.)

> *I've been on the Footy Show doing Air Guitar.*

> *My maintenance for my three children has come down to $50 a week. I was worried about the money side of things. I wouldn't like to let you down.*

> *I own my own car, a 2002 Nissan Pulsar. I am currently living with my parents again.*

> *I'm twenty-eight but I act like a five-year-old.*

I am truly handsome because I have always felt if I am to take care of another, I first must take care of myself.

I am a 36-year-old pro beach bum.

I am a soccer star and more, having coached about 40–50 schools.

I'm the smartest man I know. I am the most modest as well and see myself being absolutely made for you.

I would love to be your boyfriend. I reckon hugs and kisses are more important than sex. I would treat you like a queen with a massage when you got home.

I can help you rebuild the Ford Falcon which is for sale around the corner from my mum and dad's house for $5000.*

Reverse psychology

In what was easily the least effective approach method, one guy wanted to make it very clear that *he* would be doing *me* a massive favour if I did in fact choose to accept his invitation. I call it the 'you snooze, you lose' reverse psychology charm offensive.

You're probably thinking to yourself, stalker, freak etc. Don't get me wrong, I do have better things to do with my time besides emailing Channel 9 weather presenters.

Okay, buddy, I'll remind you that *you're* the random who wrote to a TV presenter you've never met, asking her out on a date. So it

---

*   Context required here: I was appearing on a TV commercial for the new Ford Escape at the time. Bless.

actually does appear quite likely that either you are one chromosome away from being a potato or you *don't* have better things to do with your time.

Stranger Danger

Some of the suitors wanted to assure me they weren't stalkers. Like it's completely normal to write to a woman they've only ever seen present the weather on the television and ask her out. Again, actual excerpts:

> *I am no strange person or anything. I am an executive for a large company and I am good looking.*

> *Please don't be hesitant to write or call because I really am angelic and only want what is best for us both.*

> *I can't promise you I'm normal, actually, I'm probably far from it. But I can promise you'll have a good time. No horror stories.*

Write me a poem

A few would-be Wordsworths decided the best way to woo me was to pen a romantic sonnet. And who can resist a little old-school romance? Well, me, it seems. Because I'm assuming the following were all written by fully grown adult men.

Sami, For Me Too
In this dream I get a tingle
From my dream who I hear is single
Just have to hope it's not too late
Before you're attached and shut the gate
I'm searching for my fun, my joy
Please please Sami, give me a hoy

The Sami

My Love, My God, Be True
Fortunate for Touch, I do thank, and you
I speak, I know, I trust, Pursue
You know, Sami, wouldn't you

Just a Dream

You caressed my body the way I love you to
You kissed my lips, I respond to you
You said that you loved me and said you were mine
You smiled at me and said everything is just fine
But then I awoke and you were unseen
I was on my own it was just a weird dream

WTF?

Okay, I really don't know what to say about these two, other than they
were just . . . unsettling.

> *I am your God Sami, and you are my angel. Why am I the man*
> *for you? Because I am amazing.*

> *Dear Sami, I'm not trying to blow you away, I'm trying to breathe*
> *you in.*

I was flattered by most of the propositions I received (except for
Mr Reverse Psychology and the last two WTFs). And I replied to
most, thanking each gentleman and politely declining his request.
I'm sure they got over it the moment I left their TV screens.

However, I think we can conclude from the above that some men
are mighty confused about what they think women are looking for
in a bloke. Sadly, most of them are *way* off the mark. Except for the
guy who painted my face on a rock. Because if that's not the ultimate
romantic gesture, I don't know what is.

The Millionaire Matchmaker

I was once approached by the self-proclaimed 'millionaire match-maker' of Sydney. She heard I was single and she wanted to set me up with some of her cashed-up clients.

This did not excite me.

I was seriously offended that this complete stranger assumed I was the type of woman who only wanted a man who was tall, dark and had some. So my initial response was 'Calm down, honey. I got the skills to pay my own bills!' But then she explained that some of the men who'd registered with her agency had seen me on the telly and mentioned that they fancied me, so she might as well try to give the customers what they wanted.

Okay, this *might* have been total BS from a clever salesperson who was desperately trying to fill some dates for her high-paying customers. But my ego allowed me, in that brief moment, to believe that some of her clients might have been fans. I was working on a high-profile TV show at the time, so I guess it was feasible.

I was flattered, but I declined the matchmaker's offer to meet her millionaires. Being associated in *any* way with an agency that specifically sets women up with rich dudes is just not my style.

The fact is, I don't come from a wealthy family. I've never taken money from anyone, other than an employer, and I'm proud to say that I've worked hard for every single cent I've ever earned. The idea that anyone would think I'm someone who goes digging for man-gold is repulsive. Gold diggers are clearly more interested in finding a fabulous lifestyle than they are in finding true love. They don't care whose means they live off and they don't care how they get there.

It's actually quite shameful how transparent some gold diggers can be in their pursuit of the purse. A buddy of mine once went on three different dinner dates with three different women over the course of a month and he was appalled when each of them questioned the very private matter of his financial situation, before she'd even finished her entrée. The first one asked him straight up, 'So how much do you earn?' The second asked, without even batting an eyelid, 'What are you worth?' And by the time date number three asked him how much money he had in the bank (oh yes, she *did*!) he'd heard enough to reply, 'Nothing, actually. I'm broke.' And he wasn't the least bit surprised when she excused herself just after entrée to use the bathroom, and didn't come back. Yes, this *actually* happened.

I've never specifically pursued men with deep pockets, but I have found myself in several dating situations, and even a couple of relationships, with them. So, for what it's worth (see what I did there?), this is what three decades of dating has taught me about dating men with moolah:

- They can quite easily pretend to be loaded to try to impress you, when in fact their luxury lifestyle is being funded by massive debt and incredibly irresponsible loans. If things do get serious, you'll probably be the one paying all the bills.
- They can be controlling arseholes. They think money gives them power, so don't be surprised if they end up treating you like a possession.

- Men with serious coin are desperate to own their own plane. Seriously, it's like an *obsession* with these guys. They practically give themselves orgasms just thinking about it. The *Millionaires for Dummies* handbook must rate private jet ownership as one of the ultimate measures of success but, honestly, it's just a rich dude's pissing contest.
- Private planes aside, they can actually be super tight. Which might be how they got rich in the first place.
- Money doesn't make a relationship better. Sure, it can certainly make the initial wooing process a little more exciting and glamorous. But if it's not the right fit, you'll still be having the same old arguments whether you're holidaying in a chalet in the Swiss alps or in a tent on Stradbroke Island. Once the shine wears off, even a polished turd will still always be a turd.

I'm not saying that all wealthy men are like this. But what I *can* assure you is that no amount of cash will ever guarantee you a lifetime of love and happiness.

Ridgey Didge

Only one Hollywood celebrity has ever hit on me.

Ronn Moss.

I know, right? *Who?*

The only celebrity to ever hit on me was the actor who played the original Ridge Forrester on the long-running American daytime soap opera *The Bold and the Beautiful.* Ronn Moss was on that show for literally decades before they inexplicably replaced him with another actor who looked nothing like the original Ridge and suddenly spoke with a strange foreign accent.

Ronny was quite the sex symbol back in the day. He'd been voted Hottest Male Star by *Soap Digest* magazine about a thousand times. But I'd been watching *B&B* for as long as I could remember, and I always preferred Storm or Thorne (pre-facelift) over Ridge Forrester. Ridge just seemed a little too . . . *chiselled.* There was something about that unnaturally angular jawline that scared me. That chin could cut glass, I swear.

To make this story even more tragic, my rendezvous with the one and only Ronn Moss/Ridge Forrester happened while I was co-hosting the *TV Week* Logies red carpet special for Channel Nine in 2004. (Look, for the purpose of this story, can we all agree to simplify things and refer to him by his character name, Ridge Forrester, rather than his real name? It's less complicated. And this way, everyone can play along.)

Hosting the Logies red carpet is no walk in the park. You need to be super focused, with relevant, interesting and funny things to ask the never-ending procession of actors, newsreaders and TV personalities who appear in front of your microphone. I'd just finished chatting with Delta Goodrem and Mark Philippoussis (remember when *those* crazy lovebirds were an item?) and I was mid-interview with Rove McManus, when I noticed Ridge Forrester waiting patiently nearby with his publicist. My producer politely explained to Ridge's publicist that he was actually going to be interviewed by my co-host Richard Wilkins and pointed them in Dicky's direction.

But they refused to move.

My producer came back to me and said, 'You're up, I'm afraid. Ridge is insisting that *you* do his interview.'

Luckily I was able to draw on my embarrassingly extensive knowledge of all things Bold and Beautiful (secretly relieved to know that all my years of watching the show hadn't been a *complete* waste of time after all). I managed to throw together a couple of random questions on the spot.

But it wasn't good.

As far as celebrity interviews go, it was one of my all-time worst.

To be fair, I was a little distracted. I couldn't help noticing that Ridge Forrester encapsulated pretty much everything that turns me off. Sure, he's a good looking guy who was in great shape for a fifty-year-old, but he also looked like someone desperately trying *not* to act his age. He wore sunglasses the entire time, even though the sun had long gone down. His hair was tied back in a try-hard man bun. And he was wearing one of those leather shark-tooth chokers, which look stupid on any guy over the age of twenty-one. Look, I totally respect that some gals get a wide-on for Ridge Forrester. I'm sure he's been the designated celebrity shag for lots of women over the years. But he just doesn't do it for me.

When my interview finished, I could see Nat Bass lined up for my next interview. So I hastily thanked Ridge and quickly refocused on pronouncing the most difficult celebrity surname in the history of Australian celebrities: 'Bassingthwaighte'. It's a challenge.

But when I finished my interview with Nat, I noticed that Ridge was *still* standing there with his publicist and they were both leering at me. I was pretty sure they were about to demand a redo on my crap interview. I watched his publicist go and talk to my producer again and then my producer came to me and said, 'Okay. This is a bit weird. The publicist has been instructed by Ridge to tell me to tell *you* that Ridge thinks you look really stunning in that dress.'

WTF? Did Ridge Forrester just hit on me? Via his publicist via my producer? Unnecessarily complicated, I know. I have no idea why a two-way conversation had to involve four people. Why didn't he just tell me he liked my dress when he was speaking to me, like, five minutes ago?

I guess that's how they do it in Hollywood.

I was actually more excited about the fact that someone had noticed how fabulous I looked in my frock than I was about Ridge Forrester hitting on me. The dress had been custom-made by the team at SABA and it fit me like a glove. They were literally sewing me into it twenty minutes before I hit the red carpet. But the thought of Ridge Forrester ripping that divine dress off me in the throes of passion later that night did *not* excite me. Not one little bit. So I told my producer to tell Ridge's publicist to tell *Ridge*, 'Thank you. And have a good night.' They got the hint and disappeared.

When I finished working the red carpet that night, I bolted straight to the airport to catch a flight to Singapore, where I was due to be on location for my *Today* show weather crosses the next morning. And I never saw Ridge Forrester again.

The Celery Celebrity

One of my closest friends is a guy named Galeb, whom I've known for more than twenty years. We are living proof that men and women *can* have a successful platonic relationship.

There's never been anything remotely romantic going on between us – even though some of our friends *still* think that can't possibly be true. We often share a room when we travel together and sometimes we even share a bed. But we've never been tempted. Not even by one cheeky little drunken party pash. We adore each other, but we just don't look at each other that way. He's like my bestie and my brother rolled into one. And we know that our relationship is perfect, just the way it is (even though we sometimes do argue like husband and wife).

He's my most trusted confidante and the person I call when I need advice about, well, anything. In fact, he probably knows more about me than anyone else in the world.

I know some pretty juicy stuff about him too. Like the fact that he once dated a woman who had had a fling with George Clooney. It was back in the early nineties when she was working as a waitress in a karaoke bar in Japan. Galeb didn't ask for any of the juicy details (sorry, ladies) but he is secretly chuffed to be in a two-degrees-of-separation sex situation with a Hollywood heart-throb.

*

Despite working in the entertainment industry for more than two decades, I've never had sex with a celebrity (other than Pete from *Big Brother*).

Although I have been lucky enough to *interview* plenty of hotties throughout my career – everyone from sexiest man alive Chris Hemsworth, to sexiest man alive Dwayne 'The Rock' Johnson. And lots of other sexy men in between.

The star with the most surprising sex appeal was Russell Brand. I didn't get the Brand appeal at first. He seemed like one of the *most* unlikely sex symbols – too much of a Mr Bean vibe for me. What on earth was Katy Perry thinking? But the moment I met him, I got it. He's much better-looking in person, for a start. And he gives *ah-may-zing* interview. He's whip smart and funny and charming and insanely cheeky. He was one of my all-time favourite celebrity encounters.

I've met a few duds in the line of duty, too. Hugh Grant spent the entire interview staring at my boobs. Which is actually kind of funny, because my chest is arguably my least impressive body part. As was so beautifully articulated in the complaint letter from *Today* show viewer Jo (see 'The Cashed-Up Prince Charming').

The most traumatic disappointment for me (and trust me when I tell you it hurts more for me to say this than it does for you to hear it) was Mark Wahlberg. I'm probably not supposed to mention his name. But I really, really have to. Because he seemed like such a massive tool.

I had lusted over Marky Mark and his sixpack and his in-your-face Calvin Kleins with all that bulging manhood for many many years. This guy had sparked some pretty intense hormonal stirrings in my developing teenage body. Seeing him in the flesh had been one of my greatest fantasies. But when I finally got the chance to meet him face-to-face, he had all the sex appeal of . . . a stick of celery.

I'll concede that my expectations were probably unreasonably high the first time I interviewed him. Yes, my heart was palpitating. And, yes, my excitement level was possibly a touch OTT for a professional journalist who was supposed to be doing her job . . . *professionally.*

Hey, in my defence, it's not every day you get to meet your craziest teenage celebrity crush, right?

But I was pretty shocked when the guy gave me . . . *nothing*. No witty anecdotes. No cheeky comebacks. No smile. No glimpse of personality whatsoever. He was shockingly bland. And he looked more miserable than a Kardashian without a contouring brush. The *entire* time.

After my first disappointing Marky Mark experience, I convinced myself that the guy was probably just having a bad day. I mean, we all do, now and then, right? Even movie stars with stunning wives and gorgeous kids and amazing careers who earn more money in one day than most people will see in a lifetime.

Well, I couldn't believe it when I got *another* chance to interview Mark Wahlberg a couple of years later and he gave me the exact same celery vibe. Surely he wasn't having *another* bad day? I'd seen him interviewed plenty of times since our last encounter and he seemed kind of normal in all of them. So, I don't know, maybe I just got the short end of the (celery) stick.

I guess most people would ordinarily lose their shit at the prospect of meeting their teenage celebrity crush. But I really, really wish I hadn't met mine. He was much hotter in my fantasies.

Before Sunrise

I didn't have my first one-night stand until my early 30s. And I mean one-night stand in the true sense of the term, in which I slept with a complete stranger only hours after meeting him and then I never saw or spoke to him again.

I probably should have been shagging myself stupid through my twenties on the express train to chlamydia town, but I was mostly in long-term relationships back then. And even when I wasn't happily coupled, I couldn't fathom how anyone could even think about getting naked with someone they'd only just met. That was way too many shades of wrong for me.

But just after I hit the big three-oh, I had a major shift in my attitude towards sex. It was a personal light-bulb moment: I realised I could disconnect the physical desire from the psychological one. I'm not sure if everyone has the ability to separate the two, or if some people just prefer not to. But I decided that I could most definitely be in lust with someone without being in love with them. And a shag could be enjoyed as a consensual physical interaction between two people who were:

a) wildly attracted to each other

b) horny

c) drunk

d) all of the above.

It wouldn't make me a dirty rotten slutguts if I enjoyed a spontaneous night of passion with someone I didn't have any intention of ever seeing again.

It was also around this time that I fell truly, madly and deeply in love with a movie about a one-night stand. *Before Sunrise* is my favourite flick of all time: it's that one movie I am always compelled to watch if I ever stumble across it on TV. It holds me there right till the very end, no matter how many times I've seen it.

On one level, it could be a movie about two randy tourists hooking up on a wild night out. But I see it as a profoundly romantic love story about two people from opposite sides of the globe who meet entirely by chance and discover a kickarse connection that proves their rendezvous was absolute destiny. An affirmation that the universe really is unfolding as it should be (thanks, Desiderata). I mean, what could be more romantic than that?

So it's not at all surprising that my first ever one-night stand was an unexpected, spontaneous, eerily mystical encounter with a foreigner.

It was during the 2003 Rugby World Cup, when Sydney was swept up in that fabulous festive atmosphere that happens when people from all over the world are in party-mode in your city every night. I walked into a bar in Darling Harbour and immediately spotted a guy who stood head and shoulders above everyone else in the room. He looked at me just as I noticed him, we locked eyes for a few seconds and I felt a little click in my stomach. That oh-so-subtle feeling you get when your subconscious knows something that you're not quite ready to acknowledge yet. My girlfriends were determined to drag me onto the dancefloor, though, so I gave him a quick smile and secretly hoped I'd run into him later in the night.

About an hour later, as I was standing on the edge of the dancefloor giving my tootsies a rest, I noticed an ethereal-looking Maori woman walking towards me through the crowd. She had long, dark hair and was dressed head-to-toe in black. And she was leading the tall hottie I'd spotted earlier by the hand. She walked straight up to me, placed his hand in mine, looked me in the eye and announced, 'I'm bringing him to you.'

It was all a bit weird and mysterious. But I was feeling a little tipsy so I just laughed nervously and said to her (in a very Bridget Jones kind of way), 'Well . . . *ooookay*, then. Thanks for that. Rightio, then.'

The big fella and I started chatting and the chemistry was undeniable. He was playing in the World Cup for the All Blacks. My dad is a Kiwi, so our shared background gave us plenty to chat about. I was also insanely attracted to him, even though he had a gigantic square head, no neck, very small cauliflower ears and a nose that looked like it had been broken in about forty-three places.

A couple of drinks later, the Kiwi and I were laughing about how we'd met and how funny it was that the woman had 'handed him to me'. I said she must have been a great friend, to facilitate such a unique introduction on his behalf.

'She's not *my* friend,' he said. 'I've never seen her before in my life. I thought she was a friend of *yours*.'

Nope. I'd never seen her before either.

We stared at each other for a moment and acknowledged the freakishness of the situation. Then we searched the bar for the mysterious Maori matchmaker. I was desperate to know what had possessed her to initiate a meeting between two complete strangers, but she was nowhere to be found. I started to worry that someone had spiked my drink and I was actually experiencing some kind of weird hallucinogenic episode. The big fella assured me that I wasn't tripping. The ethereal-looking Maori woman had picked him out of the crowd, led him through a packed nightclub and brought him to me.

And in that moment, I knew.

It was a sign. A sign that I must take the big fella home and shag him immediately. I was ready to embark on my first ever one-night stand!

So he came home with me. And it was spontaneous and sexy and exciting and super empowering to discover that having adult cuddles with someone you don't know very well could actually be . . . pretty fabulous! No commitment. No promises. No strings attached. No regrets.

My first ever one-night stand was more satisfying and liberating than I ever imagined it could be. Well done, me!

The morning after, however, was a complete disaster. I woke up and realised I had absolutely no idea about one-night stand morning-after protocol. I had only ever woken up naked next to a boyfriend. But there I was, lying next to a complete stranger, starkers and (shock-horror!) *makeup-free*. I raced to the bathroom and put on just enough makeup to look like I hadn't put any makeup on. Then I called him a cab, went back into the bedroom and casually mentioned that his taxi would be arriving lickity-split.

He looked a little puzzled.

In hindsight, it wasn't the right thing to do. I practically threw him out the door like a cheap plaything I had no use for any more. I would have been mortified if a guy had treated me that way. But I didn't want him to know that it was my first ever one-night stand. And I certainly didn't want to be a Stage 5 Clinger begging him to stay for breakfast and asking to swap numbers so I could wait for him to never call. So with my new-found post-one-night shag empowerment, I put my big-girl panties on, leaned in to the moment and took charge, giving him the clear message that I wasn't expecting anything more from him.

Despite our mysteriously magical meeting and crazy chemistry, I knew I'd never have a relationship with the guy. He lived in another country, for a start. Plus, he was a professional athlete. And my one and only previous attempt at having a relationship with a professional athlete didn't turn out so well.

I dated an NBL basketballer back in my early twenties. Derek would get me the best seats in the house at every game, either on the court or in the VIP area, and I'd swell with pride whenever he scored. I'd comfort him after a big loss and I'd help him rotate the icepacks when he had an injury. I remember his house always smelled of sweaty socks and wet towels and Dencorub. I eventually decided WAG life wasn't for me when I heard that my b-baller was double dribbling around town with one of the cheerleaders and it became mortifyingly obvious that I wasn't the only one who'd been rotating his icepacks.

The cab arrived and my one-night stand left and I felt a bit slack about the way I'd kicked him out, but I told myself to let it go and move on. I'd never see him again anyway.

Except I did see him again. All the bloody time. I had no idea when I shagged him that my first ever one-night stand was with a famous rugby player. For years after, I'd recognise that enormous square head whenever an All Blacks game was playing on TV. I mean, seriously. What are the chances?

We weren't destined to be together, but I do believe our meeting was destiny. Maybe a Maori spirit actually did bring him to me, because she wanted to teach me a valuable life lesson. That I could enjoy grown-up sex without being in a relationship.

But it takes a whole lot more to fall in love.

The Penguin Club

Casual sex has become an accepted part of dating for me. But so has the occasional extended sex drought.

I once mentioned to a friend that I hadn't had sex in a while and she suggested I book myself an appointment with 'The Yoni Whisperer' in Byron Bay. This Yoni expert would be able to heal any 'issues' my vajoir was holding on to, through 'external and internal vaginal mapping massage therapy'.

Side note: I prefer the term 'vaj-oir' (pronounced like 'boud-oir'). My girlfriends and I have been using it for years. It's not as clinical as 'vagina' and not as crass as 'pussy'. Confession: we do use the 'C' word on rare occasions, but *only* when referring to especially repulsive ex-boyfriends.

Anyhoo, apparently one session with the Yoni lady was all I'd need to release any pesky little vajoir related blockages, leaving me feeling empowered, connected and inspired (no mention of violated). And, most importantly, it might also miraculously break my sex drought.

Okay, so . . .

Firstly, I didn't realise vaginal blockages were preventing me from getting laid. I thought it was simply the fact that I hadn't met a guy I wanted to sleep with in months.

Also, I had no clue my poor little vajoir was so messed up emotionally (she actually sounds like a bit of a drama queen, to be perfectly honest).

But, quite frankly, I'd rather go on one of those 'Naked & Dating' TV shows than let some strange woman finger me while whispering sweet nothings to my lady bits. I don't need sex that badly. Honestly, I don't.

I'm no stranger to extended periods of abstinence. I've been a first-class passenger on the man-drought train many, many times. That's why I created the Penguin Club with a bunch of my single girl-friends back in the early nineties. And the Penguin Club is still going strong to this day.

I'd read somewhere that penguins only have sex once a year. So we decided that whenever any of us reached the twelve-month mark of a dry spell, we would call ourselves 'honorary penguins'. For a bit of a laugh.

The Penguin Club is our secret society of sexless ladies (a group of penguins is actually called a 'waddle', but that just didn't seem appropriate, given the circumstances). There have been six of us in and out of the Club over the years. When all six of us were single, there were usually two active penguins at any one time. When you're in the Club, you can be absolutely sure that all the other girls know the exact date of your penguin anniversary – i.e., your last shag. And if your sex drought does happen to roll over into a new year, you'll be comforted by messages of support from the other ladies – accompanied, no doubt, by a variety of tasteless vibrator jokes.

Membership is flexible and always, hopefully, temporary. As soon as you break the drought, you're out of the Club. Nothing warrants a bigger toast among my gal pals than when one of us announces to the group (usually over Friday night drinks): 'Girls, I'm a Penguin no more! I broke the drought!'

You're also welcome to return to the Club at any time. We were all flabbergasted when one of the girls announced that she was a Penguin again, despite the fact that she'd been married for nine years (because that's what having two kids under the age of five can do to your sex life).

The Penguin Club has given us all a lighthearted laugh about what can be a bit of a depressing situation. It's also led to some interesting chat about sex and what it means to us. Can we last without it for longer than men? (Mostly, yes.) Do women need emotional attachment before they jump in the sack? (Debatable. Refer to previous chapter.) How long can you go without sex before you have to lower your standards? (Personal choice.)

I've always refused to lower my standards. That's why I've been a penguin a grand total of *four times* during my thirty-plus sexually active years. Yes. My sex rut has lasted for more than twelve months on four separate occasions. And I'm not embarrassed to admit it.

It's actually nowhere near as tragic as it sounds. When I tell some people that I haven't had sex in a year, I'm pretty sure they just assume I'm stuck in some sad, pathetic existence where no one wants to bonk me. I've seen that look of pity in their eyes!

But what they don't realise is that *I'm* the one who's made the choice to be there.

With apps like Tinder, I could probably get sex if I *really* wanted it. I also usually have at least one ex lurking somewhere around the fringes, in case I hang the old 'open for business' sign back on my bedroom door. But, while I certainly don't shy away from the odd one-night stand when the mood takes me, I don't need to shag for shag's sake. I can quite comfortably go for extended periods without any sex at all.

This does not make me feel undateable or unshaggable or unloveable. It makes me feel proud and confident and empowered. And the best part is, when I eventually decide to make the magic happen again, I feel like a born-again virgin. So I get to enjoy all the fun and nervous anticipation of the 'first time' all over again.

My dear friend Jenna (not her real name for reasons you're about to understand) is the undisputed Penguin Club President and our

most dedicated member. As I write this book, Jenna is about to celebrate her *seven*-year anniversary in the Club.

Seven years without sex doesn't bother Jenna as much as you
might think it would (although it really does give a whole new
meaning to the term 'seven-year itch', doesn't it?) She lives quite
happily with her dog, her two cats and her extensive collection
of vibrators. She doesn't have to shave her legs, or worry about
Brazilians or ingrown hairs down there, like, ever. And she's reading the *Fifty Shades of Grey* trilogy for the fourth time. At around the
five-year mark, she completely gave up and relocated to Hobart for
a while.

When you've been a member of the Penguin Club for that long,
you probably deserve a lifetime membership. But none of us would
ever wish that on our darling friend. However, if Jenna doesn't get her
groove back by her *ten*-year Penguin Club anniversary, I'll probably
book her an appointment with 'The Yoni Whisperer'. 'Cause by that
stage, it probably wouldn't hurt to at least give it a go.

First Dates to Forget

In my tragically vast experience, blind dates are always scary. It really doesn't matter how many times you put yourself through them, there's always a very real possibility that it will turn into a horror show.

My greatest fear is that we'll run out of things to talk about and be forced to endure those excruciatingly awkward silences that make me question why I keep saying yes to blind dates when I absolutely know there's a very real possibility that this excruciatingly awkward situation might occur.

My other fear is that he'll talk too much.

I once found myself on a blind date with a pilot who had a serious case of verbal diarrhoea. Before I'd even finished my first glass of wine, he said, 'So, Sami, you know if you play your cards right, I'll put you down on my staff travel.'

I've since learned that if a guy ever uses the phrase 'if you play your cards right' on a first date, you should get up, leave immediately and lose his number. However, I didn't know this at the time, so I just put it down to nerves and his desire to impress, and the date carried on.

The date reached a new level of weird when the Pilot decided to tell me about the best threesome he *never* had. With the excitement of a kid waking up on Christmas morning, he gave me a detailed description of that time he got absolutely smashed at the races and managed to pick up not one but two hot girls, but by the time he got them back to his crib he was too drunk to get a hard-on so he passed out while the girls did their thang without him and then he had to make do with a solo flight after they left.

So that was probably my second cue to leave. But by that stage, I was so intrigued by the inappropriateness of his first-date chat, that I decided to stick around and see what other crap might spill out of his mouth.

By the time I'd finished my second glass of wine, he'd told me all the dirty details about how his last girlfriend was a swinger. He'd never done it before but she introduced him to the scene so he gave it a go and he really quite enjoyed it, but now they had broken up and he had no one to go with so he was looking for someone who might like to go to a swingers club with him now and then.

And then he suddenly stopped talking and sat there and stared at me, waiting for a reaction.

And *that* was my cue to leave.

I told him that swinging wasn't my scene and I thanked him for the wine and wished him all the best and said I really hoped he'd be able to find someone who could help him satisfy his needs, and enjoy the perks of his treasured staff travel benefits. And I left.

My friend Annie had her worst-ever blind date with a guy who hardly spoke to her at all. He'd invited her to a Liberal Party fundraising lunch, which is a fucking weird place to take someone on a first date anyway. In the limited chat they'd had pre-date, they had never once discussed their personal political leanings. Things got even more wack when she arrived at the lunch to discover they were seated at the head table with the Prime Minister. Then her date spent the entire lunch fan-girling over the PM and completely ignoring her.

Annie says it was the most boring, pointless date she's ever been on. She was even more baffled when she later discovered that the guy had paid $5000 *each* for them to sit at the head table. She was tempted to call him afterwards and tell him he should have spent the money on a Louis Vuitton bag for her instead. That would have been a much smarter way to spend 5K. And it probably would have given him a much better chance of securing a second date.

When it comes to first dates to forget, my mate Galeb wins the prize. He was suitably aroused when a girl asked him back to her place after they had shared a very flirty dinner. Things got hot and heavy pretty quickly, but he was concerned to discover a series of weird looking red lines on her stomach and at the tops of her thighs as he was undressing her. When he asked her what they were and if she was okay, she said, matter-of-factly, 'Oh no, I'm fine. I just like to cut myself while I have sex.' He suddenly wasn't feeling so aroused, so he excused himself and went home. And he never saw her again.

Putrid Pheromones

I was once turned off a guy because of his thin shoulders. I knew it wasn't his fault. He was born that way. Which, incidentally, I'm sure his mum was quite happy about. However, I couldn't enjoy having sex with him once I noticed that his shoulder width was narrower than mine. It's the most stupidly superficial reason I've ever had for putting the brakes on a new relationship, but there must have been some kind of deeper, perfectly rational psychoanalytical explanation for my behaviour. Because Jamie Dornan has thin shoulders, and I'm quite certain I would enjoy having sex with him.

Okay, let's be honest here. Superficial turn-offs are a brutal but very basic factor of dating. We've all had them. My friend Jane can't date a guy if he has a prominent Adam's apple. She's especially repulsed if the protusion in his neck moves around while he's speaking. She simply can't look at him. Another friend had to stop seeing a gentleman because of his South African accent. She cringed every time he opened his mouth. Galeb was instantly turned off when a woman turned up to a fancy restaurant for their second date wearing yoga tights. I'm not sure if it was the hint of camel toe that pushed him over the edge or just the fact that she was wearing activewear on a dinner date, which I'll agree was an especially unacceptable level of effort on her behalf.

Angie had to call it quits with a fella after he arrived at the pub to meet her friends for the first time, wearing – gasp – sandals *with socks*. Now, can we all just agree for a second that this turn-off is perfectly understandable? I mean, how could poor old Angie possibly risk being seen in public with this guy and his unsightly sock sandals ever again?

I was once on a date with a guy who told me he was turned off a girl after he heard her 'pee like a racehorse'. He'd taken her back to his place and things were getting hot and heavy in the bedroom when she excused herself and disappeared into his ensuite. She'd been holding it in for a while, poor thing, and the bathroom acoustics really weren't very kind to her that night. The guy was completely repulsed as he lay there in bed, listening to her relieving herself, loudly. Of. Every. Last. Drop (it went on for ages, apparently). After hearing that, he said he couldn't have sex with her again.

I once had to break up with a guy because I was repulsed by his pheromones. I'm not talking about your standard, run-of-the-mill morning breath or a little nasty post-workout BO. I'm referring to the guy's natural body scent, which seemed to be secreted from his pores, glide through the air and slither directly up into my nostrils, creating a reaction in my whole being that was especially repugnant.

Whenever I was in his company, the odour was undeniably nauseating. Yes, I know I sound overly dramatic but I swear it was true. It was one of the most bizarre dating situations I've ever encountered and it's the only time it has ever happened to me.

It was terribly unfortunate, because he also happened to be a really, really nice person. He was handsome, sweet and generous. He's the kind of man who would probably buy your mother flowers on *your* birthday, to thank her for having you. There was seriously nothing to dislike about the guy. Other than his au naturel eau d'odious.

I can only imagine it was some kind of chemical reaction that took place when his pheromones met mine. If pheromones are supposed to attract people in an animalistic, scientific way, doesn't it make sense that they could also have the *reverse* effect?

The situation was especially unbearable when we had sex. That foul natural odour oozing from his pores mixed in with all the funky sex sweat would literally make me gag. Which is not ideal when you're having sex with a lovely guy who you actually quite like.

I desperately wanted it to *not* be a problem, so I tried everything to overcome the issue. I'd heard the best way to combat a bad aroma is to breathe in the biggest, longest, deepest lungful you possibly can, and it will miraculously disappear. I tried that. Several times. Didn't help.

I bought him one of my all-time favourite aftershaves, hoping it would mask the smell. But the sweet muskiness of the perfume combined with his pheromones only intensified the odour from pungent to putrid.

I asked my friends if they could smell it. I once discreetly asked a girlfriend to give him an extra long hug and take a big whiff when she met him. Of course, she couldn't smell a thing. She thought I was psycho.

I hoped the smell would gradually subside if I spent more time with him. It didn't. The stench was always there. Whenever we were together. Lingering, like . . . well, a bad smell.

In the end, I accepted the fact that it was a primal chemical reaction between our bodies, warning us that we just didn't fit. I think it was the universe begging us not to multiply. So it's quite possible that he was having the exact same reaction to my body odour the whole time.

I didn't want to embarrass or upset him by discussing it. I mean, how do you tell someone their body odour is repellent? So I just broke up with him instead. And I really hope that lovely bloke has found himself a gorgeous lass who thinks he smells absolutely delicious.

Who's in My Area with Their Pants Off?

Pre-online dating, my single squad and I tried to be strategic about facilitating 'random' meetings with the opposite sex. We thought we were being proactively single by frequenting places where you would expect to find a higher ratio of men. Like the pub. Or the footy. Or the pub when an important footy match was playing on the big screens.

Didn't take us long to work out that most men who go to the pub to watch the footy . . . go to the pub to watch the footy. Not to pick up. Occasionally some loud, messy drunk would pay us a little attention after the game was over. But that never ends well for anyone.

Then Tinder came along. And men stopped paying us attention altogether. They didn't have to make *any* kind of effort at all, because they already had their Tinder hook-ups lined up for later.

Swipe right. Line 'em up. Get laid. That's pretty much how it works.

The comedian Judith Lucy summed it up best when she told me during a radio interview that it would be more appropriate if Tinder was renamed 'who's in my area with their pants off'.

I've heard way too many horror stories to ever try Tinder. Call me crazy, but I reckon an app that's used mostly by people who just want sex (stat!) is probably not going to help me meet my life partner. I know a makeup artist in LA who deals with twenty-year-old Victoria's

Secret models crying in her makeup chair over their latest hideous Tinder experiences, because some jerk hasn't bothered to message them back after they had sex. So, if a Victoria's Secret model isn't having any luck on Tinder, how the fuck are we mere mortals supposed to?

I haven't actually tried *any* online dating avenues. Unless you count my one laughable experience with a regular matchmaking service. I'd already said no the the Millionaire Matchmaker years before, but this particular agency assured me they were for ordinary folk. When they started advertising on the radio station where I worked, they jumped at the chance to help me find my match. Plus, they offered to forgo the hefty joining fee (damn, those things are expensive). I agreed to go on one date, which would be recorded for my radio show. I painstakingly filled out the extensive customer profile, so they could identify my perfect fella. At best, I thought, the expert matchmakers would find what I couldn't: the man of my dreams! At worst, it would make for a fun radio segment for our mostly female listeners.

They set me up with a nice looking fella named Jeff. We met for dinner at a restaurant at Walsh Bay in Sydney. Things seemed to go well . . . for about three minutes. Then we somehow got talking about first impressions. And Jeff told me the first thing that popped into his mind when he walked into the restaurant and saw me was, 'Geez, she's gonna be hard work'.

That was his first impression of me. And he thought it was perfectly appropriate to tell me that.

He then sculled about six beers as I tried desperately to maintain conversation (oh by the way, guys, here's a helpful tip: you should always resist the urge to scull six beers during the first hour of a first date. It's a serious dating disability).

I also discovered that Jeff and I had very little in common. He exposed the full extent of our tragic mismatch when he confessed to me that his lifelong dream was to live in Las Vegas and marry a stripper. That's actually what Jeff told me. During our date. Which was all being recorded for radio. When he saw the look of horror on my face, he tried to pretend he was joking.

I don't know whether to put his behaviour down to nerves or just the fact that he was a fucking moron but, either way, that promotion backfired spectacularly on the matchmaking agency.

Although, in their defence, I guess I got what I paid for.

Texting and Dating

Dating and texting go together like douchebags and Tinder. These days, one really can't exist without the other.

Regardless of how you meet, the initial dating process is pretty much conducted entirely via text. I can't remember the last time a man picked up a phone, called me and engaged in an actual conversation to arrange a first date. I once dated a guy for six whole weeks without ever having one single telephone convo.

It's a rude shock to my girlfriends who are re-entering the dating colosseum after marriage-kids-ugly separation-nasty legal battle-divorce. I've had numerous calls from my newly single friends, screaming, 'Honestly, Sam, I have no idea how you've endured dating in this city for all these years. It's fucking brutal out there.'

And I always reply, 'Yes, hon, dating certainly has changed heaps since you were last on the scene. By the way, it's perfectly acceptable to split the bill these days, remember. And you do know that scrunchies and butterfly clips went out in the nineties, right?'

Still, there's no established etiquette when it comes to texting and dating. And, let's be honest, men are pretty average communicators to begin with. So when you give them unsupervised access to a keypad, there's always a very real possibility that something/ everything might get lost in translation. Case in point: I gave my number to a nice guy I met at the pub, who asked if he could take me out to dinner sometime. I was understandably perplexed when I received this text from him the next morning:

> It was lovely to meet your brain.

That's it. The whole text. I have no idea what happened to the actual 'asking me out' bit. I'm no textpert, but reading between the line, I can only guess that he was trying to let me know he was more interested in my brain/personality than my looks/bits. He was probably trying to be clever or original or funny (bless), but why couldn't he simply write, 'Hey, I enjoyed meeting you last night. When are you free to catch up?' Or better still, why not just pick up the friggin' phone and *ask me out*, the old-fashioned way?

This dating/texting co-dependency often results in us ladies wasting far too many hours trying to decipher the latest cryptic text we've received. Dinner with the girls often turns into a full-blown strategy meeting, whereby text messages are discussed, dissected and decoded. Every word, every phrase, every punctuation mark is assessed and analysed from every conceivable perspective. Until. It. Friggin'. Makes. Sense.

And I'm sorry to tell you this, girls, but age does not bring clarity to this situation. It seems that men of all ages are textually challenged. Some of the smartest, most astute forty-year-old women I know have found themselves stumped by a male-derived SMS.

One guy sent me this little gem after our first date:

> Hi. Let me know when you're up for some putting practice.

Well, first things first: at least his text came with a salutation. But. The bizarre thing about this text is that we had never before discussed golf or putting in any form (putt putt included). So it left me wondering if:

a) The text was meant for someone else.

b) 'Putting practice' was actually code for something else i.e. dinner? Sex?

c) Was this was his subtle way of letting me know he wasn't interested in anything romantic and would prefer to keep things on a strictly platonic level, which may or may not include the occasional round of golf?

I didn't bother finding out. I mean, come on. Does it really have to be that difficult?

Please Don't Hehehe Me

A text can make or break the dating process, especially in the really early stages.

I was once turned off by a guy because he wrote 'hehehe' in his text message. Okay, I know it was a total bitch move on my part, but the moment I saw those six little characters sitting there on my phone, I had absolutely zero interest in having sex with him. Despite the fact that he was a super hot, insanely fit Ironman. You know, the guy who runs 50 k's, swims 20 k's and rides 1000 k's all before breakfast (or something like that). Yep, he was one of them. But when he sent me a text to ask me out and he used hehehe (*three*, to be sure), he immediately lost any sex appeal he'd had pre-hehehe. I cannot explain why I was so opposed to it, other than to say a man over the age of thirty should never hehehe.

On the flip side, a guy with good texting game can elevate himself from so-so to super sexy with a simple, thoughtful text or three. I once found myself dating a Textbook Texter. This guy sent exactly the right text. At exactly the right time. Every time.

I don't know if it was something he'd consciously studied and perfected over time, or if it just came naturally to him. But he certainly knew his way around a keypad, whether it was a post-date 'Thanks for a great night. Can't wait to see you again', or a late night 'Good night,

gorgeous girl. Sleep like an angel' or just a simple 'Missing you xxx'
completely out of the blue.

Here's the gem that really proved this guy had a black belt in text
dating. After our first weekend away together, I received this:

> Thanks for a great weekend. You had me from our first kiss on
> Friday night. I'm loving everything I'm learning about you.

Okay, if you really want me to rub it in, he sent me flowers on Monday
morning as well!

But I digress.

Until then, I had never realised it was even possible to be
wooed via SMS. It's such a simple way to let someone know you're
thinking about them. Or to say things you might not be brave
enough to say to their face. It only takes seconds to type out a message that can make someone smile for hours. On the downside,
we all know it can also be used by cowards as a pretty effective
escape clause.

My friend Lisa had been on two perfectly pleasant dates with a
lovely new fellow and was very much looking forward to seeing him
again the following weekend. But on the Tuesday night, she received
this message from him:

> I'm sorry I can't make our date this weekend, I'm too tired.

A little abrupt, for my liking. But that's not even the worst part.
How on earth was this guy able to determine on Tuesday that he
would be too tired for their date on *Saturday night*? They had only
planned to go to the movies, where you *sit down* for two hours. You
don't even have to talk to each other if you don't feel like it. It's not like
they were going to play paintball, for goodness sake.

And this brings me back to the whole texting and dating 'lost
in translation' issue. One might have easily interpreted the Tuesday
night 'I'm too tired to see you on Saturday' text as a subtle rejection. I would never have contacted the guy again. But it turns out

he was not fobbing her off. He was just being a guy. And he was *very* interested in her. So interested, in fact, that he saw her again the *following* weekend. And they ended up falling madly in love.

Embarrassing First Dates

The 'I'm too tired on Tuesday to see you on Saturday' text isn't even the most bizarre excuse I've heard to cancel a date. The best one I've ever come across is 'I can't have dinner with you because I glued my toes together.'

My old mate Ben had been pursuing a girl relentlessly for a year before she finally agreed to go out with him. But when date night finally came she called to cancel because, in her rush to get ready, she had accidentally reached for the superglue instead of the nail polish remover and glued her toes together.

Well, Ben wasn't prepared to let a silly little thing like a pair of conjoined toes prevent him from getting the girl of his dreams. He'd waited an entire year for this moment and he wasn't giving up without a fight. So he told her to sit tight while he called the poisons information hotline and begged for instructions on how to unglue those toes (make it happen, goddamit!). He succeeded, the date went ahead (all toes intact) and Ben proudly told the story, in all its hilarity, at their wedding one year later.

If an awkward or embarrassing moment on a first date doesn't send you running for the hills, it can accidentally turn into a touching bonding experience. Ted loves telling the story of his woeful first date with the woman who eventually became his wife. He hadn't realised he'd parked his car under an external sewerage line after driving into a restaurant's underground carpark. In a valiant attempt to be a gentleman, he leapt out of the driver's seat to race around and open the passenger door for his lady, but he whacked his skull on the sewerage pipe, split his head open and knocked himself out cold. They ended up spending their first date in the ER where he had his skull stapled back together. That contributed to another priceless wedding speech.

One of my most embarrassing first dates was the time I thought early menopause had hit me, in all its glory, just after entrée. I'd been a little anxious going into that blind date, but we seemed to have enough in common to keep the conversation flowing. We'd had a few laughs and the date wasn't going terribly. But sometime after the insalata Caprese and just before the ravioli, I spontaneously started to sweat profusely. I'm not talking about a delicate light mist, providing my skin with a radiant natural glow. It was as if someone had turned on a tap. Water was streaming out of my pores. There weren't enough napkins on the table to soak up the sweat dripping from my forehead. I could feel a river of it running down my back and filling up my bum crack. I was desperate to run to the loo and clean myself up but I was too scared to stand up in case I had a big wet patch on my rear, which would look like either I'd bled through a tampon or I had an embarrassing bladder leakage problem. Of course I wore the fucking silk dress that night.

So I just sat there, dripping. And pretending not to notice.

My date did a fine job of pretending not to notice as well. I'm pretty sure he just assumed he was witnessing a menopausal episode. (Yay, she's a keeper!)

The sweat tap miraculously turned itself off as soon as the date was over and it never happened to me again. Turns out it wasn't a menopausal hot flush after all, so I can only imagine it was a spontaneous uncontrollable nervous reaction.

And that particular embarrassing experience did *not* bond us. I never saw the guy again.

The Warm Sushi Escape Clause

A slice of raw fish was the catalyst for one of the most uncomfortable first dates I've ever experienced.

I was doing a fashion shoot for one of the glossy magazines when the chat on set turned to dating, and how difficult it was to meet good men in Sydney. Which is what prompted the stylist to set me up with her brother. She said he was super handsome, incredibly funny and wildly successful.

'He's a catch,' she told me, 'with a capital C!'

Well, he sounded like a catch with capital everything, so of course I agreed to a date. I didn't want to appear *too* keen, however, so when CATCH (capital everything) called to invite me to dinner, I lied and told him I already had dinner plans, but I'd be able to meet him for a quick drink beforehand.

We met at a cute little speakeasy in East Sydney. The first impression was positive and conversation flowed. We talked about work and life and family and our common passion for travel. After about an hour, he said he was really enjoying my company and asked if there was any chance I could possibly join him for dinner after all. So I fake cancelled my fake dinner with friends and agreed.

He led me around the corner to his favourite Japanese place. We had sushi and sake. We chatted some more. He seemed quite charming. But then I noticed he seemed to talk an awful lot about money. And how much he had. And about his fancy car and his big houses (yes, plural).

Well, there's no faster way to turn me off than to discuss how much money you have. Because it indicates, quite clearly, that you're a wanker. And not the one for me. So, after dinner, I politely said I had to leave and he called for the bill.

Suddenly, CATCH began flapping his hands around in front of his face. He crinkled his nose up and made strange gagging noises. Like he'd just taken a whiff of some especially odoriferous sewer gas. He said he wasn't feeling well. Said he must have eaten some warm sushi. Told me he remembered the exact piece – it was a little tepid when he put it in his mouth. And now it was not sitting well in his tum tum.

And then he got up. And he left.

Poor guy, I thought. I can only imagine that ingesting warm raw fish is not fun for anyone. I assumed he'd popped out to get some fresh air. Or throw up. Best not to go out there and check on him, I decided. Might be a little embarrassing if I appeared just as his warm sushi was introducing itself to the pavement.

So I sat there at the table, alone. And I waited . . . and waited . . . and waited. But CATCH did not reappear. After about thirty excruciating minutes I realised he must have gone home, so I paid the bill and left. The walk out of the restaurant was mortifying. I was very much aware that the other diners had watched him leave me sitting there alone at the table, like his leftovers, or a piece of warm sushi.

So imagine my *complete* disbelief when I found CATCH standing there, right outside the restaurant, leaning up against the wall, looking very relaxed and not the least bit unwell.

Major awks, as I said, 'Wow, um, I thought you'd gone. Are you okay? How are you feeling?'

And he casually replied, 'Yeah, I'm great, thanks.'

As if nothing weird had just happened.

I was shocked. Even if he had been feeling a little queasy after the alleged warm sushi, there'd been plenty of time for him to have a quick puke, get some air, suck on a breath mint or three and come back inside to check on me and, um, I don't know, maybe *pay the fucking bill*? Or at the very least, thank *me* for paying the fucking bill. Evidently he'd been standing there for the last thirty minutes, waiting for me to pay up.

Then, he *super* casually said, 'So, do you want to go get another drink?'

After my countless encounters with man morons over the years, not much shocks me any more. But this guy clearly lived on Crazy Island. Population: one. He wasn't sick at all. He was *totally* fine. In fact, I'm pretty sure CATCH had faked his little fishy encounter to conveniently disappear and avoid paying an eighty-dollar dinner bill.

The Warm Sushi Escape Clause had worked an absolute treat. I'd been had. Hook. Line. And sinker. (Forgive me, but that fishing pun has never seemed more appropriate.)

He called a few times after that, but I never returned his calls and I never saw him again. And, look, it's not even about me paying the bill. I can afford an eighty-dollar dinner. It's the ridiculous way he went about avoiding having to pay it himself. His sister might think he's a catch with a capital C, but he's actually just another A-grade loser. And, despite the fact that there really do *not* seem to be plenty of fish in the sea, this was one catch I was unquestionably happy to release.

The Player

Despite the six-star price tag, upmarket health retreats are not as glamorous as you might expect. They're basically where rich people go to get colonics. They're the only place I've been to where it's perfectly normal to sit around a dining table, openly discussing your bowel movements with people you've just met.

I'm not sure if it's the excessive fibre or the lack of caffeine, but those 'healthy' holidays have a way of doing obscene things to your digestive system. Blockages are common. And when you're in that excruciatingly unpleasant situation, with a bunch of other people experiencing similar levels of discomfort, your poo (or lack thereof) becomes a popular talking point.

Here's a transcript of an actual conversation I had with another health farm guest I had known for all of two days:

Me: This enlightened rice and kale muffin is delish. Hey, have you pooed yet?
Stranger: The Ezekiel bread is yummy too. I'm so backed up it's ridiculous. Have you been?
Me: Nope. Nothing. I'm in agony. I heard the Chi Nei Tsang abdominal detox massage can help move things along.

Stranger: I've booked one today. I'm so friggin' bloated, I can hardly walk.

Me: I'm having a colonic today after my Mother Earth Drum Circle class.

Stranger: Oh my god, I did the drum circle yesterday. I've never felt so free. If the Chi Nei Tsang doesn't work, I'll try the colonic. Hey, do you want me to grab you another dandelion tea?

And so on and so forth until you eventually poo. Which usually happens on around day five.

During one stay at the health retreat, I became friendly with a middle-aged couple who were so loaded they owned their own plane (see . . .? Rich people and private jets. I'm telling you . . . it's a *thing*). It was after yet another one of these lengthy discussions about our states of constipation that conversation turned to dating (with an obvious link there to dating shitheads, which I will avoid). The husband's eyes lit up as he excitedly said he would love to set me up with a friend of his who was a very successful professional footballer.

'Not interested,' I told him. 'But thanks anyway.'

I'm a big fan of all sports and I truly admire anyone who was the exceptional athleticism and skill to make a living out of being sporty. But let's be honest here. When it comes to professional athletes, footy players do seem to have the worst reputation. That team mentality and excessive testosterone can certainly be the catalysts for some disgraceful behavior. I know it's not fair to judge an entire group based on the acts of a silly few, but hardly a season goes by without a player being arrested for assault or drugs or public intoxication or, in at least one case that we know of (and only because poo has already featured heavily in this story), public defecation.

Delightful.

But my new friend urged me to give his mate a chance. So I checked myself for being so judgey and accepted his invitation to meet said Player.

A couple of months later, I met the Player at a fancy function after a game. He seemed polite and pleasant enough and even a little shy. He was also pretty hunky and super fit.

We spent the next couple of hours chatting and flirting and, despite my earlier reservations, I was undeniably drawn to him. I seem to be irresistibly attracted to a guy who's made it to the very top of his chosen profession, whatever that might be.

My sister was my wing-woman that night and I was also staying at her place. So when we decided it was time to leave, the Player gave me a peck on the cheek and said he'd love to see me again. We swapped numbers and I hoped he'd call me sooner rather than later.

But just when I thought I'd overcome my footballer phobia, I got a pretty nasty reality check the very next day.

My sister got a call from a mate who, coincidentally, worked with the Player's team. He said he'd heard someone at training that morning ask the Player, 'So, mate, how did you go with Sami Lukis last night?' To which the Player apparently announced loud and proud to the entire group, 'Well, boys, I took her home and I fucking slammed her', and they all erupted in cheers and laughter.

It sounded like a fearless display of Trump-style, locker room 'conquest' banter.

My sister was able to vouch for the fact that there'd been no Sami-slamming of any kind, because I'd gone home with *her*. But I still felt humiliated. And horrified, to think that a man could be so disgustingly disrespectful. It was exactly the kind of thuggery I'd been afraid of all along.

The friend who relayed the story was a decent, trusty, reliable guy who had no reason to *make up* something so foul. But a part of me still didn't want to believe it. Perhaps it was all a terribly unfortunate Chinese whispers–style misunderstanding. So rather than just promptly discarding him to the Neanderthal pile, I decided to do the mature thing and ask the Player about the reported foul play. I carefully worked out exactly what I wanted to say and how best to phrase it so that I wouldn't offend him (just in case he *was* innocent), and I rehearsed that conversation over and over and over in my head. When I finally got the courage to call, he didn't answer. So I left a message.

But I never did get the chance to confront the Player about the slamming accusation because he *never* returned my call. And I never saw or spoke to him ever again.

It was a foreseeable Game Over for me.

The Double-Pug Conspiracy Theory

A cute guy was flirting with me at a pub once and casually mentioned that he was the proud owner of two pugs. I called time out on the flirt-fest. Immediately.

My gaydar *and* my cheater radar both went into code red, alerting my inner dating detective to the very real probability that a single straight guy couldn't possibly own two pugs. Surely the pug is a gay man's dog. Or a couple's dog. Or the dog a guy inherits when he's dating a girl who already owns a pug, usually named Puggles, Peanut or Sweet Pea (the dog, not the girl).

I called the guy out on his questionable pair of pugs, but he insisted that he was neither gay nor coupled. And he persisted with the flirting. Well, that helped me rule out gay. But common sense was telling me that a single guy would never willingly own two pugs. It just didn't seem apropos. And I just knew I shouldn't go there.

My double-pug conspiracy theory made perfect sense to me. But was it ridiculous to assume a guy was a cheater simply because he admitted to owning a pair of pugs?

Sure, my gaydar was a little off that day. But if my cheater radar was broken, I guess I'll never know.

My darling friend Kate's gaydar is non-existent. She developed a major crush on a guy at yoga. He was six foot three with a rock-hard body and he was very, very pretty. He also happened to be ten years younger. Kate had just endured a super messy divorce, so she was ready and willing to take a toy boy and have some fun.

They went out to dinner a few times but whenever Kate tried to get frisky with the strapping young yoga dude, he'd back right off. Kate was keen, and she couldn't work out why he didn't want to get naked with her. She'd already noticed an impressive-looking package in his yoga spandex, so it appeared there was absolutely nothing for him to be embarrassed about in that department.

It seemed pretty obvious to everyone else that the strapping young yoga dude did not want to have sex with Kate but she was *convinced* he wanted her because, wait for it . . . He crocheted her a beanie.

Yes. He *crocheted* her a *beanie*.

So this was how our conversation went when Kate told me about beanie-gate.

Kate: He doesn't want to have sex with me. But I know he's really into me, because he crocheted me a beanie. Isn't that so sweet!
Me: He did what?
Kate: He crocheted me a beanie.
Me: Hon, he's gay.
Kate: No, he's not. Don't be ridiculous.
Me: Babe, he's gay. A straight man does not crochet. And admit it. Ever.
Kate: You're wrong. He's not gay.
Me: Babe. Listen to me. A man who likes to crochet does not like to have sex with a woman.

I'm sure we can all agree that there are various shades of metro-sexuality. From the guy who manscapes and isn't afraid to moisturise or wear pink (straight metro) to the guy who sings show tunes and can't live without his fake tan or teeth whitener (bordering on gay, possibly bi-curious). But I'm absolutely convinced that any guy who crochets has gone well beyond the bounds of straight guy metrosexuality.

After several more failed attempts to get physical with the young yoga dude, Kate realised her crush would never turn into anything more. But she kept the beanie. Apparently his crocheting skills were exemplary.

Inappropriate Crushes

My first ever inappropriate crush was on my primary school PE teacher. Mr Gibson had a porn-star moustache and a curly mullet down to his shoulders. And he wore knee-high socks with the shortest, tightest shorts he could possibly squeeze himself into. (Why were men so fond of the mammal-toe back in the seventies, anyway?)

I thought Mr Gibson was the second most handsome creature on two feet. Scott Baio was my number one. Every day during physical education class, I would desperately try to run the fastest or jump the highest to impress Mr Gibson with my physical prowess. I knew it was totally inappropriate to have those tingly feelings for my teacher, but my eight-year-old self dreamed about marrying a man just like him one day. Oh, my beautiful, mulleted Mr Gibson. With his business on the top and party in the back.

I've since realised that an improper crush can hit you at any stage in life. And there are varying levels of inappropriate, when it comes to that flicker of desire for someone you know you can't have. Like your boss, or your kid's teacher at one end of the scale. And a cousin, or your mother's new boyfriend at the other. I'm not sure where priest sits on the scale of inappropriate, but I'm willing to raise my hand and confess that, yes, I once found myself irresistibly attracted to a man of the cloth while I was holidaying in Rome with my trusty travel buddy Helen.

I had noticed two guys in clerical clothing standing behind us in the taxi queue after a delightful dinner in Trastevere. One of the guys was tall, dark and Ricky Martin–level handsome. If I'd been anywhere else but Rome, I would have assumed he was a male model on his way to a Vatican-themed fancy dress party. But considering I was practically around the corner from The Actual Vatican, I knew he was the real deal. He was hands down *the* sexiest priest I'd ever seen. Hail Mary the guy was gorge! He looked like he'd stepped straight off the pages of that annual Hot Priest calendar they sell for ten euros at gift stands all over the Eternal City. And yes, there is such a thing. (Google it: you'll be glad you did!)

It's not every day you spot a smoking hot young holy man on the streets of Rome, right? So I asked him if it would be possible to grab a photo. (Instagram would go *craaaaaazy* for this shit!) Imagine my surprise when the ravishing young holy man said, in a thick Australian accent, 'Sure! I'll do that for a fellow Aussie.'

We got chatting and I discovered they were *both* Aussies, studying for the priesthood in Rome. They were four years into their 'path of enlightenment' with one year to go, after which they planned to return to Sydney and get to work in a local parish.

Aussie Ricky Martin told me he used to be a Sydney banker wanker (he didn't actually say the *wanker* bit. I just added it, out of habit) and then one day he woke up and realised how unfulfilled he was. That was his calling from above. The other guy said he was out surfing one morning, sitting on his board at Curl Curl, when he got the holler from upstairs. Wow!

I was fascinated by their stories and in awe of their determination to find more meaning and purpose in their lives. I mean, can you imagine something so profound and life changing happening to you while you're just going about your daily business?

But mostly I was just drooling over the Aussie Ricky Martin trainee priest.

Our taxi arrived and Helen and I said our goodbyes and took off. But as we drove away, I felt an overwhelming urge to ask the driver to turn around and go back to the hot priest. Was this one of those sliding door moments? Maybe it was *my* calling. Or was it just the moment I realised I'd been harboring some weird priest sex fantasy, which was probably inspired by that episode of *Sex and the City* when Samantha flirts with a Franciscan? Either way, I knew I desperately wanted to spend more time with the smoking hot Aussie Ricky Martin lookalike.

I said to Helen, 'Um, do you think it would be massively inappropriate to go back and ask that hot priest out for a drink?'

She laughed in my face. And then, when she realised I was serious, she looked at me like I'd lost my marbles.

'I know. It's probably completely ridiculous,' I said. 'Are they even allowed to drink? I could ask him for a gelato instead. I don't care. I just feel like I *need* to spend more time with him.'

I never imagined I'd be attracted to a man of the cloth. Although to be fair, I only go to church for births, deaths and marriages so I haven't really spent much time around them. But my crush was uncontrollable. I felt compelled to return to him. I was ready to confess my sins. *All* of them.

I had no idea if Priest was allowed to date? Have sex? Get married? Was it a sin for me to even be thinking about it? Had I just scored myself a golden ticket to eternal purgatory for allowing myself to be turned on by a priest?

It was all very confusing.

Eventually Helen talked me down and convinced me to let this one go. It was already proving to be too much hard work. And, truth be told, I probably would have had about as much luck with the hot trainee priest as I would have with the real Ricky Martin. No, there was zero point in seeing the guy again. I mean, it's not like it could have seriously led anywhere. Dating a priest would kind of be like dating a married man, wouldn't it? He was already committed to someone else.

And even if they *could* get married (to someone other than the dude upstairs), I knew I'd make a really crap priest's wife anyway. I drink too much. I swear like a sailor. I'm allergic to sensible underwear. And I don't see any of those qualities changing anytime soon.

It pained me to accept that there was no future for me and the smoking hot Aussie Ricky Martin lookalike trainee priest. Sadly, we were not a match made in heaven.

Kissing Cousins

So I did worry that I might be dating my cousin once . . .

In the early stages of dating, I always enjoy discovering freaky coincidences that connect me to my new fella, via three (or sometimes two!) degrees of separation. Like finding out we went to the same school, a few years apart. Or that we both used to go to the Soho bar every Friday night in the late 90s. Or that he had already met one of my best friends in *Vancouver*, when he was there five years earlier visiting her *flatmate*, who he'd hooked up with on a Contiki tour of Europe (true story). That kind of discovery gives me a warm fuzzy feeling of familiarity. It's as if the universe was leaving subtle little signposts along my life's path, leading me, eventually, to him.

Unless the connection is a little *too* close for comfort.

Like, when the guy might be my cousin.

I guess that's, like, *minus* three degrees of separation.

I felt that familiar spark when a guy I'd just started dating told me his grandmother was Dutch. My mum is Dutch too, so I loved the idea of our shared heritage. When we dug a little deeper, we discovered that my mother's maiden name and his grandmother's maiden name were . . . exactly the same. And it's not the Dutch equivalent of Smith. Upshot being: we might be related.

Probably not *closely* related. But we could be cousins. A few times removed, perhaps.

So. There was that.

Strangely, this icky discovery did not make me want to break up with John on the spot. Look, it's not as if we knew we were related *before* we hooked up. But I'm pretty sure I could still hear the distant twang of banjos as I typed the words 'Is it okay to have sex with your cousin?' into Google (also praying that no one would ever be able to find this in my search history).

Well, it turns out that it is perfectly legal to have sex with (phew!), and even marry, your cousin in many countries. The main issue is the whole breeding scenario, but even that's not as risky as you might expect. Doctors now reckon the risk of birth defects in babies from parents who are related is around the same as for any expectant mum older than thirty-four.

John and I were nowhere near ready to procreate but, as a woman in her early forties, I can tell you I was a little insulted to know that my age would be more of a danger to the health of our kids than the fact that we might be related. No offence to me . . . but WTF?

Luckily, we eventually discovered a minor disparity in the spelling of the Dutch names, so we grasped that Hail Mary and continued dating. And enjoying stigma-free sex for the remainder of that relationship. And we never spoke of it again.

Snooping is Always a Good Idea

I'm a dirty big snoop.

If we've just started dating, you can be absolutely sure that the moment you leave me alone in your house/apartment/hotel room, I will do a full sweep of the place. I will inspect every available dresser, drawer, cupboard, shelf and surface area I can find.

I'm not trying to *steal* anything from you. It's just my way of getting to know you better. It's also my journalistic instinct. It's probably in my nature to investigate.

When I'm in snoop mode, I'm not looking for anything specific, and I've never found anything really horrific. Unlike a girl I know who reckons she once discovered about twenty polaroid pictures of different naked women in a guy's bedside drawer. It looked like the shots were taken while the women were sleeping. In his bed.

Yep. Vile!

I suggested she never see him again. And call the police. Immediately.

I did get quite a shock, once, when I found a wedding cake in a guy's freezer. We'd been on about six dates and it was the first time he'd left me alone at his place after a sleepover, so of course I had a thorough look around. I'm not exactly sure what compelled me to inspect his fridge – I was bored, a bit of a busybody and part bloodhound, perhaps? But lucky I did, because bingo!

It wasn't an entire wedding cake. It was just the top tier. You know, the piece saved by the husband and wife for the special occasion of their first anniversary. It was an elegant-looking round tier covered in traditional white icing and embellished with delicate flowers and dainty swirls. I imagine the whole cake would have been very pretty, and outrageously expensive.

The discovery of that particular slab of cake confused me, mainly because the guy I was seeing *had not mentioned he was or had been married.* We'd been dating for three weeks, so I think it was perfectly reasonable to have expected some mention of a wife by that stage. No? Apart from this sweet little discover, my snooping had uncovered no other evidence of a female living in his home.

I called him at work immediately and, as politely as I could, asked if there was any reason why he might have the top tier of a wedding cake in his freezer.

'Oh, yeah, I was married,' he told me. 'But the divorce just came through.'

Then he said the cake in the freezer 'meant nothing to him'. He'd actually forgotten it was there, so if I didn't mind, could I just throw it in the trash?

Umm . . . no!

I *did* mind, actually. I minded a lot.

'I am *not* going to throw your wedding cake in the bin,' I screamed down the phone. 'If you don't want it, maybe you should call your ex-wife and see if she wants it first, before you toss it out like some milk that's past its use-by date.'

I now assume the reason the ex did not have the cake in her possession was that she still had the very bitter taste of their marriage in her mouth. I wouldn't be at all surprised if she deliberately left it there when she moved out, hoping it would one day be discovered by the unsuspecting new woman in his life. (Which incidentally, is *exactly* the kind of thing I would do. I liked her immediately!)

This incident happened less than a month after I started dating that guy. And, in retrospect, it should have set the alarm bells off. If your new boyfriend a) forgets to tell you that he's been married, and/or b) asks you to throw his wedding cake in the bin, it's a fairly good indication that he's not a very nice fella. But I ignored the signs and it turned out to be one of the worst relationships of my life.

So I guess the moral of this story is . . . snooping is *always* a good idea.

World's Dumbest Cheater?

The only other time my snooping uncovered something really unsavoury was back in my early twenties.

I'd had this nagging feeling that my boyfriend couldn't be trusted, even though we'd been 'exclusive' for about a year. Frankie was a charming guy, working late nights at the hottest bar in town. I'd see him flirting with his female customers all the time but I told myself it was my own silly paranoia. I pretended not to notice all those times he refused to answer his phone in front of me. And I pretended not to care when he was two hours late without any explanation.

But one night, while I was staying over at his apartment, I discovered the undeniable proof that he had cheated on me. The definitive piece of evidence that proved once and for all, Your Honour, that my boyfriend was a lying, cheating scumbug who deserved to have his dick cut off.

The proof?

A long strand of jet-black hair, which I found in his – gasp! – shower. Gotcha, tiger!

Now, you might be thinking that a strand of hair in a shower cubicle is hardly undeniable confirmation of a man's infidelity. But it was, in this case, because:

a) He (my boyfriend) was bald.
b) I (his girlfriend) had long *blonde* hair.
See? A + B = C(heater).

When I questioned my bald boyfriend about the hair in his shower, he said he had no idea how it got there. But that sinking feeling in my gut told me I was onto something. He lived alone, he didn't have visitors staying and he didn't have a cleaner. The only possible way that long black strand of hair could have made its way into my bf's bathroom was if someone with long black hair had been in it.

I felt like all my fears and doubts were validated, at long last. I wasn't a crazy, paranoid, bunny boiler girlfriend after all! It was an intense mix of panic, fear, anger and relief. And my trusty women's intuition begging me to break up with him.

Yes, it seems all kinds of ridiculous to break up with someone over a single strand of hair. But that strand of hair was *everything*. I couldn't ignore what it represented. I'd been suspecting something was off for a very long time. And, finally, here was the proof.

But guess what? When Frankie realised he was about to be dumped over a strand of hair, he suddenly, miraculously, came up with a feasible sexplanation. He told me that one of his married friends was having an affair, and he'd asked Frankie if he could use his place for a little afternoon delight with his secret lady lover. So, after banging themselves stupid in my bf's bed all afternoon, they'd obviously felt the need to cool down (i.e. wash off any trace of their sordid affair) in his shower. And *that*, Your Honour, is apparently how the strand of long black hair appeared in my bald boyfriend-who-lived-alone's shower.

He begged me to believe him. Said he was sorry he didn't tell me the truth at first. But when it came down to a 'him or me' situation, he was happy to throw that filthy cheater under the bus faster than you could say, 'Hoes before bros'.

So, the million-dollar question is: was my boyfriend telling the truth? (Or was he just the world's dumbest cheater?) Maybe my fella *was* just trying to do his mate a solid by providing a clandestine sex den for the lousy scumbucket. But, it also seemed just a little too . . . convenient.

Well, a woman who really, really, really loves her man is prepared to hear *any* explanation that provides an option other than the one that might suggest he had his wang inside another woman. So I chose to believe him.

Looking back now, I realise I was dumber than a box of hair to believe that story. If I was in the same situation today, I'd be out the door quick smart. My infidelity radar is, thankfully, a little more in tune after thirty-odd years of dating.

I did not break up with my boyfriend over that strand of hair. Instead, I lived in constant fear of finding another one in his shower, in his bed, on his sofa or on his kitchen bench when I least expected it.

But from that day on, I can assure you, Frankie *always* had the cleanest shower in Sydney.

The Worst One

I fell in love once, and I ended up hating myself.

I always believed I was the type of girl who *would* never, who *could* never, find herself in an abusive situation. I was way too strong for any man to ever control me. But the truth is, there's no 'type' of girl who ends up in a toxic relationship. It can happen to anyone. And when it happened to me, I found out I wasn't as tough as I thought.

It was the worst relationship of my life. In fact, it was the worst *time* of my life. Full stop.

At first, he seemed attentive and affectionate and reliable. He launched a full scale charm offensive from the moment we met. And he made me feel special and desired and worthy. And that's all it took, really, for me to fall in love with him.

But I have discovered, after three decades of dating, that men are quite skilled at presenting the *best* version of themselves in a relationship for – oh – about three months. Then they become complacent. Or they just get tired of trying so hard. And that's when you see their *true* personality. I call it the TMT – the Three Month Theory.

This guy was no different. Right on schedule, the cracks started to appear.

Our arguments became more frequent. And more intense. I suspected that he wasn't always entirely honest with me. He seemed to be irrationally jealous of my male friends. I felt like he was angry at me and frustrated by me a lot of the time. And he tried to convince me that he *only* got angry with me because he loved me *so* much.

The verbal insults were the worst. He'd somehow worked out how to target my insecurities where it hurt me the most, and his put-downs cut through me like a machete. But I just told myself I was being overly sensitive. I was strong enough to withstand some nasty name-calling, wasn't I? Sticks and stones and all that. Unfortunately, I wasn't able to see that my self-esteem and self-confidence were both steadily being eroded away.

Besides, I had already convinced myself that we were deeply in love.

Love is such a powerful, complicated emotion. And when you find yourself in a lousy relationship, 'love' also becomes a convenient justification. You'll tell yourself that 'love' is the reason you forgive his dreadful behaviour. You'll use 'love' as your excuse for overlooking the flaws in his character. You'll blame 'love' for all of the pain and sadness and confusion you're feeling. When you've convinced yourself that you're in love with someone, you can just go ahead and blame 'love' for all your bad choices.

So, instead of breaking up with him, I went into 'rescue mode'. I thought that if I showed him more support and understanding, I could somehow earn his respect. I desperately tried to give him the best of my love, but I felt like I was walking on eggshells around him most of the time. And our fights only become increasingly volatile.

He wasn't physically abusive, but when his temper reached a scary level, I'd lock myself in the bathroom while he stood on the other side of the door, screaming obscenities at me. I would sit on the floor, sobbing. And hating myself. For turning into someone who locks herself in the bathroom to hide from her lover. And because I was too weak to walk away.

It's fairly common for anyone who hasn't been in an abusive relationship to think, 'Why didn't she just leave him?' And I hear ya, sister.

I used to think the exact same thing myself. Until *I* became the girl who couldn't 'just leave him'. I was a capable, educated, financially independent woman who still couldn't find the courage to walk away from a toxic relationship. I knew in my gut that this type of 'love' wasn't healthy, but I just couldn't bring myself to leave him.

I never spoke to friends or family about my situation, because I didn't want to play the victim. I also didn't want them to find out that my perfect life wasn't quite so perfect.

What shocked me the most about this guy was how he presented a completely sanitised version of himself to others. He was disturbingly good at putting on a saccharine-sweet display to the outside world, so everyone *else* would think he was a 'top bloke'. He just saved the worst of himself for me.

I knew I'd reached breaking point when I started to question whether I might actually be responsible for all of our relationship problems. So I took myself off to see a counsellor. And I asked her how my partner could keep *telling* me he loved me, but treating me like the enemy. Was I just too insecure? Was I delusional? Was I somehow to blame for his bad behaviour? What could I do to make it better? At the end of the session, she simply said to me, 'Sam, what on earth are you doing with this man?'

And that's all I needed to hear. I cried tears of relief.

One session with a professional had given me the clarity to see sense and the strength to take control of my situation.

Unfortunately, it wasn't the mature, private break-up I had hoped for. It happened after yet another especially heated disagreement over something ridiculously petty, which played out at a gathering in full view of some of my closest girlfriends. I was mortified to see the looks of pity in their eyes as they watched the argument unfold and saw me cringe with humiliation. Their independent, successful, outgoing friend had turned into someone they didn't recognise anymore.

Right then, I knew I couldn't do it any more. And with the help and support of my family and my beautiful, caring friends, I left him.

That was the most damaging relationship I've ever been in, but it taught me some valuable lessons about love.

It showed me that there's no place for control or fear in a relationship. Love should make you feel safe and protected and respected, not weak and afraid and insecure.

I now know that when a man treats me badly in a relationship, it's because there's something wrong with *him*, not with me. A man who tries to manipulate your emotions or push you to a point where you question your own sanity is not in love with you.

It also cemented my view that I would prefer to be alone for the rest of my life than be in another relationship that strips me of my self-esteem or my dignity.

But most importantly, that relationship made me realise: it's impossible to be in love with someone who makes me hate myself.

The Spud Gun

My gay husband Tim is one of my favourite people in the world. We have ridiculous amounts of fun whenever we're together. Aside from the time I almost got him shot.

That wasn't much fun.

I guess a little background is required before we put the bullet in the chamber. Tim worked with me at a Sydney radio station back in the early noughties and he's been my best gay ever since. It's a bit of an odd match because he's thirteen years younger than me but, I swear, we're twins separated at birth (albeit more than a decade apart). He knows all my deepest darkest secrets and I would trust him with my life. His parents treat me like a daughter-in-law and my family treat him like a son. We have the same wicked sense of humour. Except when I ask him to hand me the penis butter or the vagina mite. He thinks it's way childish and stupid. I think it's the funniest thing ever. Anyway, he makes me laugh harder than anyone I know.

Luckily, we also (usually) have very different taste in men. He's a sucker for big muscles and a cheeky smile. I'd just be happy to meet a guy who has most of his teeth, no criminal record and doesn't' say 'youse' or 'anyfink'.

Gusband Tim and I especially love to go out dancing. Well, I guess it's more appropriate to say I love to go out and watch

Tim dance. When he gets on the dancefloor after a few drinks, he reminds me of Elaine from *Seinfeld*, with arms and legs flapping around in every direction and pelvic thrusts that would make Elvis blush. And Gusband couldn't care less. He hits that dancefloor with insane levels of enthusiasm and gusto and I fucking *adore* him for it.

One of our favourite late-night venues in Sydney was the Piano Room in the heart of notorious Kings Cross. We conveniently ignored its slightly shady reputation as the rumoured hangout for drug dealers, hookers, gang members and the like, because on weekends they had a live band playing great covers of all our favourite hits and the music was ah-may-zing. We would drink and dance and sing along into the wee hours.

One night, at the slightly shady Piano Room, a guy sidled up beside me and started flirting pretty aggressively. He owned a takeaway café I'd been frequenting for years because they sell the best hot chips in Sydney. His opening line was 'So, I understand you're a regular salt, not a chicken salt, kind of girl'. Which would have been the most bizarre pick-up line ever, coming from anyone other than the guy who sells the best hot chips in town.

We chatted for a while, but I wasn't interested and eventually reached the point when I needed him to leave me alone. There was zero chance of meeting anyone else while Mr Potato Head was hanging around so I casually dropped into conversation that I was there with my 'boyfriend'. And I pointed to my gorgeous Gusband, who was dancing around like an aroused meerkat on the other side of the dancefloor.

'*That's* your boyfriend?' he said. 'Gee, he's a bit young!'

'I know! He's my toy boy,' I shouted over the music.

I think it's totally feasible that Tim *could* be my boyfriend. He's probably the straightest gay guy you'll ever meet.

But Mr Potato Head didn't believe me, so he stormed over to Tim and demanded to know if he was my lover and how long we'd been dating. Unfortunately, Tim was blissfully unaware that I was trying to ditch the guy, so he laughed in his face and said we had never done, and would never do, any horizontal dancing of any kind.

Shit! Bad Gusband.

Well, instead of just licking his wounds and letting it go, Mr Potato Head came back to me and said, 'That guy says he's not your boyfriend. So what's the deal?' (I mean, seriously, buddy? Take a hint!)

At that stage, I realised Mr Pomme Frite might have been a little unstable. So I lied (again) and told him I wasn't lying. I insisted that Tim was my pretty young boy toy. And that we were very, very happy together. Mr Potato Head promptly disappeared and I assumed he finally got the memo.

But thirty seconds later, Tim appeared by my side and said in a panic, 'We're leaving! *Now*. Let's go!' And he grabbed my hand and led me out the back door through the fire escape and onto the street. We didn't stop running until we'd flagged down a taxi and jumped in.

When he was finally able to speak, Gusband told me that Mr Pomme Frite had gone back to him and said, 'Sami says you *are* her boyfriend. And I don't like being lied to, you smartarse. So I'll tell you what I'm going to do. I'm going out to my car, right now, and I'm going to get my gun. And then I'm going to come back here and shoot you in the head.'

And Tim was quite sure Mr Pomme Frite wasn't talking about his spud gun. Oops. My bad (and a timely reminder for us all that lying is *never* a good idea).

I couldn't believe that my silly plan to shake off Mr Potato Head had backfired so spectacularly. I'd clearly been a little too blasé about the whole episode and now my beautiful Gusband was scared for his life. We managed to make it home without further incident, but I was genuinely horrified. (Almost as horrified as when I realised I would never be able to taste the mouth watering magnificence of my favourite hot chips ever again.) We never went back to the Piano Room and, luckily, we never ran into the Pomme Frite again.

We also decided the 'boyfriend' angle wasn't a good idea. Because, well, who wants to be shot in the head?

Drunky McDrunkface

Aggressive flirts are the *worst*. Some men just don't understand that flirting comes with certain boundaries. Case in point: Drunky McDrunkface.

I should have known the night wasn't going to go well when I rocked up to the bar and the door bitch looked me up and down and said, 'Oh, are you here for the body building convention?'

I immediately regretted my decision to wear the dress with the horizontal stripes. We all know they're a danger zone on anyone bigger than a size zero. But I was on holiday in Hawaii at the time, feeling tanned and fabulous and not really giving a fuck, so I threw caution to the wind and took a chance on the stripes. Turns out I looked like a weightlifter in drag.

I think it's fair to say my confidence had taken a pretty big hit before I even entered the bar. And then, to make matters worse, the only guy who hit on me all night was the drunkest guy in the room. You know the one: clearly can't handle his alcohol; swaying around, bumping into people, with no sense of personal space or dignity; slurring his words; eyes half closed (or half open, whichever way you look at it).

Yep. That guy. Ol' Drunky McDrunkface.

Sometimes drunk guys can be mildly entertaining for a while. But on that particular night, I wasn't in the mood. I apparently looked

like a man in a dress and the only guy who seemed the least bit interested was the moron who could quite possibly fall over and/or puke
on me at any moment. So when he stumbled his way over and tried
to flirt with me, I said, 'No, thank you, I'm not interested.' This
didn't deter him. He persisted with his heavily inebriated advances.
So, again, I said, 'Thank you. But I'm really not interested. I'm just
here with my girlfriends tonight.'

But he wouldn't take no for an answer. So when his manterrup-
tions reached the point of being downright annoying, I physically
turned my body away from him in an attempt to block the guy
completely. He clearly wasn't picking up on my verbal cues, so
I thought a non-verbal message might get through. My body
language was practically screaming, 'You are not included in this
conversation, buddy. I have no interest in engaging with you. This is
your opportunity to leave.'

Sadly, non-verbal cues *no comprende*. So when he tried yet again to
forcibly gain my attention, I said, 'Look, I've already told you I'm not
interested. Several times. And you're annoying me now. So *please* go
away and leave us alone.'

Which is when he looked across at my girlfriends. And then
he looked back at me. And then, very loudly, shouted, 'LESBIAN
CUNTS!'

The guy clearly didn't handle rejection well.

I was stunned for a moment, and then I looked him straight in his
half-open eyes and said, 'Wouldn't your mother be proud?' (Usually
I don't think of a suitable retort until hours after the incident!)

As Drunky McDrunkface stood there, swaying, squinting at
me and trying to remember if he *had* a mother, I leaned across the bar
and told the bartender what had just happened. And, to their credit,
I've never seen a security team act so fast. Two enormous security
guards appeared from nowhere, grabbed the pest and escorted him
out of the establishment. As he stumbled past me, I couldn't resist.
'Oh no, leaving so soon? But you had me at "lesbian cunt".'

The bartender very kindly offered us a complimentary round for our troubles and we were left to ponder what makes a guy act that way. What gives him the right to demand a woman's attention, even after she's told him she's not interested? Is it alcohol? Pride? Ego? An inherent obnoxiousness? It certainly takes all the fun out of flirting.

When a guy has no respect for a woman's space or her right to say no, it's nothing short of bullying and harassment. Parents, please teach your sons that this behaviour is not acceptable.

Bad Hair Day

I encountered another especially disgruntled Romeo while I was out with some friends at the cosy little Lord Dudley pub, in Sydney. It was one of those extremely rare occasions when a man simply walked up to me and said, 'Hi, can I buy you a drink?'

I know it was brave of the guy to just infiltrate my group of friends like that and have a crack. And sober guys don't offer to buy me drinks, like, ever! But I'll be really honest, I wasn't attracted to him. Plus, I didn't have the energy that night to flirt with, or even talk to, a stranger. I was enjoying the relaxed company and conversation of some friends I didn't get to see very often. So I said, 'Thanks so much, but not tonight. Sorry. I'm just here with some friends. Have a good night.'

He looked a little miffed but he gave me an awkward smile and disappeared somewhere behind me. I felt like a bitch for about four seconds but I didn't think about it again until he appeared out of nowhere, about half an hour later, and said to me, in a really immature, almost childish tone, 'Well, I just want to say, you've missed the *colour*. In your *crown*.' And then he walked away.

I said to my friends, 'Umm what the actual fuck was *that* about?'

I had no idea what he was talking about, until one of my friends suggested that he might have been referring to a slightly dodgy colour application on my hair. On the crown of my head, to be exact.

I need to point out that his was not a helpful gesture, like the one you might offer a girlfriend: 'Hey, darls, you've got some lippy on your teeth.' His tone suggested that what he really wanted to say to me was, 'That'll teach you for turning me down, you disgusting, colourless, fucked-up hair freak!' The comment was intended to be his big comeback after I rejected him. I can only guess he'd spent thirty minutes standing behind me, seething and staring at the back of my head, trying desperately to think up the worst possible insult he could throw at me. And the best sledge he could manage was 'you've missed the colour in your crown'.

Not quite as punchy as 'lesbian cunts', but certainly more original.

As soon as I got home, I did the double-mirror juggling act to inspect the back of my head and I was shocked to discover that, yes, there was indeed a small dark patch on my crown that was not quite as blonde as the rest of my hair. The disgruntled romeo was spot on. My hairdresser *had* missed the colour in my crown.

I guess I should have thanked the guy for pointing that out.

Note to self: find new colourist. Book appointment ASAP.

Cocaine Cowboys

I once met a notorious Sydney bachelor at a friend's wedding. We had some flirty chat throughout the night but as the wedding party ended and people started to leave, I told him I probably wouldn't make it to the afterparty. It had been a long day and I was working in breakfast radio at the time, so I was permanently exhausted thanks to my daily 4 a.m. wakeup calls.

'You should come,' he said to me. 'If you do, I'll give you masses of cocaine!'

I'd never been hit on quite like that before. The promise of *masses* of cocaine was certainly a novel approach although, sadly, it probably wasn't a unique one for this Casanova, who obviously believed the surest way to a girl's heart was straight up her nostrils.

What really repulsed me wasn't just the use of the word 'masses' (as if he was some kind of Colombian kingpin), but the realisation that the kind of girls he usually hit on were probably turned on by his generous offer. More than anything, I was offended that El Chapo thought I might *be* one of those girls. 'I'll give you masses of cocaine' does not turn me on. If you're looking for six words to impress me, try 'Would you prefer red or white?' instead.

*

It's alarmingly common for men to use nose candy to woo the ladies these days. In some circles, offering a gal a line is the equivalent of offering to buy her a vodka and tonic (top shelf, of course). I've met a few of these Cocaine Cowboys on the dating circuit over the years.

A friend offered to set me up with a handsome doctor one time when I was visiting New York. He lived in Florida but he was willing to fly to Manhattan to meet me. I didn't know much else about the guy, but the mere fact that he was willing to fly interstate for our date was enough for me to agree. When you're almost forty and single and you haven't been on a date in a while, you'll give anything a go. So what if he lived 15 000 kilometres away from me? That was insignificant, a minor problem that would be resolved after we met and fell madly, passionately and hopelessly in love.

And as I sat in my yellow cab en route to the bar of the Soho Grand Hotel, I thought to myself, 'Well, look at you. You're in frickin' New York. You're going on a date with a hot American doctor. You are so damn fabulous right now. What an amazing story this will be to tell the grandkids!'

The Doctor was already waiting in the bar when I arrived (✓). I could immediately see that he was, in fact, very handsome (✓). And when he stood up to greet me, I noticed that he was tall and he looked quite fit (✓). But about two drinks in it became crystal clear that this guy was not my Doctor Love, when he randomly embarked on some crazy story about how much he loved cocaine and how often he used blow and how much fun it was and blah, blah, blah (✗).

To be talking about illicit drugs so openly with a woman he'd only just met seemed bizarre. Maybe he was nervous, maybe he was just a complete dick, but dare I say alcohol wasn't the only mind-altering substance the Doctor had enjoyed that evening. As he went on and on and on about his penchant for the white powder, I just sat there thinking, Well, this is certainly *not* the story I want to be telling my grandchildren one day.

I'm sure this approach works for some of these Cocaine Cowboys, but when a guy offers me coke or thinks it will impress me, it's pretty much on par with him telling me, 'I've got herpes', 'I have a tiny penis' or, 'I really do think it's reasonable that women are paid 40 per cent less than men, across the board'.

Yeah, that's a no from me.

The New York Swag

New York City was also the perfect backdrop for one of my most romantic dates ever, even though that particular date took place . . . in a train station.

I really should preface this story by confessing that I love everything about New York. The sights. The sounds. The smells. The shopping. The shoes! I mean, how can you not? It's the only city in the world with a department store shoe floor so huge it's got its own postcode *and* express elevators! 'Cause when a girl needs shoes, she needs 'em stat. Am I right, ladies?

Native New Yorker Lady Gaga once said, 'New York City is like the husband I never married.' Well, your guy gets around, Gaga, because my relationship with the Big Apple feels exactly the same! I grab any opportunity I can to spend as much time with that dirty big spunk as I possibly can.

In fact, I love The City so much, I set up my own travel company just so I could host tours of New York and show off my man to other women (they all fall madly in love with him too, by the way).

On one of my frequent jaunts to NYC, I enjoyed a brief but juicy affair with an Aussie guy. We hit it off at a party hosted by mutual friends in the West Village. Despite living stateside for years, he'd maintained both his distinctive Aussie accent and his Aussie sense of humour. He had also managed to pick up a charming dose of New York 'swag'.

A guy with swag has *just* the right amount of arrogance. He's extra confident but not quite cocky. He doesn't have to be the best-looking man in the room. He's just comfortable in his own skin, with a 'life is good' vibe. The Aussie guy's swag was sitting somewhere on the scale between Jerry Seinfeld and Jay-Z, with a touch of Hugh Jackman thrown in for good measure. He was cool and confident and clever with an understated sexiness that I found really attractive and very intriguing.

So when Mr Swag asked me out on a date and told me we were going to a train station, I was initially underwhelmed. I mean, come on! Manhattan is a city overflowing with spectacularly romantic first-date options. What about a moonlit stroll across the Brooklyn Bridge? A bike ride and a picnic in Central Park would be nice. Sunset cocktails at a fabulous rooftop bar with breathtaking views of the Empire State Building? That'll do me just fine, thank you very much. But a train station. WTF?

However, the moment Mr Swag led me onto the Main Concourse of Grand Central Terminal, I got goosebumps. I looked up at the celestial mural on the ceiling. And I got it.

The place wasn't just a *train station*. It was magnificent.

I soaked up every moment as we strolled arm in arm through the iconic terminal and Mr Swag gave me the guided tour. He showed me the Whispering Gallery, where an architectural wonder allows you to whisper sweet nothings to each other from opposite sides of the room. He told me about the legend of the Kissing Room, a place set aside in the glory days of train travel for arriving passengers to enjoy that first passionate embrace with their sweetheart. He took me to a hidden bar, the Campbell Apartment, where we cosied up on a plush leather lounge in the corner and I drank champagne and he ordered a Rob Roy. It felt like we were in the New York of a bygone era. And when Mr Swag kissed me under the legendary gigantic Tiffany clock in the middle of the Main Concourse with hundreds of people madly rushing around us, I felt like I was in a movie. I'd seen this exact scene on the big screen many times before.

There is an undeniable air of romance about Grand Central Terminal and that day will always rate as one of my all-time favourite first dates. It also set the tone for a memorable Manhattan love affair.

With no job to rush back to at the time, I decided to extend my stay in New York and see where my holiday fling with Mr Swag might lead. He even invited me to move into his cute little studio on the Upper West Side, where I quickly made myself very much at home. Life in the Big Apple with my new man (and his sexy swag) was every bit as fabulous as I imagined it would be. While he was at work, I'd take a class at YogaWorks, check out the latest exhibition at the Guggenheim or shop for groceries at Whole Foods. At night we'd grab dinner at one of his favourite restaurants on Amsterdam Avenue or catch a movie at the AMC on 84th Street or meet his mates for drinks on the Lower East Side. As I realised how comfortable I felt in this incredible city, I secretly started to wonder how difficult it would be to transport my beloved furchild, Lolli, over from Sydney if I decided to relocate. Permanently. Our Manhattan love story was moving full steam ahead.

Until it unexpectedly ran off the rails a couple of weeks later.

I'd arranged to meet some girlfriends downtown for dinner. It was going to be the first time Mr Swag and I had spent a night apart since I'd moved in. But, less than five minutes after I walked out the door and left him alone in the apartment, I received a bizarre text message from him. It appeared to be some kind of poem or song verse, describing a burning desire to see someone they hadn't seen in a long time and yearning to be with them again. Mr Swag had signed off with, 'see you shortly x'.

As I sat there on the C train, I read that message over and over and over, desperately trying to understand what it meant. I didn't recognise the lyrics and it seemed a little OTT that Mr Swag was 'yearning' for me, considering I had left him only a few minutes ago.

Then I realised. Oh my god. This message was intended for someone else. And I wondered, had Mr Swag invited a visitor over for a speedy rendezvous while I was downtown with the gals? Those romantic lyrics made it sound like a passionate reunion was very much on the cards. I was crushed. And confused. And mortified to think that he'd invited someone over for a quick shag the *second* he had the apartment to himself.

Maybe I had misread our situation.

Had it been wildly premature for me to assume we were exclusive? Was he not getting enough sex? Was he still lovecrastinating over his recent ex? Had she been on the scene the whole time?

I'd heard that the dating scene in New York was brutal. But this was next level *Hunger Games* shit! Apparently men in New York like to have a few prospects on the go at all times. I just didn't realise that would still be the case when you were cohabitating with someone.

I decided not to go home and confront him straight away so I just replied, 'Hey, I don't think this was meant for me. Have fun x'.

It took him a little while to reply, but when he did it simply said, 'Of course it was meant for you.'

I didn't believe him.

My fabulous Manhattan love affair suddenly wasn't feeling quite so fabulous. After dinner I thought about checking in to a hotel, but I decided to go home and face the music (or in this case, those mysterious song lyrics). Thankfully, Mr Swag did not have company when I got home. But I couldn't believe it when he looked me straight in the eye and *swore* that the message was meant for me. Even though it made absolutely no sense.

I really wanted to believe him and carry on with my new life plan to move to Manhattan and live happily ever after on the Upper West

Side. But something didn't smell right. My trusty women's intuition was pleading with every single cell in my body to accept the fact that he was lying to my face.

That New York swag I'd found so sexy when I first met him? Suddenly not so sexy. His swag was apparently a little less Hugh Jackman and a lot more Leonardo DiCaprio than I realised. So I told him that it had been lovely to meet him and I thanked him for his generous hospitality but I thought it would be best if I moved out the next morning. And I did.

I was heartbroken. Even though the fling had only lasted a few weeks, I think I'd been more emotionally invested in the idea of being in a relationship in New York than I was in the actual relationship itself. I'd enjoyed my time with Mr Swag but I'd fallen truly, madly and deeply in love with Manhattan, the city of my dreams.

But when I got home to Sydney, I felt like New York had chewed me up and spat me out. I realised I didn't have the chutzpah to survive that kind of fucked-up dating scene.

I didn't hear from Mr Swag until about six months later, when I was back in New York. He sent me a text which read, 'I hear you're in town. Would be great to hook up. If you're up for it.'

Wow. From the most romantic first date I'd ever been on to possibly the least romantic invitation I'd ever received.

'If you're up for it'? Seriously? That's a little *too* much swag for this girl to handle.

The Love Hotel

I had my first ever overseas hook-up in my early twenties, when I was living in Japan.

It was my version of a gap year, but instead of backpacking around Europe or temping in London, my yearlong sabbatical consisted of working on a spectacular golf course at the base of Mount Fuji and partying in Tokyo every other weekend. Totally random, I know. But I thought I was all kinds of fabulous.

One night, as I was making my way through the heaving dancefloor of the legendary Shibaura nightclub, 'Juliana's Tokyo', I suddenly found myself grinding with a smokin' hot American marine. And, oh my Lordy yes Janelle, the marine could *move*. Dancing with him was basically like having sex, fully clothed. And he was gorgeous. He had a touch of LL Cool J about him, with flawless skin and dimples that sent me into overdrive. He was *insanely* fit and he spoke with a sexy tough-guy accent.

That random, amorous dancefloor meeting with the marine led to a six month relationship and the kind of steamy, sexy, unforgettable affair that every woman deserves to have with a foreigner at least once in her life.

However, it was all a bit of a nightmare whenever we wanted to play hide the sushi, because he lived on the marine base with a gazillion other marines and I was sharing a teeny tiny apartment with a nosy flatmate.

Neither of us had any money, so we couldn't afford a fancy hotel. The cost of living in Japan was astronomical back then. (I remember apples cost five dollars *each* in the supermarket.)

But we'd heard about these places called love hotels, where you can rent rooms by the hour. Now, please trust me when I tell you it's nowhere near as seedy as it sounds. Love hotels are actually a bit of a secret institution in Japan. Often used, rarely spoken about. Walls in most Japanese homes are (literally) paper thin, so if you and your new bf really need some privacy, you just zip off to the local love hotel for a quick shag. It's also the best place to go if you don't want to be seen, if you know what I mean. Yes, love hotels are a handy option for horny people having hot affairs. Oh, and for poor tourists like us who couldn't afford a room anywhere else.

I'm not the least bit ashamed of my night in a love hotel. It turned into one of the funniest nights of my life. Everything about the love hotel was discreet. No reservation system. No front door. No reception desk. The layout of the place was like a one-level country motel, with every room facing directly onto the carpark. You could drive up and park right outside your sneaky little sex den. You know the room is vacant if the light is on above the door. So we just drove up, opened the door (no key, no security code) and strolled right in.

Okay, so this is where it gets a bit weird. Not even one minute after we walked into the room, the phone rang. That was creepy. Was someone watching us? Could they see us? How did they know we were there? A voice on the other end of the phone asked if we would like the room by the hour or overnight. We said overnight, thanks. (Hey, it might be weeks before I'd get to see my smoking hot marine again!)

The voice instructed us to put the cash payment into a little canister next to the phone and then to put the canister into a transparent tube that travelled from the desk up into the roof (like they have at some grocery stores). And then *whooshka* – our cash disappeared up the chute and into the roof in 0.5 seconds flat.

And that was that. *Domo arigatou gozaimasu!* (Which translates to 'thank you very much' or in this case, also, 'now go shag yourselves stupid, you crazy kids'.) We were left to enjoy the comfort of our romantic little love nest for the next fifteen hours.

The room was bigger than most regular hotel rooms I've stayed in and it was immaculately clean. Spotless. Phew! Considering what actually goes on in those rooms, it was good to know they took their cleaning duties seriously (although I have a sneaking suspicion I would have run a mile if anyone had cast a blue light over that bedcover).

There was an enormous bed (of course), a big Jacuzzi, a double shower and a gigantic TV. (Okay, Japanese porn. *Don't.* Things get *crazy* weird in those movies.) So basically, the room was equipped with everything lovers might need for a night (or an hour) of passion. I wonder if there was even a secret vending machine somewhere that spat out *Fifty Shades*-style whips and nipple clamps (asking for a friend).

The one thing we did not expect to find in our little Nippon love shack was the karaoke machine and two microphones taking pride of place next to the TV. I mean, who wants to be singing fucking karaoke, when you've come here to, well, fuck? We laughed it off and didn't think about it again and we got busy doing what we went to the love hotel to do and then I fell asleep in my hunky marine's giant, muscly, gun-toting arms.

I was woken up at around 2 a.m. by a terrifying noise. It sounded like a piercing scream or a wailing cat or some kind of wounded animal. Or a woman in serious trouble, in the next room. I quickly woke my marine in case he needed to go save a life off-duty. We both listened for a while and then we realised it wasn't a woman in trouble or a helpless animal. It was an old man. Singing karaoke. Very loudly. And very, very badly.

He was singing in Japanese and his voice was pretty crackly but he was belting out that tune like he was on stage in front of 80 000 adoring fans. Grandpa's Viagra had well and truly kicked in. Was it a pre- or post-shag serenade? I couldn't tell. There was nothing in his voice to give it away. Perhaps it was mid-shag. Oh my god, that would have been even funnier.

I'd somehow found myself in one of the most ridiculous 'how the fuck did I get here' moments ever. The absurdity of the situation hit me, as I lay there with my American marine, in a hotel for sex pests, listening to some old (probably naked) dude serenading his lady love, with the worst karaoke tune ever. I've never laughed so hard in all my life.

The strangest thing about it all was that I could hear randy gramps in the first place. The love hotel had thought of *everything* to make your sex-escape as comfortable and anonymous as possible, except for soundproofing the walls. I mean, seriously. Of all places. A hotel where people specifically go to *have sex*. Soundproofing is kind of essential, don't you think?

A Mixtape Means I Love You

I was clearly more in lust with my sexy American marine than I was in love with him, but I was still heartbroken when the day came for me to move back to Australia and finish my University degree. I was so distraught about leaving him that I briefly considered quitting university altogether and starting a new life as an army wife on the military base in Okinawa. Thankfully, sense prevailed and I moved back to Brisbane to complete my studies. We promised to keep our love alive and tried our very best to overcome the challenges of distance. But this was the early nineties, pre-email, WhatsApp, Instagram, Facebook. No sneaky Snapchat to help keep the spark burning. Back then, staying in touch with a lover in another country took enormous effort and determined dedication.

We spoke on the phone occasionally, but it was so expensive, so we wrote letters to each other, every week. My heart would race as I'd search through the mail, desperately hoping to spot that little envelope with the familiar crooked handwriting and the US stamp and military seal.

If it was my lucky day, my marine would include a photo with his letter. It was usually a shot of him standing in the jungle in his army fatigues, all sweaty and shirtless, sixpack proudly on display, brandishing a very large weapon.

My marine was sex. On. Legs. (With a gun.)

Under all that perfectly chiseled rock-hard beefcake, my delectable marine was also a big softie. Sometimes he'd send me a mixtape – a carefully selected and personally recorded compilation of his favourite R&B love songs: R. Kelly, En Vogue, Shanice, K-Ci & JoJo, Keith Sweat, Boyz II Men. And I thought that was about the most romantic thing ever.

Sadly, mixtapes have become a lost art. But back in the day, they really were the ultimate expression of love. First, they involved a considerable degree of time and effort to compile. You'd have to cue up the song and hit record on the casette player at the exact moment the song began. It usually took a bunch of tries to get it just right. You wouldn't waste time doing that for just anyone. A mixtape also allowed you to express your private thoughts and deepest desires through the lyrics of each song. Giving someone a mixtape was basically like giving them a little piece of your soul.

I knew exactly what my man was thinking as I listened to nineties boy band Silk telling me how they wanted to lick me up and down til I said stop . . . But one day, as I lay there listening to his latest compilation and staring lovingly at an especially alluring shirtless photo he'd sent me from his most recent jungle boot camp, I couldn't help noticing a large, reddish-purple shape on his neck. It was a hickey.

A big, fat, filthy, fucking love bite. Which he didn't get from me. I hadn't seen my marine in months.

It suddenly dawned on me that while I'd returned to my boring old life as a uni student back in boring old Brissie, pathetically pining over my sexy marine, listening to his mixtapes and drooling like a bloodhound over his shirtless photos, he wasn't missing me at all. He was running around Okinawa having loads of fun receiving random hickeys from who knows who.

I was devastated. Plus, I was a bit repulsed.

I know some people think hickeys are hot, but I don't get it. There was a brief period in my late twenties where a boyfriend and I agreed to 'hickey Sundays' in an effort to understand the appeal of suck-ing on skin for the sole purpose of leaving a bruise. We'd give each other hickeys – but only on Sunday mornings and only in spots that wouldn't be visible to anyone else. We thought it was hilarious, mainly because it was our own little private stupid joke. But also because I was hosting a respectable kids TV show at the time. We gave up after a few weeks when I decided I didn't enjoy the taste of blood.

But I digress.

I despaired for days over that hickey-pic until I was able to get my marine on the phone.

Of course he told me it wasn't a hickey. He said it must have been a burn from where a gun had recoiled on his neck.

Well, I'd never dated anyone who specialised in military combat before, so I had no idea what a burn from an M40 might look like. Therefore, technically, I guess his explanation could have been true.

And even though every fibre of my being (along with a small piece of photographic evidence) told me that my boyfriend had recently received a love bite from another woman, I chose to believe his gun-recoil explanation. And we carried on.

But the relationship was never the same after that. My marine didn't send me any more photos or mixtapes. The letters became less frequent too. Until they eventually stopped altogether. Distance proved the downfall in the end. And I never saw or spoke to my sexy marine again.

But the hickey certainly left its mark. I've had a few long-distance relationships since then, and they've all failed dismally. Trust issues were always a factor.

I blame the marine and that questionable hick-pic.

The Playful Pussy

Some cheaters are especially good at manipulating their way out of potentially tricky situations. I'm actually impressed by some of the creative excuses I've heard from men in desperate efforts to deny their infidelity. It's quite a skill to be able to think up a cunningly convenient, alternative scenario right there on the spot and then lie through your ball sack to avoid confessing that your pecker has, in fact, been playing elsewhere.

I especially enjoyed the 'playful pussy' explanation presented by my dear friend Belinda's boyfriend. She'd suspected him of cheating for months but finally called him out after she discovered a woman's hair elastic on his bedside table. It wasn't her hairband. And it wasn't his. He was not, nor had he ever been, a man-bun kind of guy.

Now, even if this hasn't ever happened to you, I'm sure you can appreciate how the sight of another woman's hair accessory in the vicinity of your boyfriend's bed would make your heart sink. And your hair stand on end. And yet, when confronted about the sudden appearance of the incriminating hair elastic, he very calmly told Belinda to stop being dramatic because there was a perfect simple explanation.

It was one of his cat's favourite toys.

And that's how he explained the presence of the foreign hairband.

Bel had *never* seen his cat toying with the elastic during their nine months of dating, so she had to wonder: did he really have a playful pussy with a fondness for hair accessories? Or did he just have a playful imagination?

Put any emotions aside and, yes – like a neck burn from a loaded M40 – the story technically could have been true.

After days of gut-wrenching deliberations and self-doubt, Belinda accepted his explanation because, in the end, she decided it was so ridiculously random it simply had to be true.

She dumped him a few months later, when she discovered a stream of sexy texts to another woman on his phone. I think we can all safely assume that woman might be missing a hairband or two.

I'm glad Belinda finally dumped the dickhead, but she could have saved herself some serious heartache if she'd simply listened to her gut after finding another woman's hairband on his bedside table.

The fact is, there's no pleasant way to find out your partner is cheating on you. And your loved ones can sometimes be hiding all kinds of secrets.

I heard a story about a woman who was enjoying lunch with the girls when she recognised the pretty blue and white Country Road maxi dress on a lady crossing the street outside the café. She'd bought that exact same dress only a couple of weeks before.

And then something else caught her eye. As she glanced up, she noticed that the woman wearing the dress looked, strangely, a bit like her husband. 'Wowser, that's one masculine looking woman,' she chuckled quietly.

But then she stopped breathing, when she realised, Wait a minute. That *is* my husband.

Wearing a dress.

Wearing *my* dress!

FUCK. FUCK. FUCK.

And there he was, walking down the street without a care in the world, while her universe came crashing down around her as she suddenly discovered that her husband was a cross-dresser.

I've often wondered if this story is one of those juicy urban myths, but if it's true, well, that sure is one helluva way to find out.

The Armed Robber

One the greatest romances of my life is travel. I feel an urge, actually a longing, to pack my bags, get on a plane and explore someplace new as often as I possibly can. I'd visit every single country in this lifetime, if time and money allowed. Blame it on my wandering soul.

And possibly the fact that I find it much easier to get laid overseas. I've become quite the expert at the old 'holiday fling'. They really are truckloads of fun. Social media has made it much easier for us to keep in touch with our holiday flings these days but I always think the best way to enjoy an overseas rendezvous with a hot foreigner is to remember the golden rule, which is simply to 'enjoy it for what it is'. (I had to learn this the hard way with my American marine.)

What happens on holiday really is best left on holiday.

I've had quite a few memorable interactions abroad, like that time I unknowingly slept with an armed robber in Honolulu. I place the blame for this, quite firmly, on Gusband Tim. Who willingly let me do it. Aloha!

Bizarre things happen to Tim and me in Hawaii. The first time we holidayed on the island of Oahu, we noticed that people were looking at us strangely everywhere we went. Strolling down the main drag of Waikiki, stuffing our faces at the Cheesecake Factory, or sipping mai tais at the RumFire bar during happy hour. It didn't matter where we were. People would clock us, stare intently at Tim for a moment, glance across at me, then back to Tim, before looking away awkwardly. As if they'd looked at something that might scar them for life if they stared at it for too long.

At first, I assumed they were just trying to work out if Tim and I were a couple, as folks often do. But this was different. Rather than just acknowledging the lucky cougar and her aesthetically pleasing toy boy, these folks appeared to be so stunned by the age gap that they had to look away in embarrassment, like it was some kind of reverse Anna Nicole Smith situation. I was quite offended, to be honest. Sure, I'm thirteen years older than Gusband, but I swear to god I don't look it.

The mystery was solved on day three, when some random guy at happy hour told us he was blown away by how much Tim looked like a famous American athlete named Tom Brady. 'I swear you're his Awwzzie twin,' the guy shouted at Tim before shouting us another round of drinks.

Tom Brady is a household name in America. He's a star quarterback superbowl champion and one of the best footballers in the country. Oh, and he also happens to be married to the she's-so-freakin'-gorgeous-it-hurts-to-look-at-her supermodel Gisele Bündchen.

We googled the guy immediately and realised that Gusband does, in fact, bear an *uncanny* resemblance to Tom Brady. I, on the other hand, couldn't pass as Gisele's distant cousin's mother. Even on my best day. So all those folks staring at us thought they'd spotted the champ Tom Brady and his model wife. Until they looked across at me and thought, Wait up. She ain't no supermodel.

This revelation set the tone for a holiday that scored us several rounds of free drinks and had us crying tears of laughter, all day, every day. It was also the holiday when we refined our brother-sister cover act. We worked out that pretending to be siblings gives us the best chance of getting lucky. Whenever we meet new people, we make a point of dropping into conversation (as quickly as possible) that we're big sis and little bro. Which immediately alerts them to the fact that we're not a couple. And more importantly, it gives any interested fella the green light to go ahead and flirt up a storm with his preferred sibling, depending on sexuality.

The brother-sister cover act has always worked a treat, except for one night on our Hawaiian vacay, when we were both drawn to the same ruggedly handsome guy. We were both captivated by his cheeky personality but we couldn't tell if he was straight or gay. The situation only became more ambiguous when we found out he was in the Navy.

Well, Navy definitely seemed more focused on Gusband than me for most of the night, so I just assumed he was gay. But then, after drinks, dinner and more drinks, we all ended up at a nightclub and as soon as we hit the dancefloor, Navy walked straight over to me, put his hands on my hips and started grinding up on me like nobody's business. He pulled out a range of other dubious dance moves that pretty much confirmed he was straight.

Gusband was gracious in defeat.

The next morning, Tim and I assumed our regular sun lounge hangover-recovery positions on the beach and I provided a blow-by-blow account of my sexy little rendezvous (which is standard 'morning after' procedure with a best gay/gusband). I was describing Navy's extensive body art – all the basic nautical-style tattoos you'd expect to find on Popeye and one scary-looking tatt that stretched all the way across his collarbone – when Gusband chimed in with 'Oh, that must be his old gang symbol.'

Um, come again?

Apparently Navy had told Gusband the night before that he was once a member of a notorious gang back home in Seattle. They were in the 'break and enter' game, apparently. Armed with shotguns, apparently. He told Tim he only joined the military to clean up his act, avoid criminal prosecution and an inevitable life in jail.

So. That.

And despite knowing *all* of that, Gusband still quite happily let me toddle off to my hotel room with the armed robber in tow. He even *encouraged* the liaison, if I remember correctly. And at no stage did he think it necessary to give me a heads-up that I was about to sleep with a gangster. Not even just a cheeky little warning to keep an eye on my jewellery.

Gusband said he was 'pretty sure' I had nothing to worry about. After all, we'd spent hours with Navy and we both thought he was a bloody good bloke. (Sorry, did I mention that the guy used to be an *armed robber*?)

Well, the tough military rehabilitation must have worked, because I had around $10 000 worth of jewellery sitting on my bedside table within arm's reach of the former gangster all night while I was fast asleep beside him, and it was all still there when he left the next morning. So it was a gentle reminder for me to never judge a book by its criminal, gangster-related, shotgun-wielding cover.

The Bodyguard

The famous American ski resort of Aspen is a great place to meet men, considering two thirds of the population there, at any given time, is male. But be warned, single ladies, the local lasses have a saying about the blokes who live in or frequent their town: 'The odds are good. But the goods are odd.'

Ironically, I first visited Aspen on a romantic winter holiday with a boyfriend in my mid-thirties. I fell madly in love with the town and deeply out of love with the boyfriend soon after. And my love affair with Aspen has been going strong ever since.

The skiing is spectacular. The après is even better. I mean, for a start you're bound to run into a celeb or six while you're there. I've shopped alongside Heidi Klum and Seal (pre-divorce) at Ralph Lauren. I've tried on $3000 ski jackets I had no intention of buying in the Moncler change rooms next to Kate Hudson. I've danced in the wee hours at the ridiculously exclusive Caribou Club beside Paris Hilton (she's much prettier in person). And I once shared a ski lift with Antonio Banderas, who, incidentally, looks even *more* mackable with a couple of icicles dangling from his sexy salt-and-pepper beard.

Sadly, Antonio did not ask for my number. But I have had quite a few eventful Aspen encounters.

Like the time I was set up with Kevin Costner's bodyguard. Correct. The Bodyguard's bodyguard.

Plenty of celebs have holiday homes in Aspen. Kevvie owns a massive ranch about ten minutes out of town. Aspen is a small village, where everyone knows everyone and I've become friendly with some of the locals. So when one of my mates discovered I had a thing for tall men, he decided that a fellow local (who also happened to be one of Kev's longtime bodyguards) would be perfect for me. We were both invited to a dinner party hosted by a mutual friend, where hopefully sparks would fly.

Well, I'm pretty sure I gasped out loud when the bodyguard first walked in. There's tall, and then there's *towering* – like this guy, who was about six foot nine. He was inconveniently, uncomfortably tall. The guy wasn't fat but he was certainly big-boned, in an unnaturally gargantuan kind of way. Which made him an awkwardly tall, extraordinarily enormous human being. You might even call the guy a giant.

I was shocked by the sheer enormity of this man. Even in my six-inch heels, my eyeline sat somewhere around his nipples. Thankfully, we spent most of the night sitting down.

I wish I had some elaborate story to share with you about how I embarked on a glamorous whirlwind international love affair with Kevin Costner's bodyguard. But I do not. Sadly, old mate wasn't a big talker. In fact, he hardly spoke at all. This was especially disappointing because I'd assumed the celebrity bodyguard would have some cracking yarns up his sleeve about Kevin Costner and Whitney Houston and private planes and all kinds of fabulous and/or sordid celebrity encounters, and what really goes on in those movie-star trailers. He could have been the *best* dinner companion/boyfriend ever! But, unfortunately, he just wasn't a great conversationalist.

I tried really hard to keep the chat going over dinner, but at times I felt like I was at work, interviewing an especially tough subject. Eventually, the lack of conversation became exhausting, so I gave up.

Between the obvious communication challenges and the awkward nipple-eyeline issue, it was clear this wasn't going to work out.

To be fair, a bodyguard was probably never going to be a suitable match for me anyway. He's the guy who's trained to blend into the background and not say much. He's a professional observer. While I, on the other hand, am a professional communicator. I love a chat. And I need a guy I can talk with, not just at.

I'd also quite like someone with better manners. Turns out the bodyguard had given our hostess a box of chocolate-covered strawberries when he arrived that night. A lovely gesture from a seemingly appreciative dinner guest. Well, I guess he could tell our romance was definitely not budding, so he was also one of the first to leave, just before dessert. And on his way out, he popped into the kitchen, grabbed the unopened box of strawberries and reclaimed his gift.

Maybe he had another party to go to, or another hostess to impress? Or maybe he just decided my company wasn't even worth the price of the choccie berries.

As hilariously inappropriate as it was, it was also kind of fitting. Because if life is like a box of chocolates, I would have to say my dating life is like a box of chocolate-covered strawberries.

I love chocolate as much as the next person. But I have a tragic, on-off allergy to strawberries. I *adore* biting into a big, beautiful, sweet, juicy strawberry. But, every now and then, they give me hives. Big, red, blotchy, hideously itchy hives. Still, I can't help myself, can I? I keep going back – time after time, having another crack at yet another chocolate-covered strawberry – even though I *know* I'll probably regret it.

It's the same with love, right? Sometimes it can be sweet and beautiful and that just makes you want more, more, more. And sometimes, it just irritates the shit out of you.

The Horny Hipster

I once met Jesus in Aspen. And it wasn't after a nasty ski accident, where I temporarily crossed over to the other side.

I was enjoying a pinot grigio at the uber-fabulous 39 Degrees Lounge after an awesome day on the slopes, when I found myself chatting to a cute Mexican fellow who told me his name was Jesus. I've spent enough time in the States to know that it's a fairly common Spanish name and it's usually pronounced 'Hay-soos'. But this guy insisted that his name was 'Gee-zus'.

Jesus.

We flirted for a while but, ultimately, Jesus didn't turn me on, so that was that. I moved on.

Later that night I was very much turned on by a full-blown Brooklyn hipster. The guy was a total dude, complete with statement beard and trucker cap, checked shirt and designer dark jeans, cuffed at the bottom. He was the absolute epitome of that effortlessly cool urban look I was so into at the time. He was also tall and easy on the eye and he spoke with that sexy Noo-Yawk Brooklyn accent that makes me go weak at the knees. So, basically, he had me at his hipster hello.

He was in Aspen on business, but only for one night. So after a very entertaining flirt-fest, I ended up back at his hotel. A shag was off the menu because neither of us had condoms (#fail) but it was still fun to have a kiss and a cuddle and a bit of a snuggle and I decided to spend the night anyway. When we reached the inevitable point of sheer frustration at being virtually naked with someone you're insanely attracted to but can't have sex with, we decided to get some shut-eye.

Which was when the guy rolled over, opened the bedside table and pulled out a small box. I heard a click. And then I heard waves. The distinct sound of very loud waves. Which was puzzling, considering the nearest ocean was 1000 miles away.

Turns out the Hipster had brought the ocean with him to Colorado, courtesy of his very own portable sleep-inducing wave machine. He reluctantly told me it was the only way he was able to fall asleep.

WTF?

As I lay there in his arms, in the middle of a ski resort, listening to the sound of the ocean, I did a quick mental analysis of the situation and realised that a guy who could remember to bring his own *sleep-inducing wave machine* but couldn't remember to pack a couple of *condom*s, was probably not single. I decided to leave the hot Brooklyn hipster and his wave machine to fall asleep in each other's company. And I left.

I really shouldn't have been as shocked as I was when I Google-stalked the Hipster the next day and discovered the online gift registry for the gorgeous baby that *his wife* had given birth to, *two months* before. Yep. While this imbecile was having a romp with me (and his wave machine) in Aspen, his poor wife was home in Brooklyn with cracked nipples and their newborn.

No wonder the guy had brought the sleep inducing implement on his business trip. The new dad was desperate for a good night's sleep.

I tried to think of an alternative explanation for this situation. Maybe he was newly separated (despite having a two month old baby, nice!). Could the baby shower have been for another guy with the exact same name? Or did the Hipster just believe it wasn't cheating if you didn't actually put it in?

Well, here's what thirty years of dating has taught me:

1) I seem to be the undisputed world champion of making up excuses for cheating arseholes.

2) Most single guys over the age of twenty-five who are out of town, whether it's for business or pleasure, will be packing rubber.

3) If a guy does not have condoms, he probably should not have you in his bed.

4) And if he has a wave machine, you should run a fucking mile.

The Naughty Texans

This one time, at band camp (AKA Aspen), I met four cheeky Texans who were in town on a boys' weekend, with a clear mission statement to get drunk, get laid and party. I'm not entirely sure if skiing even factored into their plans.

We met during a rowdy lunch at Cloud Nine, which is a hugely popular ski-in, ski-out restaurant tucked away on the side of the mountain. The food is okay, but the main attraction is the wild party that happens in the dining room each afternoon. The champagne-spraying and tomfoolery kick into high gear just after lunch, when the music gets everyone dancing on the tables in their ski boots. It's a pretty small cabin with a crazy YOLO party atmosphere, so you can pretty much guarantee you'll become lifelong friends with everyone else in the room by the end of the day.

I'd noticed a table of four well-dressed guys, who all looked to be in their early to mid-thirties. One of them was tall, dark and super fine. We pretended not to notice each other for a while, but he eventually made his way over and introduced himself and my attraction to him shot into the danger zone the moment I heard his slow, smooth, Southern drawl. Now, listen up, y'all, there's a very good reason that accent is repeatedly voted the sexiest in America. There is something seriously seductive about the Texan twang that truly tickles your fancy.

I was delighted. I'd never met a Texan before. He wasn't the J. R. Ewing type, with a ten-gallon hat, gigantic belt buckle and enormous teeth. He was more Matthew McConaughey – hotter than a Texan barbecue and sweeter than pecan pie. Also, his name was Buck. One of the most Southern names you could possibly give to a boy. Well, Bucky Boy had just the right amount of swoon-worthy charm and I couldn't help wondering if he might help me discover my inner cowgirl later that night.

Lunch at Cloud Nine puts most people in the kind of euphoric mood that makes you feel like you just don't want the day (or the party) to stop. So after lunch the Texans invited a group of us to a house party back at their place. Turns out their holiday lodging was a gigantic chalet in one of the most exclusive parts of town, where the average vacation home is worth about 30 million bucks. The place belonged to the in-laws of one of our new Texan friends, and they were clearly loaded, in a Fortune 500 kind of way.

The entrance foyer alone was bigger than most studio apartments, with a ridiculously large chandelier that looked strangely out of place in a ski chalet. There was a majestic *Gone with the Wind*-style staircase and an oversized framed photo hanging on the wall. It was the typically cheesy, all-American glamour shot of the family who owned this quaint little eight-bedroom, eleven-bathroom, 15 000-square-foot mountain shack.

The party went from zero to a hundred in a matter of minutes. Bottles of champagne, tequila and bourbon appeared from nowhere and it sounded like a professional DJ had mysteriously set up when I wasn't looking. The Texans were a breed of money I'd never experienced before. Yes, they were ridiculously privileged ivy-league frat boys, having the time of their lives on a weekend away in the alpine playground of the rich and famous. I'm sure they flew in someone's daddy's private jet to get there. But there was something surprisingly likeable about them. They weren't wankers, like those repulsively ostentatious 'rich kids of Instagram'. They were just there to have a good time and share the fun with a bunch of new friends.

I have to admit, I was also a little bit turned on by it all. Everything seemed super glamorous and a little surreal for a girl who grew up in the bogan northern suburbs of Brisvegas. I felt like Alice down the rabbit hole.

They were fun guys to party with. But I sure as hell wouldn't want to be married to any of them. Our host might have been staying in the Aspen abode of his wife's outrageously loaded parents, but that hadn't stopped him from picking up two pretty young girls that afternoon and inviting them back to the party. And the photos of his gorgeous wife and cute-as-a-button kids all over the house didn't deter him from grabbing a couple of bottles of chilled Cristal from the kitchen fridge and disappearing with his two new lady friends to the outdoor spa.

That was Buck's cue to offer me a tour of the house. Conveniently, the first room we visited was his guest suite, which was about five times the size of my hotel room. The tour ended there. I didn't see the rest of the house. I'm not even going to pretend that I could ever cut it as a proper Southern Belle.

We had a fun shag but, sadly, it was nothing extraordinary. I was expecting big things from my Texan cowboy, but I guess we'll just blame the twelve solid hours of drinking beforehand. Besides, he wasn't actually a cowboy. I think he worked in insurance.

The *really* titillating stuff happened a few hours later. I didn't feel like waking up in a house full of strangers (makeup-free) the next morning, so I called a taxi around 2 a.m. and decided to get out of there. But as Buck and I were waiting in the enormous entrance foyer for my cab to arrive, two naked women suddenly appeared on the giant staircase in front of us. They were the young ladies who had disappeared with our host (and the Cristal) hours earlier. The girls didn't appear to be in any kind of distress. They were giggling uncontrollably and bounding down the stairs like they were playing an especially fun game of hide-and-seek.

The lights were on, so I copped an eyeful. Both girls were *completely* starkers. Not a stitch. And they made absolutely no effort to hide their nakedness. They skipped straight past us, in their birthday suits, before disappearing somewhere into the abyss of the Ewing mansion. It was like a scene out of a movie. Where the movie is *Gone with the Wind* meets *Animal House*. Or any film starring Zac Efron.

I was in shock but Bucky Boy wasn't surprised at all. He just kind of shrugged at me and smiled, like that shit happens to them, *all the time.*

My taxi came and he gave me his number. But I never saw him again. One wild night with those naughty Texans was more than enough for this gal from little ol' Brisvegas to handle.

An Indecent Proposal

A man once offered me ten thousand pounds to have sex with his virgin nephew in London. Yeah. So that was weird.

The day started out innocently enough. I had just flown into London with my friend Mary and by late afternoon we were both starting to feel the early strains of jet lag. But it was the first day of our holiday and we'd resolved to get the party started, so we decided to push through and head out for dinner at one of the trendiest restaurant recommendations from our in-the-know London mates. We dressed up in our sexy frocks and applied full hair and makeup, determined to show London town that these Aussie chicks were fabulous and single and ready to mingle.

However, as our circadian rhythms slowly but surely descended into complete meltdown and the jet lag took over, we suddenly both reached the point where we felt like we were about to die. So, despite every single piece of jet-lag advice that tells you to *stay awake at all costs*, we stupidly decided to take a 'quick power nap' at around 6 p.m. as a cheeky little refresher before we stepped out.

We woke up at 11.30 p.m. Because: jet lag.

As we lay there in that fuzzy jet-lag haze, where your body kind of feels like it's encased in a cement-filled coffin, we agreed that our wild night out was not going to happen. But we were still wearing the sexy

LBDs we'd fallen asleep in, so we dabbed on a fresh coat of lippy and popped across the road to the bar at the Mandarin Oriental Hotel to grab a late-night snack.

We found a couple of stools at the bar and ordered two glasses of champagne to celebrate the start of our spectacular European adventure. Two well-dressed gentlemen arrived shortly after and plonked themselves down in the stools right next to me. Which was strange, considering they could have sat anywhere in the near-empty bar.

One of the guys looked about fifty and the other was much younger. I had a friendly chat to the older fella. He was Turkish and on holiday with his nephew, who was visiting London for the first time. The nephew didn't speak English, so he just sat there quietly as we spoke.

When he could see that my glass was empty, my new Turkish friend kindly offered to buy me another champagne but I declined. I wasn't interested and I didn't want to give him the wrong impression. And that's when he very politely said to me, 'Could I offer you ten thousand pounds to have sex with my nephew?'

I sat in stunned silence, wondering if I had misheard or misunderstood his broken English. Surely he didn't just say what I thought he said? Nephew. Sex. Shitload of money.

'Pardon me?' I said, bewildered.

He leaned closer and said, in hushed tones, 'My nephew is eighteen years old and he is a virgin. I would like to pay you ten thousand pounds to provide his first sexual experience.'

I laughed in his face. 'You're kidding, right?'

But it wasn't a joke. He looked a little puzzled at first. And then he said to me, quite diplomatically, 'Would you take twenty thousand pounds?'

'Buddy, I am *not* a hooker,' I said through gritted teeth. 'And I'm *really* insulted that you think I am.'

Oh. My. God. How fucking embarrassing. I couldn't believe it. My very own indecent proposal.

Did he actually think I was a hooker? Was my dress that slutty? Sure, it was a little shorter than I usually wear, but I didn't even have my boobs out. I was mortified. Although I will admit that I was also secretly a little bit flattered that he'd offered me so much money. It would have been a million times worse if he'd only offered me a hundred pounds. Even if the guy *had* mistaken me for a prossie, at least he'd assumed I was high class.

And then it dawned on me. That's exactly what we looked like. Two high-class hookers, all dolled up in our sexy best, sitting at the bar of a five-star hotel drinking champagne at midnight on a Tuesday. We sure didn't look like two ravenous Aussie gals trying to push through a dreadful bout of jet lag.

When he realised his enormous error in judgement, the Turk seemed genuinely ashamed. I actually felt a little sorry for him when I saw the look of horror on his face. He apologised profusely and quickly gathered up his things (and his virgin nephew) and they left.

Mary and I erupted into fits of uncontrollable laughter. One of those overwhelming laughing episodes that actually makes you pee your pants, just a little bit. Amplified, no doubt, by the fact that we'd just consumed champagne on an empty stomach after travelling across seven different time zones.

'Only twenty thousand pounds?' Mary shrieked hysterically. 'Is that all? Doesn't he know you don't get *into* bed for less than six figures?'

'Well, the offer did double in about ten seconds.' I laughed. 'I probably could have got him up to fifty thousand if I'd tried!'

'You *sure* you won't do it for twenty thousand?' Mary snorted, tears streaming down her face. 'You know that would pay for our holiday! And the nephew wasn't *that* hideous. You should have asked for fifty thousand . . . and offered to teach him a couple of tricks as well!'

The story of my indecent proposal at the Mandarin Oriental in London has sparked some interesting debates among friends over the years. Some of them think I was mad for turning it down. Some girlfriends say they would have said yes to the *first* offer. They reckon it would have been the fastest ten thousand pounds they'd ever earned. It was the poor kid's first time so it probably would have been all over in a matter of seconds.

Most people agreed I did the right thing. There is absolutely no way I would have accepted the offer. Not even for a million dollars! Because we all know what happened between Demi Moore and Woody Harrelson when Robert Redford and his gigantic wad of cash got in the way.

I have no regrets. I could never have done it. Not for any amount. Being paid handsomely to have sex with a Turkish teenager was never especially high on my bucket list anyway.

Lesson learned: next time I feel like a midnight snack in London, I'm going to McDonald's.

Costa Brava

After our brief (but eventful) stay in London, Mary and I decided to check out Barcelona. Neither of us had been before and we'd heard it was loads of fun. Plus, it's the spiritual home of Zara. So, well, shopping.

But we got a lot more than we bargained for in Barcelona, when we ended up on a stranger's superyacht on the 'wild coast' of Spain. As you do.

We'd randomly befriended two lovely local lads on our first night out. Barcelona Boy #1 was a sports agent. He told us his clients were racing car drivers and tennis players, including some Wimbledon champions we'd know for sure. Barcelona Boy #2 was one of his clients, a racing car driver in the Formula Two series, which is one rung below Formula One. That was our very first experience with Spanish men, so we had no idea if they were world champion bullshit artists. We decided to believe roughly half of everything they said.

The fact that we'd only known BB1 and BB2 for a couple of hours didn't stop them from inviting us to a party on a yacht in a place called Costa Brava the next day. They assured us the party would be amazing and offered to pick us up from our hotel, drive us the two hours to Costa Brava and drop us back afterwards. They even offered us free accommodation at the party host's house, if we decided to stay the night.

It was a wildly generous offer from a couple of fellas we'd only known for half a minute. And it all sounded a little bit too suss for my liking. I told them we'd check our schedule and let them know in the morning.

We hit Google as soon as we got back to our hotel and realised that BB1 and BB2 were both who they said they were. Also, Costa Brava probably should have been on our to-do list all along. It's just north of Barcelona, closer to the French border, and it's known as one of the most stunning stretches of coastline in all of Europe. It's also renowned as one of Spain's most exclusive holiday playgrounds.

Okay, so Costa Brava was a no-brainer. But the whole partying with total strangers scenario? Well, that required some more serious consideration. On the one hand, an uber-glamorous shindig on a superyacht in the Mediterranean with a bunch of charming (and hopefully hot) Don Juans did sound quite fabulous. On the other hand, we might be taken hostage and kept as sex slaves in their friend's dungeon in the middle of nowhere in a foreign country. Not so fabulous.

We decided to take the risk. My gut told me they were decent blokes. Still, in an effort to be mildly sensible about this ridiculously nonsensical situation, we hired a car and drove ourselves to Costa Brava. That way, we could leave in a hurry if we needed to. I did google 'where to buy mace spray' before we left, but I couldn't find any, so I stole a small knife from the hotel and hid it in the glove box instead. You know, just in case.

The Spaniards arranged to meet us in a small village in Costa Brava and escorted us to their friend's house. We found them waiting in an enormous black SUV with very dark tinted windows. It looked like the kind of vehicle the FBI uses to transport the President. Which was as intriguing as it was unsettling. At that point, we did seriously consider turning around and driving back to Barcelona. But we were also *really* invested in the prospect of a fabulous party on a superyacht. So we followed the SUV through a maze of narrow country roads for about twenty minutes until we arrived at an enormous iron slid-ing gate. The gate was wedged into one of those massively oversized hedges that borders the entire property of a ludicrously expensive home. As we drove through the gate, I noticed it slide shut (and pre-sumably lock) behind us. That was officially the point of no return. We were committed. Come what may.

I briefly thought about texting my GPS coordinates to my mother back in Brisbane but I realised that might set off some major alarm bells and lead to a chain of events I could not undo, possibly involving Interpol and a very expensive international rescue mission. So I took a deep breath and hoped for the best.

When we reached the end of a very long driveway, I saw the strangest thing – two ginormous topiary sculptures. One was shaped into the number fifteen. The other was a full-sized topiary motorbike. I knew, in that moment, that we'd arrived at the home of some-one who was famous either for riding motorbikes or for owning a company that makes them. I quickly phoned my flatmate, Steven, who's obsessed with motorbike racing and asked him if he knew of a Spanish motorbike rider, who might have some connection to the number fifteen.

'Of course,' he replied. 'Sete Gibernau. Why the fuck are you asking me that? I thought you were in Europe?'

'Yep, I am. And I think I'm at his house. And, oh my god, I think he's standing in front of me half-naked right now. Gotta go. Thanks. Bye!'

There was a shirtless, delectable-looking guy standing at the end of the driveway, covered in mud, hosing down a dirt bike. We parked the car, got out, and BB1 introduced us to the hot dirt-bike dude. Sure enough, it was his dear friend, Spanish Moto GP champion Mr Sete Gibernau. Standing there covered in mud, Sete very politely welcomed us to his home and thanked us for agreeing to join their party on the yacht. He invited us to look around while he disappeared to shower and change.

It was a spectacular contemporary Spanish villa and looked like something straight out of the pages of European *Vogue Living*. As I stood there and took it all in, I thought to myself, How the fuck did I end up here?

Then I noticed some photos scattered around the living area of our host with a strikingly beautiful woman. She looked familiar. I knew I'd seen her face. Like, a lot. I asked BB2 who she was.

'That's Sete's ex-wife. Esther Cañadas. The Spanish supermodel.'

Yes. Right. Of course she is. Could this day get any fucking weirder?

They had only recently divorced but, as a couple, these guys were to Spain what Posh and Becks are to the UK. Or what Beyoncé and Jay-Z are to America. Or what Bec and Lleyton are to 'Straya. Totes Celebrity Royalty. They would probably have their own Brangelina style moniker, if anyone could think of a good one. Seteñadas? Esthernau? Giberñadas?

See? It doesn't work.

Well, things got even weirder when we arrived at the marina to board Sete's stunning yacht. And we realised that our wild party consisted of five people. Me, Mary, BB1, BB2 and Sete. That's it.

I was kind of hoping the party I'd just driven two hours from Barcelona to attend (and possibly risked my life for) might resemble something more like the opening scene of that *Entourage* movie: a bevy of beautiful people gathered on a mega-yacht, partying like rockstars, with a jacuzzi, a private DJ and copious amounts of champagne. But, instead, it was just the five of us, and some music being played off someone's iPhone in the corner.

I don't know what happened to the other guests. Or if they even existed in the first place. Maybe something had been lost in party-invitation translation. Mary and I had a good laugh about it but, to be honest, we were just excited to cruise around Costa Brava and enjoy the magnificent scenery and the company of our lovely new friends.

Just when I thought things really couldn't get any weirder, the day hit a whole new level of bizarro when I discovered, much to my horror, that there was only *one* bottle of champagne on board. And no other alcohol. I shit you not.

I would have happily brought my own, but the guys told us not to bring a thing. And, look, I don't want to appear ungrateful or anything, but how on earth did they think five people were supposed to survive on a yacht for several hours on just *one* bottle of champagne? I mean, *seriously*. Had Sete spent all his money on the topiary?

They didn't scrimp on the food, though. The most enormous dish of paella I've ever seen in my life appeared and I am not exaggerating one bit when I tell you that the dish was the size of an average car bonnet. Basically, it was a fuckload of paella. Maybe they had been expecting more people after all?

I really don't know why we were invited on the yacht that day. For a brief moment I wondered if they thought we were hookers (like that Turkish bloke in London) or if they were patiently waiting for our stripper show to start. But these guys weren't sleazy or rude or arrogant. And they clearly weren't trying to ply us with alcohol. They were total gentlemen who treated us with the utmost dignity and respect.

There was a moment when the five of us were sitting around the comically large paella dish, eating and laughing and joking and just enjoying each other's company and I remember thinking to myself, Now this is what life's about! Discovering new places. Meeting new, interesting people. And taking a chance on random unexpected experiences like this. It was a moment I'll always cherish.

I thought I noticed some subtle flirtatious eye contact from Sete on the yacht, but I couldn't be sure if he was interested. Every now and then I'd catch him looking at me and we'd share a glance and a flirty smile, but I convinced myself that it was probably nothing. I mean, let's be honest, how could the guy be attracted to a mere mortal like me, after he'd been married to a friggin' Spanish supermodel?

We cruised back to the marina and I could easily have driven back to Barcelona (I'd only had two glasses of champagne all friggin' day) but we were loving our new friends, so we agreed to stay the night at Sete's villa. We dined outdoors by the pool. A dinner party for five, and staff to serve it, magically appeared in front of us. Thankfully, this time there was no limit on the amount of wonderful Spanish red wine and I started feeling more and more attracted to our host by the second.

After dinner, we watched a movie in the private cinema (yes, of course he had a fucking private cinema in his holiday home). By that stage I had a nice little red-wine buzz going on, so when Sete came and sat down beside me, I was tempted to reach across in the darkness and find his hand and take my chances. But I was too shy (plus, I reminded myself, I wasn't a supermodel). So I just sat there awkwardly beside him, wondering if he would make a move.

He didn't.

After the movie, we all retired to our own private quarters. I had just cosied up in bed and turned out my light when I heard a knock on my door.

'It's me.' It was Sete.

And I thought, Oh my god, this is it. He's going to come in, grab me, kiss me passionately and tell me he'd been dying to do that all day. And I wouldn't resist. It would be the perfect ending to an incredible day. And who knows? Maybe it would be the start of an especially glamorous new love affair. I was sure I'd be able to make myself very much at home in this magnificent Spanish villa in Costa Brava.

He opened the door, looked in and said, 'Is everything okay? Do you need anything?'

I froze. 'No, I'm all good, thanks. Thank you again for a wonderful day.'

There was a brief pause when neither of us said anything.

Then he said, 'You're very welcome. *Buenas noches.*' And he shut the door and was gone.

The next morning when we woke up, Sete had already left. He'd asked BB1 to pass on his goodbyes. And that was that.

Mary and I drove back to Barcelona in a daze, wondering if the last twenty-four hours had actually happened.

I never saw or heard from the Spaniards again. But that encounter will go down as one of the most unexpectedly amazing holiday experiences I've ever had. And, most of all, it was a nice reminder that good, kind, decent gentlemen are out there. Even if you have to go to Spain to find them.

The 'Kinda' Guy

Single ladies, grab a pen and listen up. If you're looking for a sexy little winterlude, head to any ski resort in Austria. The skiing is sensational. The scenery is spectacular. And there are more men in those mountains than you can poke a ski pole at.

In villages like Sölden and St Anton (or 'St Man-town' as it's commonly known), the ratio during ski season can be as high as eight men to every one woman.

The guys are mostly German and Dutch. There are plenty of Poms. And Swiss. And there's always a good contingent of appealing Scandinavians – lots of Swedes and Norwegians and Danes.

And it's eight to one, ladies. *Eight* to *one*.

Maybe that's why I have no trouble meeting men during my Austrian sojourns. Or perhaps I just radiate a more carefree holiday aura of alpine abandon. Either way, I'm certainly not opposed to the occasional Wiener schnitzel.

The Euro guys I've met have all been chivalrous and courteous and considerate. They seem to take more pride in their appearance than the average Aussie bloke and they usually have a decent sense of style to match. Sometimes there's a little language barrier, but that can just make the flirtation all the more fun. (Just for the record, I reckon the Norweigens are the hottest. But maybe that's just my secret Viking fetish?)

My favourite thing about the men I meet in European ski resorts is that they're all super fit. Most of these guys could ski before they could walk, so they're not afraid to literally throw themselves off the side of a mountain and attack the highest, steepest slopes in the Alps. It's a super intense and often dangerous workout getting to the bottom, so it's not for the faint-hearted. You know how some girls are turned on by a guy's eyes or his tattoos or by the car he drives? Well, I'm turned on by a man's avalanche pack. No, that's not a euphemism. It's a backpack filled with beacons, shovels, airbags and any other gadgets one might need to survive an avalanche. If a guy is wearing an avalanche pack, it doesn't just tell me that he's an expert skier who pushes his passion to the absolute limits. It also suggests that his man energy is insanely high, with appropriately sized *cojones* to match.

I have definitely met more men sporting the avalanche accessory in the Austrian Alps than anywhere else in the world.

However.

The one thing that remains the same for me on *any* continent and at *any* elevation is that I still manage to attract my fair share of weirdos. There's clearly no translation issue when it comes to that big fat neon 'freaks welcome' sign that always seems to shine so brightly on my forehead.

Case in point: the Kinda Guy.

The Kinda Guy was 'kinda' this and 'kinda' that. And in the end, I kinda wish I hadn't gone there. I was with Gusband Tim in the ski resort of Sölden. We met the Kinda Guy in the kinda après bar where everyone was dancing on the tables in their ski boots by 4 p.m. Austrian après bars transform into full-blown nightclubs from mid-afternoon, with DJs, thumping music and flashing lights. And those Euros sure can drink. The busiest après bars in Austria sell more beer per hour than any other venues in Europe.

That bar in Sölden was mostly full of Dutchies. With our blonde hair and blue eyes, Gusband and I blended in nicely. My mum was born in Holland before emigrating to Australia as a young girl, so technically I'm half-Dutch. And Gusband is my pretend sibling, so that makes him half-Dutch too, by default.

The bar was packed, probably peaking at around 200 people above capacity. Which made it ridiculously unsafe, but also ridiculously fun. You had to do a full-on body-press with every single person you walked past anytime you ventured to the bar or the loo.

I met the Kinda Guy during one of those random, awkwardly intimate, full-frontal moments. As I squeezed past him on my way back from the loo, our body-press was enhanced by a two-second eye lock. He was cute. And I noticed he was carrying an avalanche pack.

Bingo.

The Kinda Guy was from Amsterdam. He had the quiet confidence of a man who knows he's always going to be one of the best-looking guys in the room. His bulging biceps and rock-hard chest were bursting out of his tight thermal top. He was also very outgoing and incredibly generous – always the first to shout another round whenever he noticed people's drinks were empty. I did think it was a bit lame, though, when he told me he was 'kinda' an entrepreneur.

While I'm absolutely in awe of anyone who has the skills and know-how to create their own business and forge their own success, I do think it's a bit weird when someone calls themselves an entrepreneur. I feel like that's a label you should only use to describe *other* people, not yourself. It's like Roger Federer saying 'I'm the world's greatest-ever tennis player'.

Regardless, I decided the Dutch 'kinda' entrepreneur could be a fun little holiday fling. So when he snuck in a quick peck on the lips as he handed me another flaming Jäger shot, I didn't resist. It was that unspoken green-light moment. A subtle acknowledgement that neither of us would mind terribly if this turned into something more. I didn't resist the next time, either, when the peck lasted a little longer. Or the next time, when it turned into a full-blown, embarrassingly PDA-style pash.

I blame the avalanche pack.

Then Gusband bought a *fourth* round of flaming Jäger shots and the afternoon kicked into high gear. I casually mentioned to the Kinda Guy that I was keen to visit Amsterdam one day and connect with my Dutch roots, and he got all serious and said to me, 'Look, I have to warn you about something. If you look me up on Facebook, you'll discover something about me.'

Okay, that was a leap. Just because he'd had his tongue down my throat didn't mean I necessarily wanted to friend him on Facebook. Still, my mind jumped to various conclusions about what this shocking discovery might be.

Best-case scenario: he's a famous Dutch soccer player.

Not best-case scenario: he's actually a woman.

Most obvious scenario: he's fucking married. Arsehole.

'I'm not married,' he said.

'So do you have a girlfriend?' I asked.

'Um. Kinda.'

He said I'd find photos on Facebook of him with a 'kinda' girlfriend. After having an on-off relationship for a few years, they'd recently got back together. But they had also agreed to 'explore other options'.

'What do you mean, "explore other options"?' I asked him.

He hesitated for a moment and then he said, 'Well, we can have sex with other people.'

'Ohhh. So, you're in an open relationship?'

'Well . . . kinda,' he replied.

I was fascinated to meet a real-life swinger (and a guy who was so attached to the term 'kinda'). He was shocked when I asked him to tell me how their arrangement worked.

'Are you sure you want to hear this?'

'Absolutely,' I said enthusiastically. 'No judgement here whatsoever! I only just met you so I really don't care what you do in your private life. I'm just curious to know how an open relationship actually works.'

He told me he and his 'kinda' girlfriend loved each other but they both knew they needed something more, sexually. So they signed up to a local swingers group that meets for monthly dinner parties, where partner swapping is the featured dish. Only couples are allowed in the group. And only four couples are invited to each dinner.

He told me they all dressed up in black tie for the dinners, which sounded like a superfluous amount of effort for people who are only meeting up so they can get naked. Maybe they thought the formal dress code added a level of sophistication to an evening when you're basically going to watch your partner screw a stranger?

They enjoyed a delicious three-course dinner and then the partner-swapping sex stuff happened. He said they'd been attending the parties for about six months. So far he'd had sex with three other women. His 'kinda' girlfriend had shagged five other men. And they'd also had a few threesomes with other ladies. He laughed out loud when I asked if he'd ever had sex with any of the other guys. It was a hard no on sex with men.

He said he honestly believed their relationship was stronger with the open door policy. They were both enjoying the experience and they had no plans to go back to a more traditional relationship any-time soon. Finally, he assured me that his 'kinda' girlfriend would have absolutely no issue if he slept with other women on this ski trip. And by 'other women', he was referring to me. Then he apol-ogised again. I guess he was worried I might be turned off by his alternative lifestyle choice.

I hate to admit it, but he was absolutely right. After assuring the Kinda Guy that I was not judgemental, I suddenly felt *extremely* judgey and I had zero interest in sleeping with him.

Me: Wow, that's *so* interesting. I wanna hear all about your non-monogamous, super modern, open relationship. No judgement from this totally open-minded super cool, non-judgemental gal!

Also me: Hell, no! There's no way I'm sleeping with you now. You creepy, kinky, partner-swapping nympho.

Look, I appreciated his honesty. Really, I did. And he didn't seem like a sleazebag. But, as open minded and accepting as I like to think I am (and try to be), I just couldn't go there. I think the fear of STIs was what put me off. Or maybe I'm just not that open-minded after all.

So I thanked him for the drinks and the fun afternoon and I wished him all the very best for continued fulfilment in exploring those 'other options'. He tried one last time to convince me to continue our conversation back at his hotel. But I was a hard no on sex with the swinger.

Then something kinda hilarious happened.

As I was saying my goodbyes to all our new-found après friends, I noticed that the Kinda Guy was having what looked to be a fairly intimate conversation with Gusband Tim. He was whispering in Tim's ear and they both looked very serious. Later I apologised to Tim if our new Dutch friend had been harassing him into convincing me to go home with him. But apparently Dutchie had already moved on – he had started hitting on Tim instead! Turns out the Kinda Guy was in fact 'kinda' bisexual, as well.

Of course he was.

Gusband and I laughed all the way home.

I wasn't laughing the next morning, though, when I woke up with a dirty big blistery cold sore on my lip. I guess that's what you get for sucking face with a kinda bisexual Dutch swinger. As hideously grotesque as the cold sore was, all I could think was, Thank god I didn't sleep with him. Because who knows what I might have woken up with if I had.

What Happens in Monte Carlo

After three decades of dating, scores of boyfriends and several serious long-term relationships, I'm kind of relieved to say that I have been proposed to a few times. I'd probably be a bit worried about my cred as a 'girlfriend' if not one guy I'd been with in thirty-plus years wanted to marry me.

Unfortunately my marriage proposals all came from boyfriends after a big night on the booze. The actual 'will you marry me' bit was usually slurred. And accompanied by a beer burp. I never felt remotely close to accepting any of their proposals.

No one has ever planned the whole spectacular proposal shebang for me. No shells on a beach spelling out 'will you marry me' in the sand, no skywriting, not even just a down-on-one-knee at a fancy restaurant. In fact, my most memorable marriage proposal happened in a nightclub in Monte Carlo, from a guy I'd only known for three hours. And, as far as I could tell, he wasn't joking.

Monte Carlo is best known for its fancy casino, a Formula One race and the divine Grace Kelly, who famously became a princess when she married the Prince of Monaco. I was there with some girl-friends, sitting in a restaurant bar having a pre-dinner drink, when a smartly dressed, attractive young woman walked up to me, handed me her business card for a Wall Street finance firm and offered me a job. Completely out of the blue.

'I'm actually not looking for a job,' I told her. 'But out of curiosity, why on earth would you offer a job to someone you've never met? I don't even have any experience in the finance industry.'

She said the most important part of the job she wanted to offer me was dealing with people. And she could see that I had a suitably outgoing personality. I didn't know what game she was playing at, but it all sounded pretty stupid to me.

'Thanks, but no thanks,' I said.

I was still laughing about the absurdity of the situation when the woman returned, about five minutes later, and said, 'Look, I'm sorry to interrupt you again, but I have to fess up. I'm not here to offer you a job. I would like to set you up with my boss.'

Okay. *Now* you're making some sense, pretty young banker lady.

The job offer was a ruse but the business card wasn't a fake. She did work at a financial advisory firm based in New York and she was in Monaco with her two bosses attending a conference.

She said they were all just discussing the issue of dating and she'd asked her boss Eli to describe his perfect woman, just as they entered the restaurant. Which is when, by pure coincidence, he looked up, saw me sitting at the bar, and said to her, 'There. That's my perfect woman.'

(I need to point out here that I feel like a *complete* tosser even repeating this moment. But I swear, that's what she told me. Plus, as you'll soon discover, it actually is relevant to the story.)

Of course, I wondered if it was a set up. Telling a woman that a complete stranger thinks she's his perfect woman is a surefire way to get her attention. I'd only ever made it to number thirty-one on the *FHM* Australia's World's Sexiest Women list back in the year 2000 – although that did rank me higher than Jennifer Aniston at the time (boom!).

Anyway, pretty young banker lady said her boss was too shy to approach me himself, so would I mind if she brought him over to meet me after we finished our dinner?

'Sure,' I said. 'I look forward to meeting him.' I mean, who wouldn't want to meet the guy who thinks you're his perfect woman?

I sat through dinner, wondering what this mystery man would look like. He was probably old, short, fat and bald. (I apologise to any short, fat, bald men who may be reading this, but you've got to know that's just not the description of the 'perfect guy' for most of us.)

Right on cue, as I finished my dessert, the lovely lady approached our table, accompanied by two men. One of the guys was short, fat and nudging sixty. With a combover. The other looked to be about thirty-five to forty. Tall, fit, clean cut, with a head of very thick dark hair. And he was kind of handsome, in a Jimmy Fallon way.

I stopped breathing. It's gonna be the fat sixty-year-old with the fucking combover, I thought. I just know it.

But the Jimmy Fallon lookalike walked up to me, shook my hand and very politely said, 'Hello, Samantha, I'm Eli. It's lovely to meet you.'

Inside Voice: Bingo, bitchez!

And, to my complete surprise, we got along famously. Eli appeared to be a perfectly lovely, quietly confident, kind of shy gentleman. He was a nice Jewish boy from New York City. Never married. Recently set up the fund with the combover dude.

The guys invited us to join them at the iconic Jimmy'z night-club, which happens to be one of the world's most exclusive party spots. It's where billionaires go for a boogie after they've parked their superyachts in the famous Monaco marina. Celebs love it too. You wouldn't do a double take if P. Diddy or Naomi Campbell or Prince Albert walked past. Well, actually I would do a double take if Naomi Campbell walked past me. And I'd probably follow her into the ladies and eavesdrop from the stall next door and listen out for any 'suspicious' noises. You would too. You know you would.

Unrelated. Sorry.

So somehow, I'd managed to find myself in one of the world's most exclusive nightclubs, flirting outrageously with a handsome Manhattan banker who thought I was his perfect woman. And I was loving every second! It was turning into one of the best nights of my life (and another one of those crazy 'how the fuck did I end up here?' encounters).

Suddenly we were on the dancefloor. And Eli was kissing me. And then he got down on one knee, looked up at me and mouthed the words, 'Will you marry me'.

'Yeah, sure,' I screamed over the music. 'We should totally get married! I mean, we've known each other for three whole hours now!'

Then he stood up and led me off the dancefloor to a quiet corner and said, 'I know this sounds completely ridiculous, but I *know* you're the one for me. I'm convinced that fate brought us together. So I'm asking you, seriously, will you marry me?'

'Ummm. That's completely insane,' I told him. 'I'm not Jewish, for a start.'

'You can convert,' he said.

'And I live in Sydney,' I said.

'Move to New York!'

I said I'd think about it and awkwardly brushed it off (like he'd just asked me if I felt like going to the movies tomorrow) and I dragged him back onto the dancefloor. But I couldn't stop wondering if his spontaneous marriage proposal was legit. He wasn't a big drinker, so I couldn't blame it on the booze. In fact, compared to my previous three marriage proposals, this was the most sober one yet.

I started to wonder if this was how it was going to happen for me. We've all heard those beautiful, romantic stories about love at first sight – people who *just know* from the moment they meet that they're destined to be together.

I wasn't 100 per cent convinced at that stage that Eli was my Mr Happily Ever After. Sure I was enjoying his company, but I felt like we had quite a lot of ground to cover before I committed to forever with the guy.

So I thought it best to get the ball rolling by having sex with him. Maybe *that* would help me decide.

We jumped in a cab and headed towards his hotel but I think the fresh air reconnected with my senses and sobered me back to reality because suddenly I thought, What the fuck am I doing here? I can't sleep with this guy. This *really* is insane.

I'd been so wrapped up in the glamour and spontaneity of the situation and the pure joy I felt from thinking I was someone's 'perfect woman', that I wasn't able to see what was really going on. The whole 'you're the perfect woman, will you marry me' schtick was just his way of getting me in the sack. And I *almost* fell for it. Like the complete putz that I am.

I reminded myself that I was a smart, sensible woman, who knows that shit like this actually doesn't happen in real life. It only happens in fairy tales. And fantasies.

The cab pulled up outside his hotel and just as Eli stepped out of the taxi, I leaned forward to the driver and said, 'Drive, please. Now.'

And I slammed the door and we drove away and I left Eli standing there with a look of total shock and confusion on his face.

At the time I felt like it was absolutely the right thing to do.

I wondered afterwards, if it was a massive error in judgement on my part. Was this another sliding door moment I chose to ignore? Was I too damn cynical for my own good? Had my heart been broken too many times to believe that some love stories actually can start out like this?

I thought I'd never find out. Until . . .

Three years later, I received a LinkedIn invitation from a man named Eli who lived in New York and worked in the finance industry. The guy in the profile pic looked a bit like Jimmy Fallon. I knew it was him! I accepted the invitation and sent him a message straight away that said, 'Is this the same Eli I met on a crazy night out in Monte Carlo all those years ago . . . ?'

And he never, ever replied.

I guess what happens in Monte Carlo stays in Monte Carlo. Or maybe I just wasn't his perfect woman after all.

The One

I knew I loved him *before* I met him.

It's not just a Savage Garden song.

I actually got that tingly feeling the moment I walked into the crowded bar and spotted the *back* of his head. And when he stood up and turned around and looked at me and smiled, I think I stopped breathing momentarily as my brain registered: 'Oh. Wow. He's . . . The One.'

Before that moment, I'd always wondered if the The One was just an idiotic myth. A pick-me-up fantasy for foolish romantics to cling to, in the depths of their darkest single days. I'd plead with my married friends to let me in on the big secret,

'So, how will I *know* if I meet The One?'

'You'll just know,' they'd say.

'But that's not an answer,' I'd insist, 'how will I *actually know?*'

'YOU'LL. JUST. KNOW.'

And in that moment, when I locked eyes with him, it suddenly made perfect sense.

I. Just. Knew.

We'd been set up by my friend Megan who, a few weeks earlier, had *screamed* down the phone to me (like she'd just won the lotto), 'I've met your future husband! Oh my god, he's *perfect* for you.

I've already started shopping for bridesmaids' dresses.' Usually, when a friend tells me she's found my 'perfect' guy, he turns out to be a complete dud. But this time, I decided pretty much instantaneously that Megs had picked a winner.

The invisible love current was stronger and more intense than I'd ever felt it before. And the guy was mucho handsome so there was an instant attraction on that level. But it was more than just lust at first sight. It was like a calm, cosy feeling that washed over me – a recognition that this was a person I'd been destined to meet.

We clicked immediately. Our conversation had the energy and enthusiasm of two people eagerly trying to cram their entire life stories into one very flirtatious discussion. It was the kind of conversation where you completely forget there's anyone else in the room. Or on the planet. The attraction was so intense that a complete stranger approached us after a while and said, 'I'm sorry to interrupt, but I've been watching you for a while, and I just want to tell you that I can *feel* the electricity between you two from across the room. So if you're not already together, you should be.' Then she left.

Look, maybe I was completely sucked in by a sneaky ploy designed by his friends to help him close the deal. But in *that* moment, *I* chose to believe that a complete stranger could sense the power of our attraction from the other side of the room. Perhaps that invisible love current wasn't so invisible after all.

When the bar closed and they kicked us out and he kissed me as we waited outside for our taxi, it was the most perfect first kiss of my life. I also remember thinking that it was quite possibly the *last* first kiss I'd ever have.

We fell madly, passionately, deeply in love, pretty much immediately, and we slipped into couple-mode effortlessly. I adored having a boyfriend again and doing all those cutesy coupley things. Saturday brunch. Sunday arvo museum visits. Squeezing the pimples on his back. It felt right. And it felt like *this* was what I'd been waiting my whole life to find.

So no prizes for guessing this love story doesn't have a happy ending. It was a rude shock for me to discover that meeting The One does not automatically come with a happily-ever-after lifetime guarantee.

My trusty Three Month Theory came into play, right on cue, as we spent more time together and it came to my attention that there was a third party in our relationship. Her name was Charli. And The One quite enjoyed putting Charli up his nostrils.

This was a huge problem for me. Because there is no place for drugs in my world. I'd seen how destructive recreational drug use could be. It ruins relationships. And destroys lives.

When I told him it was a deal breaker, he said that if it really bothered me, he'd just stop. Because he loved me. He *promised*.

But he *didn't* stop.

I should have walked away the moment I found out he was so fond of Charli. But by that stage, I was already *convinced* that he was The One – The One I'd waited my whole friggin' life to find. So I rationalised my decision *not* to break up with him, by telling myself that every relationship has 'issues'. Nobody's perfect. Maybe he was just going through a 'phase'? He'd grow out of it.

My biological clock had also shifted into sixth gear when I wasn't looking. And I certainly wasn't getting any younger. *Three* of my friends had bought me those age defying wrinkle busting silk pillow cases for my last birthday. *THREE of them!*

But my fairytale refused to play out the way it was supposed to. Charli kept appearing in his life regularly and that party boy could not be tamed. We argued about it constantly. And I started to wonder how being with The One could feel so very, very wrong.

This went on for almost twelve months until, in a desperate effort to try and make some sense out of it all, I booked myself in for a reading with my trusty tarot card reader, Poppy. Maybe she could see if he really was The One for me.

Or if I was kidding myself.

Poppy works out of a dingy room in the back of an op shop, which smells like mothballs and mildew and wet dog. She has wild platinum-blonde hair that sticks out in all directions, like she's just put her finger in the socket, and she draws on these giant wobbly oversized eyebrows that are a little, dramatic. She also has a reputation for being the best (if you can handle the 'thrift whiff'), and I'm quite convinced that she does have some kind of connection to the other side. I've been to see her a few times over the years and she had correctly predicted a few major events in my life. Various job offers, my dad's cancer, my grandmother's death.

As soon as Poppy started reading the cards, she saw my fella. She described him perfectly and confirmed things about him that were very specific. She also seemed quite sure that he was The One for me. And then she said, 'Wait. I see . . . Addiction. Oh no, darling. That's not good.'

Now you try telling me those tarot card readers are scam artists! How on earth had Poppy (or the spirits, or the angels, or whoever it is that passes on the messages from the other side) been able to pinpoint the one issue that had been causing me so much stress in my relationship? How did she *know*?

I went to see a therapist next. An addiction specialist. And I asked her if it was my responsibility to stand by my man, come what may. I always thought one of the most important qualities of true love was supporting each other, through good and bad.

But she told me, quite bluntly, that there was absolutely nothing I could do. My boyfriend wouldn't quit Charli or his partying ways until *he* decided he'd had enough. She said it wasn't my job to rescue him. And I should not feel guilty if I chose to walk away.

So I ended the relationship. And I walked away from the man I honestly thought I was going to spend the rest of my life with.

*

It's surprisingly easy to ignore those inconvenient little warning signals at the beginning of a relationship. It's much more exciting to get swept up in the romance of believing you've met The One than it is to listen to those pesky inside voices, screaming, 'Danger, danger, danger . . . abort!'

But in the end, it really didn't matter that *I* thought he was The One. Or that Poppy and her angel posse thought he was The One. Or that my friend Megan or a complete stranger from across the room on the night we met thought he was The One for me. My boyfriend didn't think *I* was The One for *him*. He chose the other woman, Charli.

After a massive amount of soul searching, I've decided that it really is impossible to fall in love with someone before you meet them (sorry Savage Garden, but that really is bullshit). I don't even believe in love at first sight. Fact is, you can't truly love someone until you *know* them, warts and all. That powerful reaction I *thought* I felt when I met 'The One' wasn't love at first sight. It was a cosy, comforting blend of attraction, hope and anticipation, sprinkled with a touch of loneliness.

Meeting The One is also heavily reliant on the very practical matter of timing. He quite possibly might have been the right person for me, but it wasn't the right time. I realise now that I've probably met a few *different* Ones throughout my lifetime. The trick is meeting the right *One* at the right *time*. *That's* when the stars align and the universe gets it right. And *that's* when you get your happily ever after.

Pure Love Paul

I met my first 'One' at the wise old age of nine.

I'd just moved to a new school and I was terrified of turning up on day one and not knowing a soul, but the moment I walked through the gates and laid eyes on Paul, I knew everything was going to be okay. He had the cutest dimples I'd ever seen. Big, round dimples that turned his cute little baby face into a ball of joy (and made my heart melt) whenever he smiled.

We were 'dating' before either of us knew what that even meant.

I had friends who were girls, but this was different. Being with this boy made me so happy and Paul was the one person I wanted to hang around, more than anyone else on the planet. And not just at school. We had weekend play dates and afternoon swimming dates and beach dates and bushwalking dates and movie dates with our mums. We bought matching his and hers terry-towelling shorts (that's kind of bizarre, right?) and we even had regular sleepovers. Our parents must have known it was all *totally* innocent, because they even let us sleep in the same bed.

There was no hanky panky going on. None whatsoever. No kissing. No hand-holding. No touching of any kind. I remember thinking he was a major cutie pie – oh Lord, those dimples! – and I knew some of the other girls thought he was spunkarific. I certainly felt an attraction to him, but I guess I just didn't know what to do with it. We hadn't even heard of the word 'sex' back then. But I knew I loved him. And he loved me.

Sadly, Paul was also the first guy who broke my heart. And it wasn't even his fault.

I was beyond distraught – beyond! – when, about six months after we met, he told me his family was moving overseas. This news hit me hard. I simply could not imagine my life without Paul in it.

He used every cent of his pocket money to buy me a parting gift, something to remember him by. It was a delicate sterling silver double heart bracelet with 'Samantha' and 'Paul' engraved on the back. So, so precious. Just thinking about it brings a tear to my eye, even today.

I still have that bracelet too. It was the first gift I'd ever received from a boy – a symbol of our two hearts, joined, despite the challenges of time and distance. It probably cost Paul about fifteen bucks at Michael Hill at the time but, to me, it's priceless. It will *always* be a reminder of the most pure romantic love I ever felt.

Paul was perfect. Together, we were perfect. And I know I'll never experience the purity of young love ever again. A love that isn't affected by all the crazy external pressures of adult life: family dramas, financial worries, job issues, health concerns, sex. Sex really has a way of messing things up, doesn't it? Once your bits have touched, your emotional investment in that relationship moves to a whole new, often intensely complicated, level.

Paul moved back to Brisbane a couple of years later, but things were never the same. I'd already moved on with a new 'boyfriend', and we were *French kissing*. Yep, with an open mouth . . . *and* tongues.

So, basically, I thought I was too cool for school. And way too cool for poor old Paul.

But I do wonder if that experience with Paul is somehow partly responsible for my eternally single status. After three decades of bad dates and frog-kissing and fucked-up, failed relationships, I've never been able to find a love as pure as I had with Pure Love Paul.

The Biological Time Bomb

'First comes love, then comes marriage, then comes Sami with a baby carriage.'

I loved that cute little rhyme, conditioning me to believe, from a young age, that the equation of life really is that simple. Love + Marriage = Baby.

No wonder it turns into total mind fuckery for those us who discover, as adults, that the equation doesn't always add up. Because love doesn't necessarily lead to marriage. And marriage doesn't guarantee babies. Sometimes the baby comes before love, or without love even. And what if marriage doesn't even enter the friggin' equation?

I guess I always just trusted the Universe to deliver on marriage and motherhood when the time was right. But when she didn't, I decided to rewrite the baby rhyme.

'First comes "I'm forty" then comes "and single", then comes a very different ending to this jingle'. No bugaboo in my little ditty. Just a trip to the gyno to test my ovarian reserves.

An ovarian reserves test is supposed to give you an accurate indication of your current reproductive potential – it's like a stocktake on your eggs. So, clever me, I decided forty was the perfect age to reasess how much time I had left to find a bloke and get knocked up. I honestly expected to find out that my ovaries were high-powered egg-making machines. 'Go away and stop stressing about it, you lunatic' the doctor would laugh, as he looked at my results. 'You've got plenty of time to get pregnant. Come back and see me when you're fifty!'

But that's not what happened.

The doctor told me, in a gravely clinical manner, that my ovarian reserves were frighteningly low and that my fertility was in a stage of rapid decline. And if I wanted to have a biological child, I should do something about it, stat.

So, here's the thing: 'Your fertility is in rapid decline' is one of the most terrifying things you can possibly say to a single forty-year-old woman who has never seriously contemplated the thought of a life without children. (My friend Megs was told by a doctor, at the age of thirty-eight, that she had 'lazy, ageing ovaries'. That's not fun, either.)

It was a life-changing moment for me, sitting there, alone, in my gyno's office in the Sydney CBD. It hadn't occurred to me to bring anyone along that day for emotional support. I couldn't even begin to fathom that the results would be so shocking. But there it was. The scientific proof, all neatly presented on a spreadsheet, sitting on the desk in front of me.

My biological clock had suddenly become a biological time bomb. And, at my age, my options for having a biological child were limited. I assumed freezing my eggs would be the best plan of attack. I'd just put some of those little suckers on ice until I found a bloke, thanks very much, modern technology! But the doc said egg freezing wasn't really viable for a woman 'of my age', because my eggs were possibly past their use-by date already and all that fussing about would just make them deteriorate even further. Plus, any complications with the retrieval process could result in the loss of one or both ovaries, which would mean lights out completely on the pregnancy front. While I still had the other important baby-making bits, I could at least try to get pregnant using an egg donor. I'd just have to find a super fertile young lady willing to hand over some of her super fertile young eggs.

The doc talked a bit about IUI and ICSI and embryo transfers and live birth rates. And then he told me, quite frankly, that the best option, 'at my age', was to simply get myself knocked up the old-fashioned way. My eggs were probably too fragile to deal with the trauma of IVF. So I really just needed a bit of the old in and out. Well, lots of it, actually. As soon as possible.

How ironic. I was prepared to spend thousands of dollars on the most advanced assisted reproduction technology available, but my best shot at having a baby was the one option that wouldn't cost me a cent. Not even the cost of a condom.

I drove home in a daze, trying to digest what had just happened. Why didn't I get onto this whole baby business in my thirties? Had I been so focused on my career that I forgot to have kids? Why did I waste so much time with the wrong men in dysfunctional relationships? How the hell had I fucked this up so royally?

For the love of god, why couldn't I just meet a nice guy, fall in love, get married and buy the friggin' baby carriage?

I got home, parked my car, and then sat there in the driver's seat and sobbed. It's a confronting reality check when you're forced to accept that there's absolutely nothing you can do to slow down or turn back your biological clock. And it's an especially tough pill to swallow for a woman who grew up being told she could achieve anything if she just tried hard enough or studied hard enough or worked hard enough. But there was no way to fix this. I could not simply facilitate a fertility do-over. The female reproductive system is a law unto itself.

And then it dawned on me. I was in the driver's seat here, literally *and* metaphorically. I had no other choice, but to face up to the reality and seriousness of my situation and decide what I wanted my future to look like. Were kids a must? Or was I willing to risk a life without them?

Everyone I knew with kids said it's the best thing they ever did. They all wish they'd popped one out sooner. They all said, 'You know,

Sam, your life doesn't *really* start until you have children.' Which was a little difficult to comprehend, to be honest. My life already felt like it was enjoyable and fulfilling and pretty damn exciting. I actually didn't feel like anything was missing.

Plus, I'd never been the obsessively clucky type. Sure, I go all goo-goo gaa-gaa over every cute, chubby, gurgling baby I see, but I'd never felt that intense urge to grow one in my own belly. Had I somehow been conditioned into *thinking* I wanted kids because I'd been led to believe, from the moment I was born, that my most important role in life is supposed to be . . . Mum? Still, I kept asking myself the same question: will I wake up in ten years and regret not having a baby?

I decided that a life without kids was simply *not an* option. I did not want to live my entire life without having someone to call me Mum.

And that's when my serious quest to have a baby began. I was about to turn forty-one.

With only a narrow window of time left to find new love and a baby daddy, I embarked on what I now refer to as my 'desperation dating period'. This was just before online dating really took off, so it was still old-school dating. I told everyone I knew it was all hands on deck. I was open to anything – blind dates, double dates, set-ups, dates with men I wouldn't have been open to meeting in the past. I tried to be more social. I accepted every invitation, to *everything*. And the whole time I could hear my doctor's voice: 'The best option, at your age, is to get yourself knocked up, the old-fashioned way.' I was a sperm-seeking missile with a very clear mission.

Unfortunately, my biological time bomb was a serious dating hazard. Meeting men in that mindset wasn't healthy or productive. From the moment I'd meet a new guy, he was immediately assessed as baby daddy material first, everything else second. It wasn't fair on him. And it certainly didn't give any potential relationships a fair chance of developing naturally.

My desperation dating phase lasted about six months, until I reached a point where I knew it was ludicrous to keep hoping Mr Where-the-fuck-have-you-been-all-my-life would suddenly show up, just in the nick of time. The simple fact is, there's no time limit when it comes to finding love, but I had very little (if any) time left to have a baby. Even if I had to do it on my own.

So I decided it was time to stop searching for Mr Right and start researching ways to become Miss Mum. Just because I hadn't succeeded in the game of love didn't mean I should miss out on motherhood as well.

Sami's Baby

With my biological time bomb ticking faster and louder each day, I started booking into viable options for single women wanting to have a baby. And that's when I came up with the idea for the television documentary, *Sami's Baby*.

I knew there were plenty of other woman in this situation, but very few people were talking openly and publicly about it. I hoped a program about my experience might elicit conversation about an issue that was affecting so many women of my generation. I approached Foxtel with my idea for the show and they loved it. We started shooting immediately. I agreed to let the cameras follow me as I searched for the best way to become a mum. I promised to be completely honest and open about my journey and the roller-coaster of emotions I felt along the way. Of course, it was a confronting experience for me. I'd been a TV presenter for almost twenty years, so I was super comfortable having a camera in my face. But this wasn't just another job, or some fake, scripted 'reality' show. This was my life.

On the first day of the shoot, I had to re-enact the moment I received the results of my ovarian reserves test and even though months had passed since I received the shocking news, it was just as hideous and no less painful hearing it from the doc again.

The most confronting moment of the shoot was when I asked my flatmate and one of my closest friends, Steven, if he would be my baby daddy. With no romantic interest on the scene, I figured my number-one option would be to have a child with someone I at least knew and respected. Steven was also in his forties and single. We'd been friends for more than a decade and flatmates for about six years. He's a smart guy who has a good job and he's endearingly kooky (in a charming way). He's a good man with a good heart and I thought he'd be a fine father figure for my child. I suggested that we would be able to raise the kid together in a super cool, incredibly mature and responsible co-parenting type situation. But there was absolutely no pressure if he *didn't* want to be involved after the bub was born.

He said no. To both options.

He definitely wanted kids, but he would prefer to save his swimmers for the right girl. Of course, I understood and respected his decision, but it still felt like the ultimate rejection. And it was pretty horrific having that moment caught on camera. So. Think of the most brutal 'final two' rose ceremony you've ever seen in the history of *The Bachelor*. That moment of rejection felt about as humilating for me as I imagine it was for the poor lass being dumped by Bachie on national telly.

Sadly, Gusband Tim was also a non-starter. He was the perfect candidate, but the timing was all wrong. He'd only emerged from the cosy confines of his heterosexual closet the year before and was still coming to terms with his new-found homosexuality. So boo had his hands full dealing with his own issssuuues. My bestie Galeb had just become a father to twins, so he wasn't an option either.

A friend suggested that his gay brother might be keen. He and his long-time boyfriend were desperate to become dads and share the parenting duties with a baby mama. So I was invited to a family dinner, where I met the lovely couple and we all politely discussed the very real possibility of the three of us having a baby together, even though we'd only just met thirty minutes earlier. They were both absolutely gorgeous and intelligent and successful, and they were 100 per cent committed to the cause. It appeared to be the perfect remedy for our combined baby fever. I left that dinner feeling excited that I may have finally found my baby daddy(s) and I was thrilled to know that our baby would have *one* loving mother, *two* doting dads and *three* sets of grandparents. Had I finally found a happy ending to my unconventional fairytale? Omigod the three of us would create one of those ultra modern parenting arrangements that's so damn hip it hurts.

But the more I thought about it, the more unrealistic it became. There wasn't enough time to really get to know these guys before embarking on one of life's greatest and most important journeys together. Mum gave me some sound advice on this one too. She warned me that three parents wasn't necessarily as wonderful as it sounded. When we encountered the inevitable disagreements about raising our child, it would always end up being two against one. So there was a good chance I'd always be outvoted when it came to the really big decisions in my child's life. My gut told me to listen to Mum on this one so I respectfully declined on the dual baby daddy idea. Good on you Mum – coming in strong with the vital life advice again, when I really needed it.

Somewhere along the way, I had become surprisingly comfortable with the idea of being a single mum. I just knew I would be okay if I did this on my own. With divorce rates soaring, the odds of ending up as a single mum are pretty high these days anyway. Plus, I'd seen so many of my friends marry Mr Perfect and then end up trapped in miserable marriages with men they couldn't stand. I realised I could do much worse than to choose life as a single mum.

However, I was shocked to discover the harsh criticism surrounding parents who are single by choice. Some folks say it's the most selfish thing you could possibly do. But I can't comprehend how it could be considered selfish to give up your freedom, time, money and pretty much your whole life in order to care for and raise another human being. Surely that's the least selfish thing in the world.

Also, why shouldn't a single person be able to fulfil one of the most basic human needs in life – to create a family? Married people aren't asked why *they* want to become parents. So why should a single person have to justify their desire to have a child?

I signed up with some local sperm banks and started the search for my donor, which added an entirely new level of anguish to the whole situation. The information available on each sperm donor is extensive. I found it impossible to pick a winner. I couldn't decide which of the donor's qualities I most wanted to pass on to my child: race, nationality, education, intellect, height, looks, eye colour, hair colour. It was like the best hotel breakfast buffet you've ever been to, where there's fresh fruit and five different cereals and bircher muesli and muffins and waffles and pancakes and hash browns and a chef making eggs *exactly* the way you want them and you're so overwhelmed by the choice that you end up just standing there, with your plate in hand, bamboozled by the plethora of enticing options before you.

It was frustrating to have so much information about the donor on paper, but still feel like I didn't know the man at all. The biggest hurdle was overcoming the fact that I was choosing to have a baby with someone I'd never met. I always imagined that making a baby and creating life would be an intimate process with someone I at least cared about. Not the result of a credit card transaction with a stranger. I wished I could have been more desensitised to the weirdness of the whole process. But I couldn't ignore the fact that it just didn't feel right.

And then, the unexpected happened.

I met a potential baby daddy while I was shooting pool with friends at a Sydney pub on a Sunday afternoon.

And so began my 'extreme dating period'.

Can I Buy Your Ovum

The documentary didn't end with me and my baby carriage. But it did end with me walking off into the sunset with a potential baby daddy. More about him soon . . .

The doco really struck a chord with viewers and I was deeply moved by the messages I received, both from women who had found themselves in a similar situation to mine, and from others who had been touched by my story:

Its nice 2 know I'm not the only one who struggles with the constant ticking clock. Thank u.

A great honest account of a career orientated 41-year-old girl faced with a common dilemma. Now my friends are onto the discussion of who would use a donor and by what age. Can of worms opened!!

Sami, you've scared me! At the age of 36 I still think I have plenty of time left.

Amazing journey. Gave me such a better understanding of my single friends who are going thru the same dilemma. Fingers crossed!

Great show! I'm 40, a single Mum & have never regretted it! Do it. Don't wait. Follow your heart. Bugger others opinions. GOOD LUCK!

I also received a surprising number of messages from men who saw it as an opportunity to ask me out. These are all actual messages I received from complete strangers:

Sami, you are looking for a bloke, I'm 46 and I'm not sexy in fact I'm short, fat and ugly however I'm a very loving guy.

hi sami i think it's wonderful what you are doing sorry us men let you down with mr right lol.

Hey Sami, any luck in the manhunt? cheers (some random:)

It seems we're both in the same boat, not having much luck on the dating scene. I'm an independent successful 32 yo. Hope we can chat . . . Nothing to lose! Haha

Hi Sami I would be quite happy to meet you sometime take you to dinner do you like seafood

Some fellas watched that documentary and saw it as an invitation to get their sperm onboard the Sami train, ASAP. And I was strangely touched by their eagerness to offer the one thing I was so open about needing at that point in my life.

Hi Sami. This is probably extremely forward? But I would be willing to donate sperm for you if my guys are any good? It has always been something I have wanted to do to help out people who are mad keen but can't have kids.

Could you please pass on to Sami that I would be very honoured to be the sperm donor for her baby. Of course I would be happy to have a fertility test, to make sure I'm not shooting blanks . . . haha. Please don't think I'm some kind of weirdo . . . I would be disappointed if I hadn't at least let her know.

One woman even emailed to offer me her *husband's* sperm. She empathised with me on such a primal level that she was willing to share a piece of her own hubby – a 'hot tradie', apparently – to help me achieve my dream. I declined the offer, but there really are no words to describe how grateful I was to that gorgeous couple for their generosity. (I'm assuming he was aware of the proposition.)

My favourite message came from a guy who didn't want to congratulate me on the show or ask me out or offer me sperm. He just wanted to *buy my ovum.*

Sami, I saw your video last night where you are looking for a child. I'm a 36-year-old man who's looking for a child too. I'd request you, if you don't mind donating me your ovum. Alternatively, I like to put an offer to buy your ovum if you wish to sell instead. If you are interested, we can talk more and negotiate. I am eagerly waiting to hear back from you.

While I do appreciate the fact that this request was incredibly polite, I think this guy kind of missed the point of the doco. After deep thought and careful consideration, I formulated my reply. And I can only hope that, one day, he has the opportunity to read it here:

Dear Mr Eager,

Thank you for your kind offer to rent/buy my ovum.

I regret to inform you that I am unable to assist on this occasion.

If I had any ova to spare, I wouldn't have ended up in this fucking predicament in the first place.

Thank you again for your interest and all the best.

Sincerely,

Sami x

The Sperm Stampede (Part 1)

Some men reckon they can hear a woman's biological clock ticking from three suburbs away. So when I announced to the nation, via a television documentary (and the associated press and media coverage that surrounded it), that I was forty-one and dying to have a baby, I thought men would run for the hills. I could almost feel the earth shift on its axis, as every available guy on the east coast of Australia bolted to the other side of the country.

Instead, it turned into a sperm stampede, and they were all coming in my direction! Complete strangers contacted me to offer their swimmers. And on the dating front, I ended up with three boyfriends in a row who all offered to be my baby's daddy. They were three of the most intense dating experiences of my life.

Strangely, the three successive boyfriends who offered me their baby-making services weren't even my most serious relationships. I wouldn't even say I was in love with any of them. But they were all ready, able and very willing to put their balls (literally) on the line.

Harry came first (so to speak). I met him, completely by accident, while I was still shooting the baby doco. I had planned to press pause on the search for Mr Right while I focused on finding a sperm donor, but I met Harry at the pub, he asked me out, we went to dinner and I really liked him. So we went out a few more times.

I didn't tell him about my baby plans right away. Telling the guy I'd just started sleeping with that I was making a TV show about my burning desire to get pregnant was probably TMI, don't you think? I didn't do any funny stuff either, like trick him into an 'accidental' pregnancy. I was just hiding a massive secret.

As things between us started to get serious, I realised it was straight-up ridiculous to spend so much time with a guy but *not* talk to him about the most important thing that was happening in my world. It also made the whole dating process awkward and weird. One day I had an appointment at the fertility clinic at Bondi Junction to discuss my ovulation timeline and sperm donor options, and then I popped downstairs to meet Harry for dinner and a movie straight after. It was sperm selection at four. Date with the new guy at six. Bizarre, right?

It was useless to keep dating him unless he was getting to know the real me, so I 'fessed up to everything. The documentary, my fertility dramas, the sperm donors, my baby plans. The whole complicated, inconvenient box and dice. I apologised for not telling him sooner. I said it was all unchartered territory for me and, well, I just didn't know how to handle it. And I told him I'd completely understand if he decided to stop seeing me. He dropped me home after the chat and very calmly said he'd like to take some time to process everything I'd said. I thought I'd never hear from him again.

Instead, Harry called me the very next day and said, 'Why don't you let me be your sperm donor?'

Just like that.

He said there was definitely a strong connection between us and he'd like to keep exploring that, if I would. He suggested there was no point in using an anonymous sperm donor when he was already on the scene. If we ended up together, he'd rather be raising his own kid than someone else's. And if it didn't work out between us, well, we'd just find a way to co-parent.

I couldn't believe what I was hearing. We'd only been dating for about a month. It wasn't ideal to jump in so soon, but it also sounded like a wonderfully convenient solution, with an unbelievably kind, generous, decent and respectful man. And he was definitely someone I could imagine falling in love with. One day. Maybe.

My divorced friends warned me not to do it. It wasn't worth the risk, they said, in case he turned out to be a fruitloop, or an arse-hole. After dealing with messy separations and the stress of raising a kid with someone they couldn't stand, they said it would be much smarter to go with the anonymous sperm donor option and have the bub on my own. But I'd never felt entirely comfy with the whole sperm donor situation. Plus, my crusty old eggs weren't getting any younger.

And the whole time, all I could hear was my doctor's voice, whispering in the background, 'The best option at your age is to get yourself knocked up, the old-fashioned way . . . *the old-fashioned way . . . the old-fashioned way . . .*'

So I accepted Harry's kind offer. And at the age of forty-one, for the first time in my life, I *tried* to get pregnant. It was a brand-new experience for me. I'd never had sex with the intention of trying to make a baby before. We weren't just two horny people having sex because it felt good. We were sharing something meaningful and profound and special. It felt like I was starting a whole new and very adult chapter of my life.

I assumed I'd be up the duff straight away. I knew my ovarian reserves were dangerously low, but I thought for sure there'd be a few super-fertile eggs hiding somewhere up the back of my lady parts.

But my uterus refused to cooperate. I could *not* get pregnant.

It was laughable at first. I mean, come on! I'd spent my whole life trying not to get pregnant. I'd had major panics (omigod, may-jah!) when boyfriends tried to convince me to trust the exceptional timing of their not-so-trusty pull out method.

But now that I was *desperate* to get knocked up? Fahgettaboudit. Also, I don't like to fail. I've always been a Type A personality and a high achiever. When I set my mind to something, I expect to achieve it. But the whole preggers thing? Turns out I really fucking sucked at that gig.

Anyone who's had trouble conceiving knows that your whole life turns into a revolving two-week cycle. Two weeks of waiting to ovulate and then bonking like rabbits. And then two weeks of waiting and praying and hoping. And then, when your period arrives, it's a tidal wave of disappointment and frustration. Then you start all over again. With the waiting and the ovulating and the shagging and then more waiting and hoping and praying. And then the fucking tidal wave is back, wiping out any shred of optimism you had managed to grasp onto, until you scream, 'For the love of god, why can't I just get pregnant, already?'

And then you do it all over again. And again. And again.

And the stress of failing, month after frustrating month, is excruciating. The roller-coaster of intense emotional highs and lows became too much for me to handle. I was a mess. And I took my frustrations out on Harry. I tried to fall in love with him. I really, really tried. But I couldn't, so I turned on him instead.

Suddenly it annoyed me that he insisted on the missionary position, even though he was 130 kilograms. We were having a lot of sex at the time, and every time he finished Big Daddy would collapse on top of me like a sack of potatoes, blissfully unaware that his 130 kilograms were completely smothering my 55-kilogram frame. I could hardly breathe. It was not a pleasant experience.

Then I decided I didn't want to be around him any more. He was a constant reminder of my failure to achieve the one thing I so desperately wanted. But I felt too guilty to break up with him. He'd been so unbelievably kind during one of the most stressful times of my life. So I just started acting like a bitch instead, hoping *he'd* get sick of it all and break up with *me*. My passive aggressive game was on point.

But Harry hung in there, like the bloody champion bloke that he is. Eventually I just couldn't do it any more. He deserved better. I told him it was over.

My friends were right. I shouldn't have rushed into it. We somehow took that relationship from zero to one hundred in Ferrari record time. And we certainly didn't have the strong foundations required for a couple sharing such a stressful experience. But I honestly thought Harry was my last shot at the title. Surely there weren't too many guys out there who would willingly try to have a baby with someone they barely knew.

I had no idea at the time that I'd meet *two more* after Harry. My extreme dating period had only just begun.

The Sperm Stampede (Part 2)

You'd think I would have learned my lesson after rushing into it with would-be baby daddy #1, but I had a non-refundable ticket to the maternity ward and I was *not* getting off that baby train until it reached the birthing suite.

Would-be baby daddy #2 appeared on the scene about six months later and he jumped on board with the whole baby-making process surprisingly quickly as well. We'd been set up by a close friend, so he was already well aware of my situation. He was also very keen to settle down and have kids, so we kind of just fast-tracked the relationship and skipped over most of the normal getting-to-know-you stages. The usual early dating chat of, 'Tell me about your job, do you have any siblings, what's your favourite movie?' was replaced by, 'Hey, I'll be ovulating on Wednesday so could you pop over during your lunch break for a quick shag?'

I'm not even kidding. (And all the while I could still hear the doctor's voice, over and over again: 'The best option at your age . . .')

So, before I knew what I was doing, I was back on the emotional roller-coaster of the two-week baby-making cycle. When the trusty ovulation kit told me I was good to go, we'd have sex four times a day. Somehow he always managed to report, ready for duty. And afterwards, I'd lie on my back with my legs up the wall, hoping that might give his sperm an express pass to my cervix. My life revolved around peeing on ovulation sticks, having sex and lying with my legs up the wall.

My close friends knew I was having a tough time, so they offered all kinds of 'helpful' suggestions to expedite a conception.

Karen gave me a bag of rose quartz fertility stones, which would give me special fertility powers if I carried them on my person at all times. Didn't work.

Helen helped me research all the best sex positions for baby-making. Tried them all.

Angie suggested I pray to St Gerard, the unofficial patron saint of motherhood. Did that. Repeatedly.

Tina said if I bought myself an item of newborn baby clothing and put it in my bedside table it would will the baby into existence. I gave that one a miss. I was actually worried it might jinx me.

I did, however, spend a small fortune on appointments with the Chinese herbal acupuncture fertility specialist, Lily Liu. Lily is famous for her miraculous ability to help even the most fertility-challenged women fall pregnant. I remember sitting nervously in the waiting room before my first appointment, reading all the touching messages on her wall of thank you cards from all the new mums and satisfied customers, *praying* that there would be a card from me up on that wall one day. But all the acupuncture, weird herbs and putrid-tasting potions did not put a baby in my belly.

The monthly disappointments became harder to handle as my dream of getting pregnant looked more and more unlikely. I'm not trying to be dramatic when I say I could actually feel my uterus ache whenever I saw a baby. Any woman who's ever been in my situation knows that feeling. And I truly hope that anyone who has ever managed to fall pregnant effortlessly, without a clue as to when she even ovulates, knows what an absolute *miracle* that baby is and how incredibly blessed she is.

Life became even more unbearable when I discovered that would-be baby daddy #2 and I were not compatible. At all. It took me a while to realise he actually wasn't even a very nice guy. He was incredibly insecure and his ego was out of control. I think the fact that he couldn't knock me up made it even worse. We argued a lot. It was awful. So I broke up with him as well.

I thought that was the end of my baby journey. But again, I was wrong.

The Sperm Stampede (Part 3)

Would-be baby daddy #3 was the handsome German architect I met on one of my crazy ski holidays in Austria. It was initially just a regular holiday fling (with protected sex, of course), but we broke the golden rule of holiday flinging and kept in touch afterwards. We agreed to meet up in Thailand a few months later for a tropical shag-fest.

As we got to know each other a little better on that holiday, I opened up to him about my baby dramas. And he said, quite matter-of-factly, that he'd be very happy to be my sperm donor. We'd spent a total of three nights together on the ski holiday and six nights on our Phuket fuck-fest, with a few Skype sessions in between. And I thought, Oh my god, here we go again, with a guy offering to impregnate me after I've known him for, like, five minutes.

We both knew there was no guarantee that this fling would develop into any kind of relationship. The German said he had no intention of moving to Australia anytime soon and he had no interest in helping me raise the kid. So he really was just offering to be my (non-anonymous) sperm donor.

After the spectacular failure of my attempted relationships with would-be baby daddies #1 *and* #2, I had planned to renew the search for a sperm donor anyway. And, on a purely superficial level, the German was about six trillion degrees of hot, *way* better-looking than any of the guys I'd seen on the donor list. Maybe someone upstairs had been listening after all. This guy really *was* the answer to my prayers.

So I said yes to the German sperm, and I embarked on Mission Baby: Round 3. This time, however, I knew the process had to be different. It was time for IVF. The old-fashioned bonk-a-thon just wasn't working for me. Plus, the 16 000 kilometres between my uterus and the German's pecker was going to be a major problem.

The German went home and had all the appropriate testing done at a local fertility clinic, with the intention of sending his swimmers to me in the mail, or one of those cute little temperature-controlled mini-eskies. But then, instead of letting the fertility clinic send me his sperm in the cute little esky like he was supposed to, the German announced that he would very much like to come and visit me in Sydney, and deliver his sperm, in person. His swimmers weren't going Down Under without him.

Sure, I said. Even better! And we booked his flights to coincide with my ovulation calendar. Yep. That happened. We booked his flights. To coincide. With my *ovulation calendar.*

Can we just accept for a moment how utterly ridiculous that is? A guy I've spent less than two weeks with books his first trip to Australia to align with my menstrual cycle. I mean, holy shitballs. That's weird, right? At the time, it seemed perfectly reasonable to me.

I booked appointments for the sperm donation and egg retrieval at my fertility clinic in Sydney. I saw a lawyer to make sure we were both covered legally. I didn't want the German trying to steal my baby or sue me for maintenance down the track. I also wanted him to know that all I wanted was his sperm and I had no intention of hitting him up for child support. I upped my appointments with Lily Liu to twice a week. I was on a mission to be the most fertile woman in Australia by the time Ze German landed.

Everything was in place and I was ready. But within twenty-four hours of his arrival in Sydney, I realised I'd made the mother of all mistakes.

Things with Ze German did not go as planned.

That Time I Turned Down Brad Pitt

A word of warning ladies: just because your fertility is declining rapidly and you meet a guy and he's about a trillion degrees of hot and he offers to be your baby daddy, doesn't necessarily mean you should agree.

I had to learn this the hard way.

I'd endured so much heartbreak on my quest for motherhood, but the day Ze German arrived in Oz, I felt like I'd won the baby daddy jackpot!

He was super excited to be in Sydney as well. Australia is such a long way to travel for most Europeans, who can jump in the car and drive to Prague or zip off to Paris for the weekend. To them, the idea of sitting in a plane for twenty-four hours to get, well, *anywhere*, seems ridiculous. So I was really grateful he'd made the effort.

After some pretty wunderbar, 'we haven't seen each other for a couple of months and you've just travelled to the other side of the world to help me make a baby' sex, we went out for lunch.

Sadly, two incidents that afternoon put a major fizzer on things.

Fizzer number one: he saw a spider and shat himself.

I'll never forget the moment I turned around and saw Ze German standing there on the footpath, frozen on the spot, because he'd noticed a spider in a web about five metres above his head. I told him it was *totally* okay to walk underneath it, because the spider was not going to leap out of the web and kill him.

But he shook his head and refused to move. He was too petrified to even speak.

'Babe, it's fine!' I laughed. 'It's *not* going to hurt you! Just walk under it.' But he clenched both his fists in tight little balls under his chin and crept, tentatively, like one of those cartoon character villains, *across* the road, where he could put enough distance between him and the arachnid to safely walk down the *other* side of the street, before crossing back to me, about two metres past the spider's web.

(Inside Voice: Da Fuck?!)

So. I *know* those lucky Germans don't have to deal with the kind of lethal wildlife that we do Down Under, but seriously, buddy, fucking grow a pair. Or at least *pretend* to! Watching a grown man carry on like that over one teensy weensy spider was a *major* turn-off.

Still, I tried not to let it bother me. Because, well we had a baby to make.

Fizzer number two: he didn't have any money.

We went to an ATM after lunch so he could get some cash out, but his card didn't work. This didn't really surprise me. ATMs can be quite temperamental about which foreign cards they'll accept. So we just tried a different ATM. But the same thing happened. Then we tried another ATM, and another. But not one single bank would give him any funds. Strangely, he didn't seem too fazed by it, even though he hadn't brought any cash with him either. No euros. No Aussie dollars. Not one single cent.

Look, maybe it was an oversight. I always forget to pack something when I travel. Either my sunblock or my toothbrush or my power converter (I *always* forget the friggin' power converter). So this guy just forgot to pack *money*.

I told him not to worry because he'd be able to use his credit card for most things. But he said he only had a work credit card, which he wasn't allowed to use for personal expenses.

Then I suggested he could go online and transfer some money into my account so I could withdraw the cash for him. But he said he didn't know how to use internet banking.

As a last resort, he said he'd just borrow the cash from me and ask a friend to somehow transfer it to me later. And we left it at that.

However, I did struggle to understand how a 38-year-old man could travel to the other side of the world, where he only knew one person and he intended to stay for three weeks, with no cash, an ATM card that didn't work, an unusable credit card and no access to any funds of any kind.

Okay, I'm just going to go ahead and say it. That *did* set off some pretty big alarm bells.

But I really, really, *really* wanted to give him the benefit of the doubt. Because my biological clock was on its final countdown, locked and loaded on its very handsome target.

We had about a week before our appointment at the IVF clinic, which gave Ze German some time to explore Sydney before we got down to the business of making babies. Unfortunately, I wasn't able to play tour guide. The timing of his visit had worked in perfectly with my ovulation cycle. But I'd also just started a new radio show and the three hours I spent live on air each morning was the easy part of the job. The five-hour meetings every day *after* the show were excruciating!

In radio land, if you start a new show and it doesn't rate its arse off immediately, the bosses start to panic. Sadly, our show was not having much of an impact in the competitive breakfast market, so we had to endure these unbelievably tedious meetings every day going over *every single thing* we'd said on air that morning and discussing *every single thing* we were planning to say on air the next day. And it was not fun. Not one little bit.

While I was stuck at work, Ze German spent his days sight-seeing. But of course he didn't have any moolah. So each morning, I'd leave him a hundred bucks on the bedside table, as I raced out the door. And I couldn't decide whether it felt like I was leaving tuckshop money out for a small child before Mummy left for work. Or if I was paying for a cheap hooker who'd spent the night. I dunno. You decide.

Ze German would come home every day and tell me what an amazing time he'd had. Climbed the bridge. Went to the zoo. Took the ferry to Manly. Went to the aquarium. Taxied himself down to Bondi for a swim and a picturesque lunch on the beach. Not bad for a guy who arrived in Sydney *without a fucking cent to his name*. And the whole time he didn't seem to be making any attempt to work out how to do that online transfer.

I didn't tell him how much it was bothering me, but I was silently seething. The thought had crossed my mind that I was being scammed. I just didn't want to believe it.

I also started regretting the fact that I'd turned down an interview with Brad Pitt, so I could take Ze German away to the Great Barrier Reef.

Yes. Let me repeat that: *I turned down Brad Pitt.*

I had just booked the romantic weekend getaway when I got a call from Event Cinemas asking if I'd be available for a one-on-one chat with Brad Pitt, on that *very same* weekend.

SHIT. SHIT. SHIT.

It was the first time in my twenty-year career I'd been given the opportunity to meet the hottest man alive. And I knew it might never happen again. How could I possibly turn that down?

But if I said *yes* to Brad Pitt, I would have to cancel the weekend away with Ze German. He'd understand, wouldn't he? He could see the Great Barrier Reef another time. Or, like, never.

It was a tough decision, I won't lie.

And in what surely has to be the *ultimate* example of sacrificing my career for my personal life, I turned down Brad Pitt.

I know, right? Me = idiot.

So I don't know if it was a serious case of Pitt Remorse or the questionable money situation that finally pushed me over the edge.

Things went downhill pretty quickly after we arrived in Port Douglas. I decided to speak up over dinner on the first night and I told him how uncomfortable I was feeling about everything. How could he possibly think it was okay to travel all this way without access to any money at all? Was he *really* that irresponsible? Or was he playing me? And was he ever going to pay me back?

He cracked it! He took his watch off and furiously threw it across the table at me. 'Take it! As security! If you think I'm not going to pay you back. Take it. *Take it!*' he screamed. 'How dare you accuse me of such a thing!'

Oh my god. I'd never seen him angry before. It was scary.

And suddenly it all became too much for me. Between the insane pressure of my new job, the ongoing disappointment of failing to get pregnant, the stress of worrying that Ze German was scamming me, and missing out on my moment with Brad-fucking-Pitt, I just couldn't take it anymore.

A little voice inside me screamed, '*Schnell, schnell!* Get out of this nightmare immediately, you *dummkopf.*'

Something in my subconscious told me it would be incredibly foolish to make a baby with this man. To be completely honest, I think a little part of me knew it was fucking ridiculous to accept his non-anonymous sperm donor suggestion in the first place.

So I told him I was really sorry, but this had all been a big mistake and I was going to cancel the IVF appointments and it would be best if he returned to Germany. I booked myself on the first flight out of Cairns the next morning but I suggested he stay for the weekend and enjoy the luxurious hotel and the spectacular Great Barrier Reef. I couldn't get a refund on the trip anyway.

To this day, I don't know if I read the whole situation wrong with Ze German. Maybe he *was* playing me the whole time. Or maybe he thought he was doing me a massive favour by offering to be my sperm donor, so he just assumed I would support him on his holiday in return.

Okay so please don't judge me too harshly for what I'm about to tell you.

When I woke up the next morning in Port Douglas and rolled over and saw my hot German lying there in the sheets, looking all smouldering and delicious, I decided I would quite like one last shag for old times' sake before I left him.

It was a fitting farewell.

But just before I walked out the door, I left my penniless German with all the cash I had in my wallet. Four hundred and fifty dollars. And this time, it really *did* feel like I was paying for a hooker.

My 'baby-brain' had lasted for, oh, about three years. And in my desperate effort to fall pregnant at all costs, I momentarily lost my mind. But try as I might (and oh how I *tried*!) I could not fall pregnant. My fertility declined just as rapidly as the doc had warned and my crusty old eggs weren't up to the challenge. Then, at the age of 43, I also found out I had chronic endometriosis, which had been making it virtually impossible for me to fall pregnant all along.

So, I guess it really just wasn't mean to be.

A little part of me will grieve for the baby I never had for the rest of my life. However, the transition from trying so desperately to make a baby, to realising I wasn't going to have one was surprisingly less painful than I imagined it would be. I accepted the fact that these were the cards I'd been dealt. I forgave myself for wasting way too much time (and my fertility) in dysfunctional relationships with the wrong guys. I made peace with it all. And I just got on with life.

My trusty tarot card reader Poppy suggested that the reason I don't have kids is because I was a mother of *ten* in my *previous* life and

I'm giving myself a well earned, lifelong 'mummy-time-out' in this incarnation. I have yet to see proof that my soul has somehow been reborn. But if Poppy's right and I did have ten rugrats in my *last* life, that would probably explain my aversion to cooking and cleaning and my affection for foot massages, sleep and gin in *this* life.

Sexual Bucket List

(Hey, heads-up, Mum and Dad, you might want to skip the next couple of chapters.)

I think we've already established that I've had a decent amount of sex in my three mostly-single dating decades, so far (especially during my panicked baby trying years). But I've never been into any of the kinky stuff. So I'm either a bit of a sexual straighty-one-eighty or I've just never been in a relationship that's lasted long enough for us to seek out freaky new ways to peak the passion.

I once found out that a guy I'd dated briefly had his own 'Jungle Room', a *Fifty Shades*–style secret sex dungeon he'd custom designed for his newly renovated house. I was never invited into the Jungle Room so I'm not exactly sure what goes on in there. But I'm really glad I never found out. You, Tarzan . . . me, definitely not Jane.

The most adventurous stuff I've ever done is to join the dots in some unusual locations. When people ask me, 'Where's the weirdest place you've ever had sex?' I have a few options to choose from.

Like that one time with a boyfriend in his hospital bed. Oh, and I should probably mention that he had a collapsed lung and a breathing tube sticking out of a hole in his chest at the time.

I'd never fantastised about a hospital romp (other than with Dr Jackson Avery in the on-call room like they do on *Grey's Anatomy*).

But my boyfriend was surprisingly frisky when he ended up in the hospital only two months after we started dating. We *could* blame his spontaneous horniness on the mind-altering pain relief he was on at the time, or the fact that he simply wanted to finish what he started. You see, his lung had actually collapsed mid-shag, the night before.

I'd like to tell you it was a night of wild chandelier swinging that caused the pneumothorax. But, in fact, he was just a prime candidate – tall, slim and in his thirties. That being said, I'd still really much prefer that it hadn't happened while he was inside me. He says he'd felt a weird click in his chest while we were getting busy, which put an unexpected halt to proceedings. But instead of investigating further or seeking medical attention, Mr Tough Guy decided to ignore it and we both just fell asleep. We woke up the next morning to the alarming and rather unsettling sound of a loud rattle coming from somewhere inside his chest cavity. He said it was probably just a chest infection and not to worry, but when he left my place that morning, he panicked and drove himself straight to the hospital, where he was rushed into surgery immediately.

I raced to the hospital that afternoon to find my poor fella lying there, with a tube extending from a hole in his chest into a machine next to the bed, which was helping him breathe. He looked terribly unwell. I had brought him chocolates and flowers and all the latest issues of his favourite motoring magazines. But he told me there was only one thing that would make him feel better.

Boyfriend was horny.

I thought he was high on drugs and out of his freakin' mind when he suggested a little hospital-style how's-your-father. And he was very insistent. I guess I did feel somehow partly responsible for the collapsed lung, so when the sicko reached the point of practically begging, I reluctantly obliged. I closed the door (it was a private room, thank god), pulled the curtain securely around his bed and then I carefully climbed on top of him and maneouvred myself into a position where I hopefully wouldn't knock the breathing tube out of his chest.

He thought the whole thing was hilarious. I felt sick. There was no pleasure in the experience for me. At all.

It wasn't the kind of dangerously naughty 'maybe we'll get caught' sex. It was just dangerous, period. It could have ended with a horribly awkward conversation with his parents: 'Yeah, it's nice to meet you and all, but look, I'm really sorry, your son suffocated because the tube helping him breathe accidentally popped out while we were having intercourse in his hospital bed six hours after his emergency surgery. My bad.'

The parents didn't even know I existed at that stage. Boyfriend had told his folks the lung collapsed while he was changing his duvet cover. Which actually does seem quite plausible, because you know how violently you sometimes have to shake those things to make sure the doona reaches every damn corner of the cover.

His mates all thought I was tops, by the way. From then on, I was forever known as the shag who sent him to the ER. Something to be proud of? Not sure. But it was certainly a notable introduction to his friends.

Sex with the patient (and his breathing tube) was a complete disaster. And, of course, the nurse also managed to walk in on us. Unfortunately I was still sitting on top of him at the time. She popped her head through the curtain, quickly assessed the scene and asked him, 'Are you okay, sir?'

To which he replied, 'Yeah, I'm good, thanks.'

She smiled knowingly and said, 'Rightio then, I'll come back later. Be careful.' She seemed alarmingly calm about the whole situation. Perhaps the horny patient thing happens more often than we realise? I was *mortified*.

Turns out that particular boyfriend was quite fond of expanding his sexual experiences beyond the bounds of the traditional bedroom workbench. He was also the guy responsible for my initiation to the mile high club. I had never been able to understand the appeal (or logistics) of two bodies and eight limbs having intercourse in an aeroplane toilet. It seems physically impossible, for a start. Plus, it's got to be one of the least sexy locations for getting hot and heavy. What with the foul stench, the disgusting drops of wee all over the floor, the dirty shit stains in the bowl and someone else's spit frothing in the basin, it's downright feral.

So I was quite relieved that my MHC experience didn't happen in the loo. Boyfriend and I were on a long-haul flight to London and we were already ecstatic about being unexpectedly upgraded to the pointy end of the plane. Then, Madame Bollinger here wasted no time sculling around twelve glasses of vintage French from the comfort of her fabulous first-class seat. (I do not adhere to the 'don't drink alcohol on a plane' theory. If it's champagne. And it's free. You can feed it to me on a drip. Thanks.)

So I thought it was an absolutely splendid idea when the boyfriend suggested, somewhere over Uzbekistan, that we were at an altitude to remember.

Now, I should point out that this was well before the introduction of the outrageously expensive luxurious first-class suites they have these days, which come with their own privacy doors and double beds. Those things are like mini-apartments. We were on a plane that still had the exposed open cabin with the old-school, povo first-class seats (how's that for the ultimate oxymoron?), but we discovered that when reclined into their flat-bed positions, the seats were just wide enough for two people. So boyfriend jumped in, snuggled up behind me and we pretended to watch a movie. And with the assistance of some dim cabin lighting and a rather large blanket, I discovered that it really wasn't that difficult to receive my on-the-spot membership to the MHC. No toilet-sex gymnastics required.

I'm sure no one saw us. There were only three other passengers in the first-class cabin on that flight and they were all asleep (or pretending to be). And the staff were all on a break (or pretending to be). However, I would like to apologise to anyone who has been seated in 2E in the first-class cabin of that particular jumbo jet anytime since 2009.

If the mile high club is on your sexual bucket list, outdoor sex is probably there as well. Theoretically, outdoor sex should be the easier of the two to achieve. I guess when most people consider a public tryst, they're aiming for a private, secluded spot on a deserted beach or someplace nice and warm (preferably without the risk of arrest). I don't think too many people hope to get their gear off on an open communal rooftop, in one of the most densely populated cities on the planet, in sub-zero temperatures in the middle of winter.

Which is what I did. On a New York rooftop. On New Year's Eve. Because, New York. Also, New Year's Eve.

I know the idea of outdoor sex is a turn-on for some. But it never has been for me. I'm not an exhibitionist. In fact, I'm a bit of a prude. The idea of being caught in the throes of passion with my pants down doesn't turn me on. So I really have absolutely no idea what came over me on that chilly New Year's Eve in New York City.

Except, New York. Also, New Year's Eve.

A boyfriend and I were invited to ring in the new year at a friend's Midtown apartment. We joined the other residents and their guests on the rooftop, where we had a direct line of sight to the famous ball drop in Times Square. We all made the obligatory toast at midnight and slurred along to 'Auld Lang Syne', but I've clearly been spoiled by too many spectacular firework celebrations on Sydney Harbour over the years, because I thought the whole Times Square ball drop business was a little . . . underwhelming.

Still, I was determined to have a NYC NYE to remember! So, in my overjoyed 'I'm in friggin' New York on New Year's Eve, bitchez!' state of mind (encouraged, no doubt, by the internal warmth I was feeling from the three vodka shots I'd consumed just before midnight), I suddenly had the urge to be naughty. That sparkling Manhattan skyline was practically screaming at me to have sex in its glow. When all the other ball watchers retreated to the warm confines of their apartments at exactly three minutes past twelve, I convinced my fella to stay on the rooftop and join me for a spot of midnight delight. 'Cause even if the big ball drop doesn't excite you, maybe you've just got to grab life by the balls yourself, right?

One of the things that makes a public tryst feel so damn naughty is the risk of being caught out. But I'm sure the only reason I even considered it was because I was fairly certain we *wouldn't* be interrupted. Folks couldn't get off that ice-cold roof fast enough after the midnight celebration (it was about two below zero). We also managed to find a small ledge to hide everything that was going on below the waist. So, in the city that never sleeps, we were mostly protected from the prying eyes of any nosy neighbours.

It was bitterly cold, terribly awkward and certainly not the ideal spot for an outdoor interlude, but we gave it a bloody good go. And I have to admit, it was an unexpected thrill to throw out the inhibitions and do something entirely spontaneous. It was one of the most memorable New Year's Eve experiences I've ever had.

Major kudos to my fella, by the way, for managing to perform under extreme conditions that night. That's one auld acquaintance who will certainly never be forgot. And yes, he and his manhood were both able to escape the encounter frostbite-free.

Choke and Poke

Ideally it would be nice to find a partner whose sexual bucket list is more or less on par with yours. And one who respects your limits.

I accidentally discovered that one of my hard limits is choking.

I say accidentally, because the first time a guy tried the old choke and poke on me in the bedroom, it took me completely by surprise. He certainly hadn't asked if I'd like some subtle asphyxiation with my shag. I was totally oblivious to what was going on. I only noticed something wasn't quite right when I started feeling pressure around my neck. And because I didn't resist immediately (um, I was trying to process what the fuck was going on), Mr Chokeypokey interpreted that as a green light and started to squeeze my neck a little tighter and press down on my windpipe a little harder. That was my cue to physically remove his hand from my throat and tell him I was not comfortable with that particular manoeuvre. Thanks very much.

What shocked me even more about this situation is that it happened while I was having sex with the guy for the very first time.

Sure, I understand that some people enjoy a little erotic asphyxiation. But I imagine that's something you'd only choose to explore if you're in a secure, trusting relationship with a partner you feel completely safe with, even at your most vulnerable. It seems wildly inappropriate to try it out on someone you're getting jiggy with for the first time. Especially without asking their permission. Or discussing it first.

If that wasn't already the most disturbing thing that had ever happened to me between the sheets, I couldn't believe it when I found myself in the exact same position on two other separate occasions.

The second time it happened, I assumed the guy was taking a little breather and he just hadn't realised that his hands (and his full body weight) were pressing down on the base of my neck. But then he started to slowly tighten his grip around my throat and I realised I'd found myself in the sack with another cheeky choker.

On the third occasion, I was able to swat the guy's hand away from my neck the moment I sensed where it was heading. Third time is definitely *not* a charm.

After this happened to me *three* times on *three* separate occasions with three different men, I had to wonder if I was out of touch with some new bedroom craze and blissfully unaware that choking had somehow crept its way into most people's sexual repertoire.

I asked my girlfriends if they'd ever experienced it. Most of them said they'd encountered a random bum slap or a surprise hair pull now and then, but none of them had ever been exposed to the old sex strangle.

As ridiculously bizarre as it sounds, I know these guys weren't trying to assault me. I guess it might be an intense form of domination for some men and I reckon they were probably even hoping it might 'pleasure' me. But what it actually did was force me into brief moments of non-consensual submission and vulnerability I'd never felt before. And there was nothing pleasurable about those experiences for me. On any level.

It's most definitely a hard limit for me, Mr Grey.

Here's another thing that shocked me about these encounters: each of the stranglers was about ten years my junior, which put them all in their early thirties (despite my occasional cougar tendencies, I generally adhere to the motto 'if I can make you, I can't date you'). So I wonder if these guys only attempted the choke and poke because they assumed I was the experienced older woman, who had seen and done it all before? Or has choking just become a commonplace sex act among the younger generation?

It saddens me to think that young women embarking on their first sexual encounters might actually think this is normal behaviour or, worse still, that it's what's expected of them. Hey, if choking floats your boat, go for it. But please remember girls, sex is supposed to be enjoyable for *both* people involved.

And to be perfectly honest, most guys would just be pretty damn thrilled with a good old-fashioned blow job.

All the Good Ones are Taken

My two besties decided to hire me a gigolo for my last birthday.

I am not making this up.

Galeb and Gusband Tim were having great difficulty deciding what to get me. 'She's so hard to buy for,' they agreed. 'She really doesn't need anything,' they said. 'What's the *one* thing she would really, really like?' they pondered.

And there was only one answer.

A root.

Yep. Delightful.

When my darling friends were able to stop laughing about how hilarious this idea was, it suddenly dawned on them that, actually, a little wham-bam-thank-you-Sam would be the perfect birthday gift for their single, 47-year-old friend. They even discussed how they'd present it to me. They knew I'd never go for it if they just handed over the fella and said, 'Hon, meet Giovanni. He's all yours! Oh, and we paid for the overnight package, so take your time.' They knew it would have to be a clandestine operation.

So they planned to bring him along to my birthday dinner disguised as a 'friend' and seat him at the end of the table, under instructions to make eyes with me all night. Given enough subtle flirt-ing (and champagne), I might just go home with him. And they'd only tell me the truth the next day, well and truly after I'd blown out the candles (so to speak).

My outrageously thoughtful buddies did not go ahead with my birthday surprise in the end. But when they told me later that they had seriously considered paying for sex for me, I nearly died. I was horrified.

Gusband Tim said he even researched some options online, but then realised it was all a terrible mistake as he perused my choices and saw how overly manscaped the male prostitutes all seemed to be. I believe 'Oh, no, darls, there was way too much vegetable oil in those profile pics' were his exact words.

So, would I have done it?

No fucking way! I still can't even bring myself to try online dating!

I only know of one woman who decided to pay for sex, a successful businesswoman in her early fifties, who was devastated to discover that her husband had been cheating on her for many years. After a messy, drawn-out divorce, she was too emotionally exhausted to even think about dating. She just didn't have the time or energy to deal with the mind games, bullshit or complications of any of the dating apps. But she really, really, really just wanted to be touched. I'm not sure if she ever actually went through with it, but in some cases, I guess a professional who knows exactly which buttons to push is a more time- and cost-effective way of attending to one's needs.

I'm not mad at Tim and Galeb for wanting to pay for me to get some action. I know they had good intentions. And I hadn't been on a date in *months*. God knows, they've both heard me whinge enough about how hideous it is out there on the forty-plus singles scene.

If you ever want to truly understand the meaning behind the saying 'all the good ones are taken', try dating in your forties. That'll sort it out for you pretty quickly.

I don't want to be a Debbie Downer or anything, but I have had very few positive dating experiences so far this decade. In fact, it's proving to be my least favourite dating decennary. Even dating from the ages of zero to ten was more fun than this.

Technically, it should be less complicated when both parties are over forty. We've lived. We've learned. We've loved. Right? We're supposed to have our shit together.

We're more mature. So we shouldn't have time for silly games. We're wiser. So we shouldn't be bothered by any of the insignificant crap. We're more experienced. So we shouldn't waste energy on people who aren't on the same wavelength. And we're more confident and self-assured. So we should know what we want and we shouldn't be afraid to ask for it (also, the sex should be better).

But I have sadly discovered that dating in my forties is rife with all the same dilemmas as my previous decades. Plus there's a whole *bonus set* of new, complicated, *grown-up* issues to throw into the mix as well. Yay.

For example:

- Kids: Most guys over forty have them. So if things do get serious, you won't just be bringing him into your life, you'll also be bringing his kids. And the kids' mother(s) too. They aren't all necessarily going to be happy about it – or you.
- Baggage: We're both going to have it, guaranteed. But more often that not, the combined baggage is so inconveniently big and bulky, it just gets in the fucking way.
- Bad habits: You can't teach an old dog new tricks. Full stop.
- Peter Pan syndrome: A man who's forty-plus and coming out of a ten- or twenty-year marriage is ripe for a midlife crisis, which will possibly involve the desire to date much younger women. Which means any woman over the age of thirty-five won't get a look in.
- Online dating: Older dudes are mad for it. After years with the same partner, they suddenly realise that the

smorgasbord of sex available to them through these dating apps is mind-blowing! It makes them feel like Hugh fucking Hefner (RIP). And they embrace it wholeheartedly. It's Dating Disneyland for these dicks.

Which brings me to the biggest issue of all: All the good ones really are taken, or gay.

At my age, there are definitely *not* plenty of fish in the sea. In fact, I wouldn't even call it a sea. It's more like one of those inflatable kids' pools. That's sprung a leak.

Look, I'm sure there are still some good ones left. But from my experiences and the experiences of all my single forty-something girlfriends who are also out there on the frontline (please refer to any of the following stories), the number of good, decent, honest, mature, available (emotionally and physically) men for us to date is in alarmingly short supply.

I've even heard it suggested that my best option now is to find myself a grieving *widower*. For realz. A man who has suffered the heartbreak of his beloved spouse's untimely death is my best chance at finding love with a man over forty, because he's not single *by choice*. So he might actually still be a decent bloke. Yep. Men with dead wives are now my target demo. Isn't that a comforting thought?

Actually, come to think of it, maybe I will grab Giovanni's number. You know, just in case.

The Lawnmower

I didn't discover until my early forties that one of the worst guys you can possibly date is a chronic snorer.

Sleeping beside John sounded like there was a lawnmower, on crack, doing laps of the bedroom, *all night.*

I quite liked the idea of sleepovers and special cuddles and falling asleep in the arms of my lovely new boyfriend, but instead I'd just lie there, wide awake, while he trumpeted along beside me. I tried everything to drown out the noise. Earplugs. Headphones. Meditation. Sleeping tablets. Nothing worked. Smothering him with a pillow seemed like the only viable option.

It didn't help that I was working in breakfast radio at the time and my alarm was already set at 4 a.m. each day. The ongoing quest to get a decent amount of sleep was the single most important issue in my world, but I realised that would be hopelessly unachievable while I was sleeping beside the lawnmower.

To make matters worse, John was a snorer in denial. He refused to accept that it was an issue, because it didn't bother him at all. And, look, I totally get how this happens. The offender is sound asleep and blissfully unaware of the incredible kerfuffle they're making and the angst and chaos they're causing their partner. So he never made any real attempt to remedy the problem, and the snoring continued. Night after night after night after night. Which basically meant I was always grumpy and tired. And irritable and tired. And frustrated and tired. And JUST. FUCKING. TIRED. Allthefuckingtime.

It reached a point where I could no longer sleep in the same house as him. So I stopped seeing him altogether during the week and limited the number of weekend sleepovers. Not an ideal situation for a blossoming relationship.

Well, do you know what's worse than having a boyfriend who's a chronic snorer? Agreeing to go on holiday with one. Dumbest relationship decision of my life! Because – here's a tip – a chronic snorer does not miraculously stop snoring just because he's on holiday. Or in another country.

I must have had a major brain freeze when I invited John to join me on the ski trip I'd booked with Helen a month before I met him. On the first night of our romantic getaway, I didn't sleep a wink. He snored just as loud and hard and long as he did back home. Of course, the resort was fully booked, so I couldn't just move to another room. I was trapped in bed with Darth Vadar, on the other side of the world. On what was supposed to be our relaxing, rejuvenating, romantic holiday.

I reached peak frustration on night two, at around 2 a.m., as I lay there and realised I had *two weeks* of this nightmare ahead of me. My vacay was well and truly fucked. By 3 a.m., I couldn't deal with it for another second. I shoved John to wake him up and turn him over and I begged him, for the love of god, to – please – *shut up* so I could get some damn *sleep*!

Which is when he told *me* to shut the fuck up and stop acting like a selfish princess. Then he rolled over and went back to sleep. And pretty soon it sounded like Darth Vadar was on crack, riding a lawnmower, doing laps of my hotel room.

That's when I snapped. I was livid.

It wasn't the 'princess' accusation that upset me. I'm pretty low maintenance most of the time. But I *can* teeter into a princess territory occasionally. Sure, I refuse to drink sparkling wine, because, well, if it's not champagne, why bother? I *always* put on makeup before I go to yoga. And I never take the train (unless I'm in New York or Paris). You are more than welcome to call me a princess for any of the above.

However. I could not cop being called 'selfish'. The basic human need for a restful night's sleep does *not* make me selfish. Look, if I really cared about the guy, maybe the snoring wouldn't have bothered me so much. And if he really cared about me, maybe he would have tried a little harder to find a solution. But he didn't, and I guess I didn't. So instead, we found ourselves at a snoring impasse somewhere near the Brenner Pass, in the Austrian Alps.

Darling Helen came to the rescue with a generous offer to swap rooms. John could move to her room, which was, thankfully, on a different floor on the other side of the hotel and Helen would move to my room and sleep with me (we'd shared a room countless times before on our travels without any drama). I could still visit my fella before lights out and tuck him in and read him a bedtime story (nudge nudge, wink wink) and then leave him to snore loud and proud, while I went back to my room to sleep in peace, alongside Helen. Then we could *all* get some sleep.

It was a perfectly rational solution to a really unfortunate problem. I'd paid a lot of money to fly to the other side of the world to ski on some of the most magnificent slopes in Europe. Why should my holiday be ruined when there was a simple solution at hand?

But when I presented the proposal to John he acted like I'd asked him to cut off a fucking limb. He only reluctantly ageed to the move when he wasn't able to offer an alternative solution. But I think his ego had been bruised.

Because he found a way to get his revenge that night at dinner, in what I like to call 'mash-gate'.

Mash-gate

Helen and I had spent a couple of weeks exploring Italy together before John and his mates met up with us. Our Italian adventure had turned into a two-week pasta odyssey. We ate as much pasta as we could, as often as we could – usually for lunch *and* dinner. And it was *delizioso*!

I can cope with brief spurts of intense carb-loading, thanks to a pretty high metabolism, but my jeans were definitely starting to feel snug. And by the time I met up with my boyfriend, after not see-ing him for a few weeks, I was feeling a little uncomfortable about the appearance of a mini-muffin top. Look, I'd probably only gone from a size eight to a size ten, so I didn't lose any sleep over it. But I was already a little self conscious whenever I was naked around him, especially during sex. That stupid cow gravity had started forcing some of my forty-year-old body parts in a rather unflattering south-erly direction and I didn't like it. I couldn't even recognise my own boobs anymore.

So when all of us went out to dinner on that third night of our holiday I ordered a healthy salad. But when John's plate of steak and mash arrived at the table, that fluffy white mound of potato and butter looked so damn good. I did what any girlfriend is well within her rights to do, and reached across towards his plate, with the intention of stealing one innocent little forkful of mash.

Just one forkful, to taste, because I'd ordered the dumb salad.

Well, John must have clocked what was about to happen and before my fork could get anywhere near his mash, he sprang into action and wrapped his arms all the way around his plate as if he was protecting something incredibly valuable. Then he said to me, loudly enough for everyone at the table to hear, 'Do you *really* think you need that, Sam?'

And he glanced down at my waist and raised his eyebrows and then looked back up at me as if to say, 'The answer is *no*. You most definitely do not need the mash.'

Oh yes he did. My boyfriend fucking *mash-shamed* me! He protected that mashed potato behind a double-arm wall, so I couldn't get near it.

It's kind of weird that I can still recall that moment, from all those years ago, so vividly. But I remember feeling humiliated and belittled in front of his friends, and in complete shock that a grown man could act so childishly. Plus, come on, how could I ever forget the one and only time I've ever been publicly mash-shamed?

I tried to convince myself that I'd misread it. Maybe he was just trying to be funny. At my expense. But the next night at dinner I ordered the pasta. And after I'd finished every last delicious piece of penne on my plate, John turned to me and said, 'Geez, you polished that off, didn't you?' Again with the face and the snide little glance down at my muffin top.

So it turned out my boyfriend wasn't just a mash-nazi. He was a carb-nazi too. (Oh, and a total fuckwit.)

I'm happy to report that his malicious little comments did not send me into an unhealthy spiral of starvation and bulimia. I just broke up with him instead.

There were a bunch of other issues in that relationship anyway, so my fuck budget was already running pretty low. Aside from the chronic snoring (I could never have married the guy, let's be honest), his ego was a little too inflated for my liking. Plus, we'd been arguing, a lot, about everything. And I'm pretty sure I caught him lying a few times. I was tempted to break up with him before the holiday, but it would have been way too messy to cancel everything, so I stupidly decided to ignore our problems and just go away with him, have some fun and reassess the situation when we got home.

But when he started with the fat-shaming, I just ran out of fucks to give. About him and the relationship. Mash-gate was my out.

When we got back to the hotel after dinner, I told him I was done. The relationship was over. It was day four of our holiday.

We managed to mostly avoid each other for the rest of the trip and I thoroughly enjoyed my holiday without him. In fact, the very next night at après-ski, I met a smoking hot guy who made me feel like the sexiest woman alive, pasta belly, saggy boobs and all. And we embarked on a pretty intense rebound and holiday fling (combined), which helped me move on from the snoring carb-nazi pretty much immediately.

Neville No Pay

I'm so over the whole 'who should pay on a first date' debate. Should the guy pay? Should you always go Dutch? Are you an anti-feminist and a traitor to all women if you let a man pay for your meal? I know Mars and Venus have been arguing about this since the dawn of time, but I've reached a point where I'm chemically incapable of giving a fuck about this topic any longer. The guy and his Warm Sushi Escape Clause is probably what pushed me over the edge.

I actually know plenty of women who refuse to split the bill on a date. *Ever*. These women are all hard-working, independent, successful chicks, but if they're out with a man and the bill arrives, they don't even go for the fake wallet reach. If the guy doesn't insist on paying, in full, they lose his number. Immediately.

Look, I have to admit that it does impress me when a guy picks up the bill in the early stages of dating. I think it shows some old-school gentlemanly character. It indicates that he might be a good bloke in other ways – kind, considerate, courteous, generous. Those are all qualities I look for in a partner. But I don't have an issue with going Dutch. If the fella doesn't *insist* on paying, I'm not going to kick him to the kerb over it.

It only becomes an issue if he *never* pays. Which seemed to be the case when I found myself on a series of unfortunate dates with a forty-something-year-old guy my friends have affectionately named 'Neville No Pay'.

As his moniker suggests, Neville did not like to pay. He wasn't even fond of going halfsies. When the bill came, he would usually just fold his arms, sit back and watch me hand over my credit card. We went on a total of six dates. I paid for four of them.

To be fair, Neville did pay for our first coffee date. The bill was around nine bucks. On our second date, I just automatically threw my credit card on the table when the bill arrived after dinner. He didn't offer his, so I paid for it in full. I was a little surprised that he didn't even offer to split the bill, but I just assumed it would naturally evolve into a 'take turns' situation from then on. Sadly, it did not. Neville let me pay. In full. On every date thereafter.

I asked the girlfriend who set us up what the fuck was going on. Was he broke? Had his ex-wife taken him to the cleaners? How could a guy in his forties be so totally clueless?

She was shocked. He apparently ran a very successful business and, as far as she knew, he was quite comfortable financially.

I tried to think up excuses for his behaviour. He'd recently divorced after twenty-something years of marriage, so maybe he was confused about modern-day dating protocol. My friends quickly called bullshit on that excuse. They reminded me that the last time he'd dated, back in the dark ages, there was absolutely no confusion about who paid the bill. The man *always* paid.

We all have that one friend we can count on for a brutally honest answer to any question. Anywhere. Anytime. That friend, for me, is Nicole. She's truckloads of fun, she's got a heart of gold and she has a more finely tuned bullshit meter than anyone else I know. She has no qualms about voicing her opinion, even if she knows it's the one thing I really, really, really don't want to hear. So when conversation with Nicole rolled around to the Neville No Pay dilemma, her advice was blunt.

'The guy's a tight-arse,' she told me. 'Get rid of him!'

You might be thinking that my six dates with Neville were possibly four dates too many. But I honestly wanted to give him the benefit of the doubt. And I do think a simple bill can give a guy mental whiplash in the financial department. If I *do* pay, will she think I'm a controlling misogynist? If we split the bill, will she think I'm cheap? Blah de blah blah.

The last straw with Neville No Pay came after a meal with four other couples. It was a big, boozy dinner so it was a pretty hefty bill. It was agreed that the bill would be split evenly between the couples and all the men put their cards on the table. Except Neville. I waited a while, but he didn't move. So eventually I added my credit card to the others so we could all pay up and go home. Neville pretended not to notice. But someone else did.

When the waitress came to take the cards and process the bill, one of his friends reached over, removed my card from the bunch, handed it back to me and then turned to Neville and said, 'Buddy, don't be an idiot. Give me your fucking credit card.'

It's the only time a man has been *forced* into paying for a date with me. It was humiliating. I stopped replying to his texts and calls after that and eventually he got the hint. I never slept with Neville, or even kissed him, on any of our six dates. But I hung in there, hoping the attraction might come if I developed feelings for him. I now wonder if that was the reason he never paid. Maybe he wasn't into me, or maybe he just wasn't prepared to fork out until he knew he was guaranteed a return on his investment.

Sperm on his Business Card

I once went on a few dates with a gynaecologist. Yep. The guy looked at vajayjay, all day long.

Thankfully, I didn't meet the Gyno at his office. We met at mine. We got chatting at a sales event for the radio station where I was working. He seemed lovely. He was smart (obviously), successful, easy on the eye, interesting. And very, very interested.

I accepted his invitation for a date but I couldn't help feeling a variety of uncontrollably irrational 'dating-a-gyno' concerns. Like, what makes a man (a human without a vajoir) want to become a gyno in the first place? It's clearly a very female-focused field. And how well can you *really* understand the ins and outs of a body part when you're not actually in possession of one? If we were to become a couple, wouldn't it be rather unpleasant knowing my boyfriend spent his days at the office looking at female genitalia very, very closely? Oh, and let's remember that he wouldn't just be looking at them. He'd be prodding them and poking them and touching them and putting things inside them and generally analysing other women's bits for eight to ten hours each day. Before coming home to me and *my* bits.

Is it reasonable to wonder if your fella's job as a gyno could somehow ruin his passion and enthusiasm for the home vag? We've all heard the analogy of the chef who spends all day in the kitchen. The last thing he wants to do is come home and cook you dinner. Isn't it same-same, but different?

Also, what if a gorgeous supermodel comes into your boyfriend's surgery with the prettiest little vajoir he's ever seen? Will he feel disenchanted when he comes home to yours? We all know no two are the same, but have you ever wondered how yours compares? The Gyno could certainly tell you the cold hard truth, if you really wanted to hear it.

A male gyno once told a friend of mine that she had a 'beautiful' vagina. During a pap smear! This made her incredibly uncomfortable. Not just because she was twenty at the time and her gyno was an old man who reminded her of her father, but also because that surely belongs in the category of 'most inappropriate things you could possibly say on the job'.

I had one other small concern about going on a date with the Gyno. Which is . . . he had sperm . . . on his business card.

It wasn't fresh jizz. Let me clarify that right away. It was cartoon sperm. For a fertility specialist, his name conveniently contained the letter 'O'. So he (or someone he had probably paid way too much to come up with the idea) thought it was clever, or cute, to design a business card with drawings of wriggly little sperm swimming towards and around the 'O' in his name, capturing that magical moment of conception.

Now, here's my concern about that: just because you're a fertility specialist, and you happen to have an 'O' in your name, doesn't mean it's okay to have sperm on your business card. Isn't it a little flippant? I couldn't decide if the sperm on the Gyno's business card was clever, cute or crass. And I couldn't decide whether or not to date him.

Luckily, when you host your own radio show and you're facing any of life's big dilemmas, you can just ask your listeners for advice. It provides entertaining content for your show (✓). It fills precious air time (✓). It gives you helpful advice (✓). And it allows you to hear other perspectives that you may not have previously considered (✓).

So I put it out there, and the listeners loved it. The segment was hugely popular and very entertaining. They were divided on the issue, though. Plenty of callers said they could never see a gyno romantically, because it would just be too weird (for precisely the same reasons as me). Others reminded me that the guy was a professional, doing his job, so there was no weirdness about it whatsoever. Quite a few callers suggested that he would probably be an amazing lover, considering he spent so much time around the female anatomy.

In the end, I decided to overlook the dodgy business card design, be an adult about it and give the Gyno a go. I mean, how could I not? This guy might just give me the best orgasm of my life.

For our first date, he took me to dinner at the super-fancy Icebergs restaurant in Bondi. Dinner was delightful, conversation flowed and it was a relief to be able to talk to him so openly about my own recent fertility struggles and numerous heartbreakingly painful attempts to fall pregnant. He told me he didn't have kids but he'd love to have his own one day. He paid for dinner. He dropped me home. And he very politely asked when he could see me again. As far as first dates go, it was perfectly lovely.

For our second date, we shared another delightful dinner at another fancy restaurant. And we talked at length about our careers. I talked about working in radio and he talked about what it was like working in the booming fertility industry and he casually mentioned that there might still be some options I could look into, if I wanted to have another crack at getting pregnant. And I was a little bit confused about whether he was suggesting this as my potential 'Doctor' or as my potential 'Partner'. Either way, it all seemed a bit too much, too soon. Sure, buddy, I realise it's your area of expertise and all, but I'd really like to get through at least two full meals with you before we start making plans with my uterus.

We finished dinner and he dropped me home. A gut feeling told me not to kiss him. Something didn't feel right. I just couldn't put my finger on it. We'd enjoyed two perfectly lovely dinners and he seemed like a perfectly lovely guy. But as I lay in bed that night, thinking about our date and trying to work out what was missing, I accepted the regrettable fact that there was an obvious lack of chemistry between us. The Gyno did not make my vajoir flutter.

Which really sucked, actually. Because I knew it would be incredibly convenient for *this* guy to be my Mr Happily Ever After. A smart, successful fertility expert certainly ticked *all* the boxes (and then some!) for this fertility challenged woman on the wrong side of forty.

I agreed to a third date, *determined* to locate that missing spark. We decided on a movie and he chose Sacha Baron Cohen's *The Dictator*.

Sadly, that movie only made our disappointing lack of chemistry even more obvious. He thought it was absolutely hysterical and he roared with laughter from start to finish. I thought it was the worst movie ever made. I didn't laugh once. Not *once*!

The Gyno dropped me home after the movie and after some not-so-subtle ghosting, I never saw him again. I possibly could have dragged it out for a few more dates and kept my fingers crossed that the spark would somehow magically ignite. But honestly, why delay the inevitable?

Maybe I'm desperately searching for any reason to explain why I didn't fall madly in love with the smart, successful, handsome fertility doctor, but I would actually like Sacha Baron Cohen to accept some of the blame for this one.

Because there are two types of people in the world. There are those who think *The Dictator* is pure comic genius and a witty social satire. And people (like me) who think that movie was about as funny as a terminal disease. And I really believe that these two types of people should never date. They are not, and never will be, a match.

In the end it wasn't even the fact that he had other women's vajoirs in his face all day that turned me off. It was something as simple and primal as the Gyno's sense of humour (also explained the sperm on the business card).

Sure, laughter is the best medicine, but *only* when you're laughing at the same things.

The Doggie Deal-Breaker

Love me, love my dog. Or don't waste my time.

For most of my dog's furry little life, it's been just the two of us: Sam and Lolli. Two badass bestie bitches, *Thelma and Louise*–style. The Brad Pitts have come and gone in our story, so for the most part, it's just me and the pooch. She's been my one constant companion for more than eleven years. Naturally, my dog sleeps on my bed. Well, she sleeps wherever the hell she wants, to be honest. But, mostly, she likes the bed.

Unfortunately, Lolli does not curl up in a compact fluffy ball at the end of my bed. Oh no. Most nights I find the princess stretched out, diagonally, across the middle of the mattress, taking up as much surface area as a canine possibly can. It's as if she makes a conscious effort to lie in the most inconvenient spot she can find. So, despite the fact that I have a smallish dog and a gigantic king-sized bed, I usually find myself curling into whatever limited space I can find on the edge, like a Cirque du Soleil contortionist. If I want to let sleeping dogs lie.

The furchild's complete and unashamed dominance of my bed really doesn't bother me, and it has only ever led to issues in my dating life on a few occasions. Like the time a guy told me about halfway through our our first date that he could *never* be with a girl who let her dog sleep on the bed. 'It's a dating deal-breaker,' he said, rather sternly.

I laughed out loud and yelled jokingly, 'Cheque, please!' But my date did not think I was funny. He didn't even crack a smile. Instead, he made it very clear to me that he *could* not, and he *would* not, ever be in bed with a dog.

So I decided to make it very clear to *him* that my dog *did* always and *would* always sleep in my bed, which presented an uncomfortable conversational crossroads for a few moments, before we moved on to other topics. It was wildly premature to be discussing our bedroom routine at that stage, anyway.

After dinner, I was a little surprised when he said he'd like to see me again. It seemed pointless getting to know him better. You don't have to be an expert matchmaker to realise that a man who hates dogs and a woman who loves hers like the child she never had are probably never going to make it down the aisle.

I was understandably confused by his mixed messages, so I did what any self-respecting content-hungry radio host would do, and turned it into an on air segment. The next morning, I explained his no-dogs-on-the-bed first-date deal-breaker to my listeners, who were already well aware of my boundary-less relationship with my pooch. And I asked them if it would be foolish of me to accept his invitation for a second date.

Some callers said I should give him another chance. They assured me that he'd change his tune as soon he met my adorable furbaby. But most warned me not to waste my time. Well, I didn't even have to make the decision in the end, because about thirty seconds after I came off air, I received a text message from the guy that read, 'I heard your show today. I think it's best that we don't see each other again. Take care.'

Boom! Just like that. He'd sent *me* a one-way ticket to the doghouse. Where, quite frankly, I realised I'd be much happier anyway. Still, I honestly don't know what his problem was. My dog is a non-shedding, non-allergenic bichon frise toy poodle mix who gets professionally groomed once a week. She's probably cleaner than some of the women he's slept with.

Plus, whenever I have had a home-ground dalliance in the bedroom, Lolli always plays ball with the girl code. She knows exactly when to remove herself from her preferred position on the bed. As soon as things start getting hot and heavy, she relocates to a different spot, underneath the bed. She somehow understands my need for privacy and uninterrupted access to the full scope of the mattress. Or she's just hiding down there covering her ears with her little paws, begging for it to be over.

I actually think she was emotionally scarred early on when she took it upon herself to investigate the strange new game that Mum and her man-friend were playing on the bed. She crept up behind the guy while he was on top of me, and licked his balls. The poor fella got the fright of his life. It didn't take him long to work out that it wasn't me down there.

So, yep, that was a terribly awkward situation for everyone. Probably worst of all for Lolli. She's never tried that move again.

There was only one other embarrassing occasion, when Lolli wanted everyone to know that she was really pissed about sharing her bed (and/or her mum). I had invited a guy back to Villa Lukis for the first time on our third date. We had a fun groping sesh on the couch before relocating to the bedroom. Unfortunately, Little Miss Intuitive must have already sensed where things were headed because, while we were still mid-make-out on the couch, Lolli had popped into the bedroom and peed on the floor . . . on his side of the bed.

As if that wasn't awkward enough, I woke the next morning to discover that, during the night, Madam had also urinated right next to his clothes, where they'd been sitting in a crumpled heap on the floor (I never told him but I'm pretty sure I also spotted a little splashback on his shoes).

All dog owners know that dogs don't pee where they sleep or eat, so I can only imagine Lolli really wanted to make a point that night. The first pee was probably just marking her territory. But the second one, next to his clothes, was a warning shot. Doggie language for, 'And don't *ever* come back. Next time, you won't be so lucky.' The guy was a good sport about it all. But I never saw him again.

There have been a number of men in my bedroom since then and Lolli has *never* done it again. So maybe she was trying to tell me something. Maybe she did me a favour by scaring that guy off.

I can only imagine the kind of almighty mess she would have made if I'd brought home the guy with the no-dogs-on-the-bed deal-breaker.

The Flirty Frenchie

The Vin de Champagne Awards is my favourite event on the Sydney social calendar. Guests enjoy a gourmet five-course meal matched with no fewer than fifteen fabulous tastings of (mostly vintage) champagne. Yes, it's every bit as extravagant as it sounds and it's pure heaven for a champagne lush like me.

Unfortunately, one year, the event left me with a bad taste in my mouth.

After quaffing glass after glass of Bollinger, Pol Roger, Dom Pérignon, Krug and Cristal, I had left the event and was on my way to the taxi rank when a well-dressed, middle-aged man suddenly appeared alongside me. In a deliciously seductive French accent, he said he'd also been at the champagne awards and we struck up the kind of flirty conversation you might expect to have with a handsome French stranger after you've both just sampled fifteen different spectacular vintage champagnes.

In the five-minute exchange as we walked to the taxi rank, he bombarded me with flattery: 'I notice you ze moment you arrrive', 'Zat dress is spectacularrr', 'You were ze most boooootiful woman in ze room'. The intensity of his flirting was actually verging on the ridiculous. But I told myself to relax and accept the compliments graciously. It was probably just the way of the flirty Français, after all. *Oui, oui*!

We arrived at the taxi rank and he said he would very much like to take me out to dinner sometime. He gave me his business card and urged me to call. I accepted his card, said goodnight and got into the back seat of the taxi. But as I slowly started to drive off and I sat there, trying to process what had just happened in that brief but intensely flirtatious interaction, there was a knock on my passenger window. It was the flirty Frenchie.

He leaned in and said, '*Excusez-moi*, but I really like to spend more time wiss you, *s'il vous plaît*. Can I join? Perhaps I drop you at your house and take ze taxi on to my home after? *Oui?*'

It was as if the guy had made a split-second decision, in that sliding door moment, that he wasn't prepared to risk letting me simply drive out of his life. It was all incredibly charming and I'd already been swept away by his avalanche of flattery. I was feeling slightly euphoric after the champagne so I said yes. And he jumped in, and we drove off.

As we chatted in the back of the cab, I started feeling that warm glow you get after you've met someone you're attracted to and you realise you're feeling a rapport with them as well. I also noticed that Frenchie was really, really, really good-looking. He had a touch of Emmanuel Macron about him. I wondered how I hadn't noticed him earlier in the night.

One of the things that makes the French language so provocative is not just hearing it, but watching someone speak it as well. Mainly because they need to round the lips for that 'ou' sound (for the *vous*, *nous*, and *tous*), which gives them a subtle 'blue steel' look. It can sometimes look like their lips are preparing for a kiss.

I noticed that Frenchie's lips looked *very* kissable. And I didn't resist when he gently reached over for my hand and intertwined his fingers with mine. It was all starting to feel rather romantic. I started feeling those wonderful butterflies of attraction and antic-ipation, wondering if this could possibly be the start of something quite fabulous.

As the taxi weaved its way through the city and Frenchie sat there holding my hand, he explained (in his super cute broken English) that he'd just moved to Australia for the job in Sydney. He said he had three children under eight. Alarm bells!

I quickly glanced down at his left hand. After decades of being on the singles scene, I pride myself on having ninja-like precision when it comes to spotting a wedding band on a potential. But I was pretty sure I hadn't clocked one on this guy. I was right. His ring finger was bare. Then, as he stroked my hand, Frenchie asked if I was single.

'Of course I'm single,' I said, before hesitantly following up with, 'Are you?'

Cue awkward silence.

'Errrr, no.'

'Oh. Are you . . . separated?'

'No.'

Another awkward silence.

'Are you . . . married?' I asked without really wanting to hear the answer.

'Errrrr, *oui*,' he said with a cheeky smile.

Frenchie wasn't the least bit fazed. He calmly explained (as he was seductively stroking my forearm) that his wife of nine years was also the mother of his three children. And they were all very happily living under the one roof close to the beach at Manly. The kids really loved the beach, apparently.

I pulled my arm away and said, 'So what the hell are you doing in the back of this cab with me?'

And he told me, very matter-of-factly, that he 'just couldn't help himself'. As if it was perfectly normal for a married man to flirt so aggressively with a woman who was not his wife. I asked him if his wife was aware of what he got up to while she was at home tending to their *enfants* and he just shrugged his shoulders and gave me a look that said, what do you think?

This clearly wasn't Frenchie's first rodeo.

I'd heard about these guys and their uber-relaxed attitudes to marriage and fidelity but it was the first time I'd been the direct target of a real-life French philanderer. The champagne goggles had well and truly worn off by this stage and I suddenly felt enormously embarrassed for allowing myself to be seduced by this sleazebag. Had I actually become so desperate and vulnerable that all it took was a French accent and a couple of corny compliments (oh, and a bucket of champagne)?

I felt like a fool.

We sat in awkward silence for a few minutes and then we arrived at my apartment building. I got out of the cab and couldn't believe it when the frisky Frenchie made one last-ditch effort.

'Please call me. I vould love to see you again.'

'No, I will not call you. Ever,' I said. 'Go home to your wife.'

The Other Woman

I have been the other woman. Twice. That I know of. (Okay, three, if you count the horny Brooklyn hipster.)

I was eighteen when it happened the first time. I'd been lusting after Matty forever. I was totally besotted by him. He looked just like Andrew McCarthy from *Pretty in Pink*: cute little button nose, shaggy hair that fell over one side of his face, a bit preppy. He always wore a polo shirt with the collar flicked up. He was so dreamy.

Sadly, Matty had been going around with his schoolyard sweet-heart, Linda, for years. I also knew Linda. We played in the same water polo team. From what I could tell, Matty and Linda seemed very happy together. So I kept my distance and just admired my dream-boat from afar (silently praying for the day when he would dump Linda and realise it was me he wanted all along).

I lost my *shit* when Matty called to say he'd broken up with Linda and his parents were out of town and he had the place to himself and would I like to come over and watch a movie? I was in the car, with the pedal to the metal, and at his house, on the other side of town, in about six minutes flat.

It wasn't exactly the romantic rendezvous I'd been dreaming of. His mate Toby was there as well, so we all played video games in the rumpus room for a while. Boring! Eventually, Matty invited me upstairs and through the doorway to heaven (i.e. his bedroom) to fool around and, yes, it was every bit as wonderful as I'd imagined it would be. I was more convinced than ever that Matty was my one true love and that we'd live happily ever after. Hell, we might even invite Linda to the wedding, after she realised he was meant to be with me all along.

We were onto our third shag – we were teenagers, remember – when Toby started banging on the bedroom door. Linda had just turned up at the house and she was standing at the front door, asking to come in. And Toby needed to know what Matty wanted him to do.

Well, Matty panicked. That's what he did.

He told me he was really sorry but he actually hadn't broken up with Linda at all. They'd just had a big fight.

I think I had a sneaking suspicion all along that this might be the case. Because I didn't even argue when Matty kicked me out of the house. Well, he didn't actually kick me out. He asked Toby to sneak me out the back door so Linda wouldn't see me.

With my shoes, handbag, some exceptionally unsightly JBF hair and an unhealthy dose of guilt, I followed Toby outside and onto the adjoining golf course. He escorted me all the way up the seventh hole fairway and showed me where I could pop back out onto the street and sneak down to Matty's house, where I could find my car. And escape. Like the scandalous, filthy, rotten ho that I was.

Sure, I got the prize momentarily but I felt like a thief. Stumbling around a suburban golf course half-naked, like I was an extra in some C-grade Seth Rogan movie was a suitably humbling experience. It wasn't worth it. I swore I would never be the other woman, ever again.

It didn't take long for the rumours to start spreading like wildfire through the Brisbane water polo community. Linda told everyone that she'd gone over to Matty's place on Saturday afternoon after their big fight, to find my car parked there, right outside his house. Linda knew exactly what my car looked like. She saw it every week at training. But when she asked Matty why my car was parked outside his house, he played dumb and pretended he had no idea what she was talking about. So everyone assumed I was a stalker.

Thanks, Matty. You dick.

Maybe I should have told Linda the truth. That her boyfriend had invited me over and that we'd had sex. Three times! But I didn't say anything. I just kept my mouth shut, because I didn't know which was worse: having everyone think I was a stalker or that I'd been the other woman.

It was another twenty years before I realised I was the other woman again (and sure, there may have been a few other times in between that I'm not even aware of). I was holidaying in my favourite ski resort of St Anton. As I've mentioned, they say the ratio of men to women during ski season there is about eight to one but the reality is, the ratio of *single*, *available* men to every woman is nowhere near that high.

I met a fetching English fellow who flirted with me outrageously, even though he appeared to be wearing a wedding ring. I say 'appeared to be wearing a wedding ring' because the whole ring thing is a bit confusing over there. Some European guys wear their wedding band on their right hand, instead of on their left, like they do in Australia. So I can never really be sure who's married and who's not. Basically, you just have to hope he comes clean.

Well, the Pom told me it was a wedding ring, but that he and his wife had separated only a month before and he just wasn't ready to take it off yet. He seemed quite sweet, so I conveniently believed him. Plus, he was there with a group of eight mates. Surely if the wife was still on the scene, one of the friends would have given me some kind of heads-up or tried to stop their buddy from going home with me. But they didn't. So he did.

I had a second night on the town with the English lads and they were bloody good fun. Again, none of his mates seemed bothered by my presence and nobody mentioned the wife. So I have absolutely no idea what prompted me to ask him, post-shag, on the second night, 'You're not really separated, are you?'

And he very calmly replied, 'No, I'm not.'

(Note to self: your gut *always* knows what's up. Trust that bitch.)

I didn't immediately throw the Pom out into the hotel hallway in a fit of rage and invite him to go fuck himself. Instead, I had a really open, fascinating conversation with the naked married man I'd just slept with, about why he was there, in my bed, cheating on his wife.

He told me he loved her and he always would. But he wasn't 'in love' with her like he used to be. They'd reached a point where they were more committed to their children than they were to each other. He didn't have the heart (or balls) to leave her but he thought he probably would, when the kids were a bit older. Also, they hadn't had sex in about six months, which is probably, in all honesty, what led him to my hooha.

So it left me wondering if the guy was a lying slimebag and a bloody good actor, or if he was a mostly decent guy in a passionless marriage, who cheated on his wife in a moment of weakness.

It also made me reconsider some things I'd always assumed about cheaters. Maybe they're not all fucking arseholes. Yes, cheating is a violation of trust and a terrible, *terrible* thing to do to a partner. But maybe it doesn't mean you're a terrible person if you do it.

The fact is, sometimes people *do* cheat on the people they love. At the end of the shag, he's the one who has to go home with his guilt.

I still felt like shit, though, knowing that I'd just slept with someone else's husband. I couldn't stop thinking about that poor woman, sitting at home with their kids.

The only thing that made me feel 0.001 per cent better about the situation was knowing that if it wasn't me, it probably would have been someone else. I would never be a threat to the wife or her family. I'd never track him down, and turn up at her door bunny boiler–style. And I'm not the type of person to contact the wife to let her know that her husband just had sex with me. I feel uneasy when I hear stories from friends who have done this. It's kind of like punishing the poor woman for her husband's actions.

It's also not my business to get involved in other people's drama. You never know what's going on in other people's relationships anyway. Maybe she already knows he cheats on her. And she doesn't care. Maybe she's cheating on him too. Plus, did she really need to know? I sometimes wish I'd never found out about the guys who cheated on me. Ignorance can actually be bliss in some situations.

When he left – yes, I did kick him out – I lay there and wondered a) how many other boyfriends had cheated on me, b) how often, and c) how many times I'd been the other woman.

I'm guessing the answer's not zero to any of the above. And I'm absolutely sure I'll never know for sure. I suppose, in the end, you've just got to believe that karma really is a bitch. And hope that she always shows up when it counts.

Pashing War Zone

I can vividly remember three first kisses in my life. My first-ever pash at the age of ten (thanks, Kylie), my first kiss with the One (which I thought would be my last ever first kiss), and the absolute worst first kiss of my life, with the Foreign Correspondent. Which didn't actually happen until my mid-forties.

I met the Foreign Correspondent when we were both holidaying in the Austrian ski resort of (yep, you guessed it!) St Anton. He worked for a German television news network so we had plenty in common and lots to chat about. He was fiercely intelligent, really interesting and seriously attractive. Plus, he seemed like a genuinely lovely fella. A gentleman. The kind of guy I could imagine having a relationship with, if we lived in the same city. Or even just on the same continent.

At the end of the night, we found ourselves standing outside my hotel, fairy lights sparkling all around us in a charming alpine village, snow starting to fall – and I knew it was time for *the kiss*. As far as romantic situations go, this one was pretty spesh. It was all systems go.

But then, as his face moved slowly towards mine and I readied myself for the magical moment of our first kiss, my romantic little fairytale turned into a Wes Craven nightmare. He had very hard lips, almost like they were pursed. And there seemed to be too many teeth. I hadn't noticed that about him before. When our mouths met, there was a significant amount of enamel clicking and clacking. But the worst part? His tongue, and the way it darted in and out of my mouth. Very hard. And fast.

All I could feel were those thin, hard lips, and that thin, hard tongue. Darting. In and out. In and out. Hard and fast. Fast and hard. Like a woodpecker trying to locate my tonsils. And I remember thinking, Um. Can you fucking not? Please.

All those years ago, Kylie had taught me that a kiss should start off soft and slow and gentle. (How in the name of Aphrodite did she know this shit?) But the Foreign Correspondent went straight in there, without warning. All tongue. And all kinds of crazy aggressive, desperate desire. I felt like my face was being assaulted. Methinks the Foreign Correspondent had spent *way* too much time in war zones.

Still, I persisted, hoping the tongue action would eventually subside. It did not. That's when I spontaneously laughed out loud, mid-kiss. Which prompted him to disconnect and draw breath for a moment.

Thank god that's over! I thought to myself. Surely he felt it too. It must have been just as bad for him. How embarrassment!

But he wasn't laughing. He looked a little puzzled at first. Then he looked longingly into my eyes and, before I knew it, his mouth was coming at me again. I made the split second decision *not* to turn away. By that stage I was kind of invested in the idea of a fun little Austrian fling with the German foreign correspondent, so I told myself it couldn't have been *that* bad, and puckered up for another try.

It wasn't just bad. It was face-numbingly bad. Again with the tongue, poking, and violently thrusting into my gums. A little voice inside my head started screaming obscenities, begging for this horror show to end. It was undoubtedly, absolutely, the most excruciatingly ghastly kiss of my life.

Another guy I dated many years before produced excessive saliva whenever we kissed. Every time we locked lips, my mouth would fill up with his spit. I felt like I needed one of those suction tubes the dental assistants use to remove excess fluid, just so we could keep kissing. (Yes, it was every bit as gross as it sounds.) And, sadly, it wasn't half as bad as this guy and his savage, stabbing lizard tongue.

The kiss with the Foreign Correspondent was so bad, it completely turned me off the idea of having sex with him. So I told him I wasn't feeling well, said goodnight and left him standing there outside my hotel.

I spent most of the next day dodging him and analysing the situation with my girlfriends, trying to rationalise and understand how a man in his early forties could possibly be such a horrendous kisser. Should I accept some of the blame? It takes two, after all. But I'd never experienced anything like it before. And I'd never had any complaints. Plus: Kylie.

There was some lively debate about whether I should bother to see the Foreign Correspondent again. If everything else about him was so great, was the kissing part really that important anyway? And is a terrible kisser guaranteed to be just as clueless between the sheets? I decided not to risk it. Engaging with the Foreign Correspondent at snogging level had proven to be way too much of a hostile environment for me already.

The Shithead

Dating in my forties has presented me with a surprising variety of 'never have I ever' scenarios: the Gyno, the worst kisser, the snoring mash-nazi, the choke and pokers (plural) and, my least favourite so far, the Shithead.

I'd been dating this guy for a few months but after a strong initial attraction, things weren't really going anywhere. He'd just become a part-time single dad after his wife of ten years left him, so I was willing to account for the fact that he was in a major period of readjustment. Another serious relationship probably just wasn't a priority.

But even on his child-free weekends, he didn't seem especially keen to spend time with me. There'd be an overnight stay and maybe a smashed avo the next morning but he'd always have to rush off to the gym or lunch or drinks at the pub with mates. And I was never invited. I hadn't met any of his friends, I'd never been to his place and I'd never met his kids.

I resigned myself to the fact that he was only interested in some obligation-free slap and tickle and decided it was probably time to be letting this one go.

And then he suddenly offered to come over and cook me dinner. I took this as a promising indication that he may have made it through

the adjustment period and was ready for something a little more serious. (Or I was desperately clinging to anything that might suggest this
guy actually gave a shit. I don't know. You decide.)

Anyone can make a dinner reservation. (Or ask their secretary to
do it.) But it's a thoughtful, romantic gesture to plan and prepare a
meal for your lover. Isn't that supposed to show that you care?

Sadly, things went from romantic to rank on the day he was supposed to come over and cook for me. He left a message on my phone,
asking if he could email me the recipes for the dishes he was planning to cook, so I could go to the supermarket and buy all of the
ingredients for him.

What the actual fuck? Isn't the whole 'I'll cook you dinner' experience meant to be an all-inclusive deal? A guy had never before offered
to cook me dinner, only to *ask me to buy my own ingredients*. Sure, it's
something you might ask of a partner if you've been together for a
really long time, someone you're comfortable enough to pee in front
of. But we'd only been dating (shagging) for a few months, so I did
not feel comfortable enough to a) let him watch me pee or b) buy
his groceries.

Also, I really wanted him to make the effort. Actually, at that
stage, after months of very little effort, I *needed* him to make an effort.

I happened to be having lunch with another trusty truth-telling
friend when the message came through, so I asked her opinion. Was I
a bitch for expecting the guy to buy his own groceries? Did that make
me high maintenance?

'No way!' she screamed. 'Tell him to buy his own fucking groceries. Or to get fucked.'

Solid advice from a straight-shooting girlfriend. Who doesn't
love that? So I sent him a text and said, 'Hey, I'm not going to
the supermarket. If you're too busy to cook, we can eat out, no
problem x'.

He immediately replied, 'haha thought you might say that ☺.
See you at yours, 7ish'.

So the guy knew he was being naughty by even asking in the first place! That annoyed me. Along with the blatant abuse of the smiley face.

I don't want to sound like a total punish here, but the meal was not quite as fabulous or romantic as I'd hoped. Some plain spaghetti with a little garlic and onion and some feta cheese on top. Minimal effort on his behalf. It was probably one of his kids' favourites. I added some chilli. Actually lots of chili. So I could taste *something*.

I let him stay the night. Dinner was a letdown, but I was determined to enjoy my 'dessert'.

The morning after, he disappeared into my bathroom for a very long shower before leaving for work. But when he gave me a good-bye kiss, he asked if my stomach was okay. 'I think you added a little too much chilli to the pasta last night. My tummy doesn't feel great.' He laughed awkwardly, as he rubbed his belly.

'Oh god, I'm sorry,' I said. 'I feel fine. Hope you feel better.'

And off he went to work and I went back to sleep. But later, when I got up and entered the bathroom, I was appalled to discover a scene of absolute carnage in my commode. The guy didn't just have an upset belly. He had a complete diarrhoeic explosion, the remnants of which were splashed *all over* my toilet bowl. I'm not talking about a cheeky little skid mark on the bottom of the ceramic here. There was shit everywhere! It must have been some kind of upward projectile diarrhoea, because it had sprayed up under the rim and the seat and there was poop in remote corners of my toilet I didn't even know existed.

Mr Spray and Go had flushed (thank god!) but he'd made no effort whatsoever to clean up the aftermath of the horrific crime scene. A guy with that kind of monumental bum burst had to know he'd made an apocalyptic mess. So why on earth would he just leave it there, on full display, in my loo? There was a friggin' toilet brush sitting right there next to the toilet. Why didn't he use it?

I couldn't believe my eyes. It was fucking foul.

After more than thirty years of dating, no man had ever done this to me before. I had a male flatmate for *six years* who never left this kind of destruction in our bathroom. It was, to quote my all-time favourite line from Samantha in *Sex and the City*, 'a real shit-motherfucker-fuck-shit situation'.

To make matters worse (and I do realise it's difficult to think of anything that could make this situation worse), the poo had solidified on the bowl, because it had been sitting there for a while. So I did what any other independent woman would do in this shit-motherfucker-fuck-shit situation. I grabbed the toilet brush, the bleach and a pair of industrial-strength rubber gloves and I got down on my hands and knees and got to work.

As I sat there on the cold tiles, scraping his solidified shit off my toilet bowl, I knew that I would never see him again. I was disgusted. Then I was angry. Then I was sad. That a man could show me so little respect. Then I laughed out loud when I realised I had actually spent more time cleaning his shit off my bowl than I had enjoying my 'dessert' the night before. *So* not worth it.

I was done making excuses for this guy. It was rude, inconsiderate, thoughtless, downright shitty behaviour. Plus, I couldn't help thinking, if that's how he treated a woman he'd only known for a few months, imagine how he treated his poor wife of ten years!

I once heard Priscilla Presley in an interview talking about how to keep the magic alive in a relationship. She said there are certain things you should keep to yourself. Like a bare face. Elvis never saw her without makeup. He even told her he didn't want to watch her getting dressed because it might ruin the mystery and romance of the relationship.

Well, kids, here's something else you should keep to yourself: your shit stains. Especially the ones on *my* toilet. You can definitely keep those to yourself. Particularly if you want to have sex with me, ever again.

I never told the Shithead the real reason I stopped seeing him. I thought about taking a photo of the bowl and sending it to him with a note saying, 'It's not me, it's you'. But I knew there was no point. The guy really couldn't give a shit. Or, maybe he could. Just not where it mattered.

Chanel Can't Buy You Love

Okay, so, my Mr Big story. Please forgive the *Sex and the City* reference, but he literally was my Mr Big. He was six foot five, which is about as tall as a fella can get before it's weird.

He also happened to be loaded. Seriously loaded. In a 'let me fly you to Fiji for our first date' kind of way. While the offer to whisk me off to the South Pacific after knowing me for less than thirty minutes was certainly the most glamorous first-date invitation I'd ever received, it was also the most ridiculous. I told him he was dreamin'.

He promptly suggested Hayman Island instead. And I could tell he wasn't joking. Now, I love a tropical island getaway as much as the next gal, but my wanker radar was peaking in the red zone with this guy, so I graciously declined his unnecessarily generous (i.e. ridiculous) offers and wished him all the best. And then I watched the tall handsome stranger speed off in his brand-new Maserati.

Fast forward seven years (no itch!), to when I ran into Mr Money Bags again. He was way more relaxed this time and much less desperate to impress. He also seemed more mature and, um, how should I put this, less of a dick. His life had changed considerably since we'd last met. He'd been married, had a couple of kids, got divorced.

So perhaps that experience had given him a more grounded perspective on life.

When he asked me out again (no bells and whistles or private jets this time, just a simple dinner at a restaurant of my choice), I decided to give it a go. I hadn't been on a date in six months so I figured I had nothing to lose.

Dinner was wonderful. He was great company and we laughed heaps. He was pleasantly self-deprecating about the whole 'let's fly to Fiji' fiasco and there was no hint of the flashy, brash personality that had turned me off seven years earlier. So I agreed to a second dinner. And then another. And another. And the whirlwind romance took off.

I've dated a few men who were a little more cashed up than the average bloke but no one came close to this guy. He spoiled me in a way I still can't quite believe. There was all the lovely stuff a man with a healthy bank account can easily afford to woo a lady. A gigantic bunch of flowers delivered to my home every week. A driver to chauffeur me to every lunch and dinner date at all the finest restaurants. He upped the fab factor on our fourth date, when he took me by seaplane to Sydney's exclusive Jonah's restaurant for lunch. That, by the way, is about as perfect as a lunch date could possibly be.

I realised I might be drifting into *Pretty Woman* territory when he gave me a Chanel purse on our *fifth* date. It was exquisite soft leather with delicate white stitching embroidered in the familiar Chanel criss-cross pattern. I adored every impeccable millimetre of it but I knew I couldn't possibly accept it.

You know how you say 'it's the thought that counts' when someone gives you a crappy present? Well, I'm not sure it works the same in reverse. Because I'm a gal who knows her Chanel accessories and I was well aware that sublime little purse had set him back around 2000 bucks. Which was way too much to be splashing out on me. On our fifth date.

Maybe I should have just said thank you and accepted the wildly expensive gift with grace, but instead my guard went up. I went all proud, independent woman on his arse, launching into a full-blown lecture about how I was not a gold digger and he would never be able to buy my affection. When I finished berating the poor bloke, he looked genuinely offended. He wasn't trying to buy my affection, he calmly explained. He gave me the purse simply because he saw it and it was beautiful and he thought I would like it. That's it. He said I was making a big deal out of nothing. And if I didn't know how much the purse had cost him, would it have been an issue? The value of the gift really shouldn't matter.

He had a point. So then I just felt like an ungrateful bitch.

I did accept the gift but for some strange reason, I couldn't bring myself to actually use it. I left that divine leather pouch wrapped perfectly in its crisp embossed white tissue paper in its elegant black gift box in my top drawer. And I made a pact with myself that I would only take it out of the box and start using it if things between us became serious. If it didn't work out, I would just return the wallet to him, untouched.

Well that's how I rationalised it, anyway.

The next outrageous display of excess came when he organised a car for me to drive while mine was being serviced for a few days. It was a kind gesture. Except, after calling in a favour from one of his car dealer mates, he sent me over a $450 000 Bentley. Which is the car of choice for Saudi billionaires, American rappers and Lisa Vanderpump from *The Real Housewives of Beverly Hills*.

I was too scared to drive the beast so she mostly just sat in my parking spot at home – what on earth did the neighbours think? Plus, the four-door Bentley Flying Spur is roughly the size of a small country, so she's a bitch to reverse park.

Gusband Tim begged me to take her out for a spin one night. So I drove us down to the local shops. In a half-million-dollar vehicle. In our activewear. To buy hot chips. (Tim still counts this as one of his life's greatest achievements.)

I managed to return the Bentley without a scratch. But Gusband had guzzled the hot chips in the car on the drive back to my place so

I was paranoid that the stench of those greasy French fries had permeated the bespoke leather upholstery and lush wood-grain interior (#firstworldproblems). We still laugh about it today, like naughty schoolkids.

Mr Money Bags' most extravagant gift was an all-expenses paid trip to Mexico, after we'd been dating for just two months. I was excited about the idea of a romantic holiday with my new boyfriend but I felt really uncomfortable about letting him foot the bill. I told him I'd only join him if I could pay for my own flights. He said that wasn't an option.

My girlfriends eventually convinced me to stop stressing about it and just give in to the reality of having a boyfriend who could afford to spoil me.

'He knows you're not a gold digger, Sam.'

'He knows you could pay your own way.'

'For the love of god, please just go and have hot sex with your gorgeous boyfriend in a stunning resort in Mexico. At least do it so we can all live vicariously through you!'

And so, for the first time in my life, I broke through that wall of pride and independence I'd been steadily building over the last forty years and I allowed myself to be spoiled by my man. Elaborately, magnificently, luxuriously, splendidly, spoiled.

We stayed at the most exclusive resort in Cabo San Lucas, the place where paparazzi snap pics of Jen Aniston and Courteney Cox chilling on their BFF getaways all the time. This place was off the charts ah-may-zing. The sand was pure white and the water was aqua blue and our spectacular oceanfront villa came with three private butlers, available at our beck and call twenty-four seven. I mean, who the fuck needs *three* butlers? On holiday! Who even needs two? Ridic, right?

I didn't argue when he organised a sexy speedboat to zip us around the crystal-clear waters off Cabo. I didn't flinch when he popped open a bottle of champers at lunch. I didn't resist when he booked me in for a three-hour spa treatment. I'll stop now, because it's seriously nauseating. But you get the picture, right? It was pure heaven (with the best guacamole ever!).

The holiday hit a snag when Mr Money Bags arranged a romantic private bonfire for us on the beach and presented me with a small blue box. Tied up with a perfect white ribbon. My heart stopped momentarily as I mentally prepared myself for things to get super awkward. I wasn't ready to marry the guy. We hadn't even said the 'L' word yet.

(Inside voice: 'Please don't get down on one knee. *Please* don't get down on one knee!')

As I tentatively opened the box, I was blinded by the sparkle of diamonds. A plethora of spectacular, shiny, brilliant diamonds. Now I really did feel like *Pretty Woman*. It was a drop-dead gorgeous Tiffany & Co diamond bracelet. (No ring – phew!)

Ordinarily I would go all deliriously bizonkers at the sight of a Tiffany & Co diamond anything. But not this time. I'd already agreed to the all-expenses-paid lavish overseas holiday. Diamonds were *not* in the brochure.

I tried to explain to him (again) that I really didn't care about the material things he could give me. I was more interested in the things money *can't* buy, like honesty, loyalty, manners and respect. And if our relationship had any hope of reaching the next level, he needed to show me the real him, and not just the enchanting lifestyle and all the pretty sparkly things he could so clearly provide.

He assured me, again, that he wasn't trying to buy my affection. He just enjoyed spoiling me. Because he could. And he looked so sincere and vulnerable when he said it.

That's when I checked myself.

Maybe I was already seeing the real him. Sure, my boyfriend was wealthy. But he also appeared to be kind and caring and fun and funny and outgoing and my friends all loved him. He always called when he said he would. He (or the driver) always turned up on time. He was safe. And dependable. And he never let me down. He was the kind of man I could fall in love with. Maybe he was the kind of man I *should* fall in love with.

So I decided to stop sabotaging the relationship and punishing the guy because of his financial status. I put that divine diamond bracelet on my wrist and, I have to say, it was the most spectacular piece of jewellery I've ever worn. I felt pretty fabulous whenever I caught other women admiring my four carats from afar. You know how they say Tiffany diamonds shine brighter than any other? Well, it appears that's absolutely correct.

And just when I finally gave myself permission to nudge that chip off my shoulder and allow myself to fall in love with the guy, things turned to shitsville when we returned to Australia and the monster-in-law entered my life. And put her big fat fucking Louboutins in it.

Monster-In-Law

We've all heard horror stories about the in-laws from hell. There are even online forums dedicated to advice on how to deal with the worst ones.

Stories about interfering in-laws also make great radio content, by the way. I had a listener call in once to proudly explain how he put his mother-in-law in her place by buying her a cemetery plot one year for Christmas. And when she asked him why he didn't buy her anything for Christmas the *following* year, he told her, 'Well, you still haven't used the present I got you last year.'

So naughty. (Also: hilarious!)

I hadn't even met my fella's mother yet, but turns out she was very much alive and very much involved in her only son's life. Every. Single. Aspect. Including his love life. She knew all about the weekly flower deliveries and the Chanel wallet and the sojourn on the seaplane and the shag-fest in Cabo. Oh, and let's not forget the $30 000 Tiffany & Co diamond bracelet. And she didn't like it.

The dra-mah only came to light when a friend of mine ran into mother dearest and casually mentioned how thrilled she was about the budding relationship between her son and little old *moi*. Which is when the monster-in-law snapped and screamed, 'That Sami Lukis! She's a *gold-digging whore!*'

Ummmmmmmm . . . Say what?

My friend tried to explain that she was seriously barking up the wrong tree with the whole gold digger accusation. But I think she was already convinced that I was only dating her son so I could get my greasy little hands on his big fat bank account.

OK, so I've been called plenty of disparaging names over the years. Having a public profile makes some people think they have the right to be as mean to you as they like. People make assumptions about me all the time. Mainly that I'm a blonde bimbo. But I don't let it get to me. Sadly, it comes with the territory.

The only label I can't cop is 'gold digger'. (Look, I wasn't exactly thrilled with 'whore' either, to be honest. That was completely unnecessary, don't you think?)

I called my fella to relay the story and tell him how insulted I was but instead of apologising for his mother's outburst, he defended her. He told me she was only protecting him. And that maybe she had a point, actually, because, come to think of it, I hadn't really seemed that interested in him until he paid for the five-star trip to Mexico.

Big mistake, buddy. Big. Huge.

I had let him know from the very start that his outrageous generosity made me uncomfortable. And the *one* time I let my guard down and allowed him to spoil me, he used it against me. I couldn't fucking believe it.

If that was even a glimpse of what a future with him might look like, I wanted *out*. So I thanked him for showing me his true colours and for making it easy to break up with him. And I promptly returned the Tiffany bracelet and the Chanel wallet (still perfectly wrapped and untouched since the night he gave it to me).

Of course I wondered afterwards if I overreacted. He was, mostly, pretty wonderful to me. And being single in your mid-forties *can* get a little lonely at times. Is a potential mother-in-law who doesn't appear to respect me, and a boyfriend who won't always have my back, a small price to pay for not being alone?

Simple answer: no.

Because that would mean doing the *one* thing I have steadfastly refused to do for the last thirty years. I would have to settle.

And that? Well, I'd rather be alone. And buy my own damn guacamole.

Unfortunate Breakups

As a professional dater, I really should have mastered the art of breaking up. But, honestly, I don't think I ever will.

If we've only been dating for a few weeks (or sometimes months), my go-to method of indicating that I'm no longer interested in seeing you is to 'ghost' you. Yep, I'm the witch who just stops replying to your calls and texts. I am she who inexplicably disappears. I know it's rude. It's immature. And it's downright selfish. As a reasonably intelligent, somewhat sensible adult person, I should know better.

But it's also, by far, the easiest option for someone who prefers to avoid awkward conversations and potential confrontations at all costs. I'm just going to go ahead and blame this hideous behaviour on the emotional scars from an especially traumatic breakup with the first boyfriend I ever had sex with. We were each other's 'first', so it was achingly passionate, crazy teenage love, but when I tried to break up with him, he threatened to drive himself off a cliff. Of course I couldn't dump him. I was seventeen and terrified of feeling guilty about his death for the rest of my life. I tried calling it quits with him again when I thought he was stable enough to handle it, but he turned on the same emotional blackmail, so I ended up being held hostage in that relationship for a year longer than I wanted to be in it.

When I finally decided to risk eternal guilt and dump him, he did not attempt any self-harm. Praise be.

In an ideal world, when a relationship comes to an end, it would be lovely if you could both politely agree that it hasn't worked out, accept that not every person who walks into your life is meant to be there till the end, close that chapter and move on. C'est la vie! You might even promise to stay friends, with cries of, 'Catch up soon for a latte, babe,' and double air kisses as you leave.

Yeah, nah. In the real world, splitsville is just not that pretty.

My serious relationships never end well. There'll inevitably be floods of tears, amid a series of long, drawn-out, heart-wrenching debates over who's right and who's wrong. There'll probably be raised voices, harsh words and some unsavoury name-calling as we each try to blame the other person for the failure of the relationship. If I find myself singing along (with gusto) afterwards to Beyoncé's 'Best Thing I Never Had' then I know *he's* to blame. And I feel infinitely better.

Break ups can be all kinds of brutal. Comedian Steve Harvey's ex-wife sued him for sixty million dollars when he opted out of their marriage. She said he 'murdered her soul'. That's a woman who loved her man so intensely, she ended up hating his goddamn guts. Now, while I do think sixty million bucks is a bit ridiculous, the whole 'you murdered my soul' schtick? Well, I kind of get it. The pain of a broken heart can absolutely feel like someone has pulverised your life force.

But let me tell you something. You find yourself in an especially horrific hell when you break up with someone while you're on holiday together. I should know. I've done it three times. Before Ze German in Port Douglas and mash-gate with the snoring carb-nazi in Austria, there was also Thailand.

It was the last night of what had been an otherwise idyllic holiday on a tropical island with my boyfriend. After a few too many sunset cocktails at the beach bar, my tipsy, loose-lipped beau accidentally confirmed my suspicions that he'd cheated on me a few months earlier.

There's probably some wonderfully prophetic metaphor I could use here about the sun going down on my relationship in that moment blah, blah, blah, but the only way I can describe it was an overwhelming sense of relief. The relationship had been going downhill for a while, but I'd hung in there, clinging to the whole 'I'd rather stay and argue with you than be with anyone else' messed-up theory. That theory is not healthy, by the way.

So the revelation that he'd been unfaithful was my 'come to Jesus' moment. And I knew I had to end it, right then and there, on that stunning beach in Phuket. Emotionally, I knew it was over. Logistically, it wasn't so simple. We were twenty-four hours and 7000 kilometres from Australia.

The journey home the next day was excruciating. We sat in stony, miserable, awkward silence the entire way. It wasn't the flight from hell. It was the flight *in* hell. Crashing would have been less traumatic than having to sit next to my cheating ex for ten hours. I don't recommend it.

My all-time favourite breakup was the guy who managed an act of stealth revenge after I dumped him. We'd been together for about six months before I painfully accepted that he just wasn't going to be my Mr Happily Ever After. A few months later I decided to use the gift voucher he'd given me for my last birthday for a weekend away at a beautiful golf resort just outside of Sydney. I was desperate for a mini-break at the time, and a golf weekend was just what I needed, so I called the resort to book it in. But when I quoted my voucher number over the phone, the receptionist said, 'I'm sorry, Ms Lukis, that voucher has been refunded.'

The little shit had called the resort to cancel my gift voucher and demand his money back after I dumped him. I guess nothing says 'fuck you, bitch' quite like *reclaiming* a gift voucher. Although that really is the gift that keeps on giving.

Mr Happily Ever After

I knew a girl who could walk into any bar, restaurant or party in Sydney, and be confident that she had slept with at least two men in that room.

That's a big call.

It's downright scary for most of us to run into *one* guy we've slept with. Anywhere. Anytime. So imagine knowing you'll be coming face to face with at least *two* men who've seen your lady bits, pretty much anywhere you go? Heidi didn't say it with a bragging-about-the-shagging, 'notches on the bedpost' kind of vibe. It was more matter-of-fact. Like she was just stating the obvious. And, from what I observed when I was with her, she *wasn't* exaggerating.

We would easily run into at least two former fornications on any given night in any restaurant in Bondi. We once walked into a friend's engagement party and immediately identified three men she'd shagged. We went to the footy one afternoon and she pointed out two past lovers, who were both on the field, playing in the *same* team.

Look, I think it's a fair assessment that Heidi has been pretty active on the local dating scene. But I don't want you to judge my friend. She's a great girl. She's funny, clever, outgoing. She's sexy as hell and a natural flirt. Men love her. And she loves men. And she enjoys sex. Nothing wrong with that.

Still, I think if *I* reached the point where I couldn't go anywhere without having intimate knowledge of at least two penii in my immediate vicinity, I might start to wonder if I'd perhaps dated *too* many men?

I was unexpectedly forced to ponder this very question when I experienced two 'Heidi' situations of my own.

The first time it happened, I walked into the Four in Hand pub in Paddington and was immediately confronted by the fact that I had slept with three men in the room. *Three!* There was Skinny Harry, the guy I was meeting at the pub for our fourth date. (Yep, awkward.) There was Fat Harry. The guy I'd broken up with about six months earlier. Aha, same name, *very* different body shape. And there was the Eternal Student. The lovely guy I'd had a brief fling with a few years earlier. (My friends called him the Eternal Student because the guy was in his mid-30s but he was *still* studying. I think he was onto his third degree).

And there it was. My sexual past colliding with my sexual present. In a cosy Sydney pub, on an otherwise lovely Sunday afternoon.

If this had happened while I was out with the girls, we would have all laughed our tits off about it. They'd be like, 'Three in the bush at the Four in Hand', 'Ha ha ha ha', 'Ménage à quatre, anyone?', 'There are three men in the front bar who've all seen your front bum', and that kind of ridiculousness. But I didn't have any of my girlfriends there for support. Because I was on a *date*.

Of course I didn't mention it to Skinny Harry. He didn't need to know that he was in close proximity to two other men who'd been in my bed. I'm sure he didn't think I was a virgin, but I'm guessing that's not something a guy wants to hear from the woman he's just started dating. I told myself I had nothing to be ashamed of anyway. I'd been in relationships with Fat Harry and the Eternal Student after all.

But I couldn't help wondering if it was some kind of sign, that I might be getting dangerously close to reaching my Sydney dating limit.

I conveniently didn't give it any more thought, until it happened to me *again*, a couple of years later. Only this time it happened in Aspen. The ski resort. In Colorado. USA. On the other side of the Pacific Ocean.

I was enjoying a cheeky pinot grigio in my favourite après bar, when I spotted a guy I'd been on one date with in Sydney a couple of years earlier. It was the naughty surgeon who went out with me, even though (I later found out) he already had a girlfriend.

There are plenty of Aussies in Aspen during ski season, so I wasn't at all shocked to see him there. But I had to do a double take when Neville No Pay walked into the same bar five minutes later – I'd only dated him a few months earlier. I knew he loved to ski but he'd never mentioned an imminent trip to Aspen. Strange. (Side note: it wasn't lost on me that the guy couldn't pay for one fucking rice paper roll the whole time we dated, but he could suddenly afford a trip to Aspen.)

Okay, so here's the freaky bit: Neville No Pay and the naughty surgeon didn't know each other. But they both lived in the same Sydney suburb of Bronte. And I'd been on dates with both of them. And now they were both *here*, in the same bar as me, 14 000 kilometres from home, on the *other* side of the world. What a crazy coincidence! It might have been the pinot grigio talking, but I decided it must have some profound meaning. This time, the Universe was definitely trying to tell me something.

Had I finally reached my official dating quota?

Was I meant to give one (or both) of those guys a second chance?

Should I consider moving to Bronte?

The whole thing was pretty funny at the time. But the more I thought about it, the more it rattled me. And it forced me to face some home truths about all my years of dating.

Most people remove themselves from the dating scene once they've met and settled down with their forever person, right? But what happens if, after *decades* of dating, you still haven't found your person?

Am I supposed to just keep dating, endlessly, until I die? Or at some point, will I be forced to conclude that there is no Mr Happily Ever After out there for me, throw in the towel and become one of those women who invite all my friends and family to a lavish celebration to watch me marry *myself*?

(That would *never* happen, by the way. Even though furchild Lolli would be *the* cutest ring bearer ever.)

After reading about my unfortunate dating disasters, you might agree that I have been exceptionally unlucky in love. Or maybe you're thinking I don't have a hope in hell of ever meeting Mr Right because I have unrealistic expectations about men and relationships.

But hey, if my expectations *are* high, I'll thank my parents for this one. After being set up on a cheeky little blind date, they're still happily married more than fifty years later. It's blatantly obvious to anyone who meets my folks that they were made for one another. To this day, they still hold hands, everywhere they go, whenever they're close enough to touch. They share the kind of 'til death do we part' love that most of us would like to find.

So here's what I've decided.

After riding this crazy dating roller-coaster for more than three decades, I'm well aware that it *can* be daunting, dumbfounding, disappointing, demeaning, depressing and downright laughable. But I've also discovered along the way that dating can sometimes be exciting and inspiring and bloody good fun. And most importantly, full of promise, that I might just find the kind of love my folks have.

Hell, maybe it's even time for me to finally throw caution to the wind and give online dating a go (despite my reservations, fears and overwhelming anxiety about the entire process).

I have no idea how many Mr Wrongs it will take to find my Mr Right, but I'm not ready to bow out just yet.

I'm also inspired by a couple of crazy kids named Gertrude and Alvin from Middletown, New York, who were ninety-eight and ninety-four years of age when *they* got hitched, just as I finished writing this book. See? It *is* possible to find love, at any age.

I hope my Mr Right is a kind, decent, honest man who respects me and loves me, despite my flaws. Someone who makes me smile. And makes an effort. And has my back. I hope he loves to travel as much as I do (and if he wears an avalanche pack, well, that would be an absolute bonus).

I love the idea of being with someone who knows the exact spot where I like my arm tickled (inside bicep) and exactly how I take my coffee (strong, soy capp). And I would really like to be with a man who doesn't care that I lick the chocolate off the inside of my takeaway cappuccino lid. In public. In broad daylight. I am well aware that licking *anything* in public is not appropriate behaviour, but I just can't help myself. My Mr Happily Ever After will know that about me, and he'll love me anyway.

But until I find *that* guy, I'll be quite content to remain – happily, hopelessly and hilariously – romantically challenged.